Privatization in Eastern Germany
A Neo-Institutional Analysis

T0271974

PRIVATIZATION IN EASTERN GERMANY
A Neo-Institutional Analysis

HERBERT BRÜCKER

FRANK CASS
LONDON • PORTLAND, OR
Published in association with the
German Development Institute, Berlin

First published in 1997 in Great Britain by
FRANK CASS & CO. LTD.
Newbury House, 900 Eastern Avenue,
London IG2 7HH

and in the United States of America by
FRANK CASS
c/o ISBS
5804 N.E. Hassalo Street
Portland, Oregon 97213-3644

Transferred to Digital Printing 2004

Copyright © 1997 GDI/Frank Cass

British Library Cataloguing in Publication Data

ISBN 0-7146-4335-1

Library of Congress Cataloging-in-Publication Data

Brücker, Herbert, 1960–
     [Privatisierung in Ostdeutschland.   English]
     Privatization in Eastern Germany : a neo-institutional analysis /
Herbert Brücker.
          p.   cm.
     Includes bibliographical references.
     ISBN 0-7146-4335-1
     1. Privatization—Germany (East)   I. Title
HD4180.5.B7813   1996   96-39063
338.9'2—dc20   CIP

Contents

List of Figures

List of Tables

Acknowledgments

The present study was written while I was research fellow at the Department of Economics of Johann Wolfgang Goethe-University in Frankfurt/Main. With their critical comments and numerous suggestions, my colleagues and friends were instrumental in the production of the study, although I myself am of course responsible for its shortcomings. First of all I am grateful to Armin Bauer, Petra Kachel, and my wife, Martina Schmiedhofer; they put forward many ideas, devoted great care to the reading of the manuscript, and their constructive criticism was a crucial factor in improving the study. To my two advisors, Professor Tamás Bauer and Professor Jiří Kosta, I owe a great deal of my knowledge of planned economies and the transformation of the economic systems in the countries of Central and Eastern Europe. I am grateful to Paul Knowlton for his excellent translation. Sylvia Combelle-Ahl, Bettina Koltermann, Waltraud Phaneuf, Gisela Rau, and Kerstin Wilke provided excellent assistance in preparing the study for publication. My special thanks go to Jörg Meyer-Stamer for his generous support and valuable comments on the English version of the study.

The Vereinigung für Wirtschaftlichen Fortschritt e.V. awarded the study its CEPES Prize in 1994. I would like to take this opportunity to express my heartfelt thanks to the prize's sponsor, Peter Schuhmacher, the board of the Vereinigung für Wirtschaftlichen Fortschritt, the jury, and Professor Peter-Michael Schmitz for honoring the study in this way.

The German Development Institute (GDI) sponsored the translation and publication of this study. I am indebted to the GDI, especially to Klaus Esser, Hans-Helmut Taake, and Professor Peter Waller for this generous support.

Frankfurt/Main, June 1996

Foreword

Since the late 1950s the leadership elites of the former Eastern Bloc were at pains to reform the poor performing systems of planned economies. But not even market-oriented economic reforms of the type of Yugoslavia's self-administered socialism or Hungary's "New Economic Mechanism" proved able to overcome constantly recurring economic crises. The concept of a "socialist market economy" in the form of a link between collective or state ownership and a market-economy type of control tuned out in the end to be a flawed construct. Even insider economists (Kornai, Balcerowicz, and others) increasingly came to the insight propagated by neoliberals in the 1920s (von Mises, Hayek) and western institutional economists, in particular the property rights school: without a dominance of private ownership there can be no efficient economy.

In the present study Herbert Brücker underpins this thesis, which is hardly in question among the mainstream of contemporary economists, not only with the aid of new theoretical approaches, he at the same time analyzes empirically the privatization process in Eastern Germany against the background of the theoretical framework developed here. To my knowledge, this is the first study on privatization in the literature on economics that is at the same time so well founded in both theoretical and empirical terms.

In the first, theoretically oriented part of his book, the author builds above all on theses developed by the New Institutional Economics (Coase, Demsetz, Furubotn/Pejovich, North, Olson, Williamson), enriching these approaches with positions developed by Hungarian economists (Bauer, Kornai) and the social philosopher John Rawls. The author's theoretical point of departure is the thesis that it is only a link between market economy and private ownership that guarantees the "coherence" and the efficiency of an economic system to the extent that only in this case will the postulate of the necessary "incentive intensity" and the existence of a "hard budget constraint" be fulfilled.

The study's theoretical section is centered around the question of the comparative advantages or disadvantages entailed by the choice of a given privatization procedure. The transaction-cost approach is drawn upon to answer this question. Privatization - the author argues - runs up above all against the restrictions posed by the limited financial endowment and competence of bidders. Under the given conditions facing the transformation of the socioeconomic systems in the countries of the former Eastern Bloc, the problem is now to allocate as efficiently as possible the scarce factors of capital and economic competence. The author deepens his comparative examination of these two constraints by developing in detail three criteria, viz. (1) the alternative: dispersion vs. concentration of property rights, (2) the requirements posed by bidder financial endowment, and (3) the type and complexity of the information needed to make privatization-related decisions.

It is under these aspects that the author discusses the choice of alternative privatization strategies - informal bargaining, management buyout, auction, stock exchange, vouchers, restitution. Based on a great number of arguments for and against each potential procedure, the author points to the option (realized by the Treuhandanstalt) of informal direct bargaining with bidders as the one most advantageous in relative terms. He bases this judgment on the existing "high asset specificity of capital", in other words, fixed capital that was invested in connection with previous industrial strategies and cannot simply used for alternative purposes (arms, heavy industry), and the "above-average size" of the enterprises concerned. The author's conclusions on the advantages of this privatization procedure also find support in the possibility of reaching agreement on additional specific conditions (investment, employment). On the other hand, the author concedes that auctions can make sense in cases in which small service firms are concerned (artisans, retail trade, etc.) and possibly also in privatizing certain larger-sized firms (e.g. hotels), where asset specificity is low and the requirements placed on bidder financial endowment and competence are not unduly high. Privatization by vouchers (à la coupons in the Czech Republic and Slovenia), the author argues, can make sense when the conditions required for informal bargaining are not given (e.g. in the face of a lack of sufficient private bidder capital), although he doubts that in this case the firms concerned will prove able to operate efficiently.

Proceeding from the position put forward by Rawls, the author develops his views on the highly controversial issue concerning the extent to which, in terms of distributional and welfare criteria, privatization procedures keyed to the interests of managers (the old "nomenclature") and foreign investors are acceptable. This strategy, frequently criticized in the debate from the view-point of "justice", is regarded here as fully justified to the degree that those who are "less well off", i.e. wage earners or nationals, are placed in a better position than they would be without privatization or if another privatization procedure were selected. As the author convincingly argues, employees also stand to benefit, due to the higher efficiency to be expected in this case, more from privatization via management buyout (or the commitment of foreign capital) than they would if this method of privatization were not used.

On the basis of his theoretical considerations and his empirical analysis, the author comes to the well-founded conclusion that the construction of Treuhandanstalt privatization was basically the most adequate method available to come to grips with Treuhandanstalt's task of building an efficient private sector in Eastern Germany. Nor is the author in any way blind to the errors and flaws that actually occurred in the course of the privatization process, though this in no way changes the Treuhandanstalt's record of success now that the task with which it was entrusted has been completed.

The conclusions that Herbert Brücker draws can only be endorsed. The reasons are not merely the impressive figures on Eastern Germany's privatized and newly established private firms, they also find support in the extent of the takeoff experienced since 1992 and, presently, three years on, the sustained strong upswing of the economy in Eastern Germany.

June 1996   Jiří Kosta

1   Introduction

At the turn of the year from 1994 to 1995 the Treuhandanstalt was dissolved. It had, all in all, completed its task of privatizing Eastern Germany's stock of enterprises. Eastern Germany is thus one of the first transforming economies of Central and Eastern Europe to have completed the process of privatizing the core stocks of the state-owned industrial sector. Privatization was in Eastern Germany - as it is in the other transition countries - part of a sweeping transformation program aimed at decentralizing economic decision-making and denationalizing broad segments of economy and society. A privatization process so broad in scope, one extending not only to individual enterprises and sectors but to the core areas of the economy as well, is historically unprecedented. In view of the dramatic cutbacks in production capacities and employment in Treuhandanstalt and former Treuhandanstalt enterprises, the agency's privatization strategy continues to be controversial: the pace of privatization, the choice of privatization procedures, and the decision to refrain largely from investing in rehabilitation measures are, even today, the topic of a controversial discussion.

The focal point of the present study is an investigation of the comparative advantages of various privatization strategies and procedures. Instead of restricting itself to an analysis of the procedures practiced in Eastern Germany, the study also deals in general terms with the theory of the privatization and transformation of planned economies. It is for this reason that the study makes reference not only to the privatization strategy familiar from Eastern Germany but also includes the privatization procedures practiced and discussed in other countries in the process of transformation. Any generalization of findings obtained in a study of the privatization process in Eastern Germany must of course reflect the particular initial conditions defined by the German economic and monetary union and the unification of the two German states. While it is true that the transformation of the institutional systems in the other countries in transition likewise led both to an inflow of international capital and drops in production and employment, the scope of the influx of public and private capital was nevertheless much lower in these countries. These differences must be noted in the choice of privatization strategies. On the other hand, a study of the privatization process in Eastern Germany offers the chance to observe the problems and the results of a process largely completed, one, it is true, whose pace will differ but which will, in many respects, run in similar channels.

The starting point of the study is the hypothesis that the choice of a privatization strategy has a lasting impact on both the efficiency of the enterprises concerned and the distribution of income and individual life-chances in the economies affected. The assumption that the structure and distribution of property rights constitute a central factor explaining the behavior of economic agents is by no means uncontested. For the classics of political economy from Adam Smith to Karl Marx, the structure of ownership relations was still the focal point of economic theory. But one implication of the transition to Walrasian microeconomics was that it sapped the ownership question of some of its significance as a theoretical category. It was the representatives of the Austrian School, above all Friedrich von Hayek, Ludwig von Mises, and Joseph Schumpeter, who again and again stressed the eminent significance of private ownership for the functioning of market economies. Only when the New Institutional Economics began to develop its diverse approaches did the question of ownership experience a theoretical renaissance. It has been property-rights, transaction-cost, and principle-agent theories that have subjected the incentive and sanction structure of ownership rights to an in-depth analysis. In many areas the theoretical findings and models of the New Institutional Economics share common ground with the empirically based analyses of reform economists in the transition countries. In attributing the problems faced by market-socialist reform programs to the specific incentive and sanction structure of the state business sector, these economists crossed the Rubicon separating reform and the transformation of an economic system.

In analyzing different privatization procedures and strategies, this study draws upon the framework provided by the New Institutional Economics. Not unlike transaction-cost and property-rights theories, the study is grounded on the assumption of bounded rationality. Individual rationality is not only bounded, it is also unevenly distributed. If the traditional assumption of perfect rationality on the part of economic agents is abandoned, the issue of the efficiency of the allocation of property rights through privatization is no longer trivial: the highest bidder must no longer necessarily have the most productive use for a firm. The efficiency of privatization depends on how the two scarce factors of capital and economic competence are allocated.

Not all of the sections of this study are based on the realistic assumption of bounded rationality. In a discussion of the problem of restricted bidder competition (Chapter 3.4), the principal-agent problems involved in the granting of rehabilitation subsidies (Chapter 7), and the question of rehabilitation by the Treuhandanstalt (Chapter 8) are, in keeping with the formal apparatus involved, based on the more restrictive assumption of perfect rationality. Since both cases entail an analysis of the problem of imperfect and asymmetrically distributed information, the conclusions are, in my opinion, not impaired fundamentally by the unrealistic assumptions of rationality.

The study's line of argument is developed in three steps. The investigation starts out by inquiring into the theoretical grounds on which the privatization of the state economic sector in the transition countries is based. Two aspects are distinguished in dealing with this question. The first is addressed in a discussion of whether private ownership constitutes a necessary condition for the *coherence* of a market economy. The second involves an examination of the theoretical arguments that speak in favor of the assumption that the structure of ownership relations has an influence on the *efficiency* of enterprises (Chapter 2).

The allocative and efficiency effects of different privatization procedures are analyzed in the second step. Proceeding from the hypothesis that privatization gives rise to nontrivial transaction costs, the *allocative effects* of the most important privatization procedures are subjected to a comparative analysis (Chapter 3). Privatization not only influences the efficiency of an economic system, it also affects the *distribution* of social wealth and individual life-chances. Privatization is therefore, in all of the countries in transition , the focal point of a political debate as fierce as it is controversial. Based on the normative criteria of John Rawls' theory of justice, the study discusses the most important arguments posed by this debate and analyzes the distributive and welfare effects of different privatization strategies (Chapter 4).

The third and final step looks into the Treuhandanstalt's privatization strategy in Eastern Germany. The success of a privatization strategy depends on the *economic* and *institutional framework* involved. The study thus looks straight away at the consequences of the German economic and monetary union and the transformation of Eastern Germany's legal system for the privatization of Eastern German enterprises (Chapter 5). The analysis of the Treuhandanstalt's privatization strategy is based on the theoretical arguments developed in Chapters 3 and 4. Chapter 6 looks into the capital requirements of privatization resulting from the value of the assets held by the Treuhandanstalt, the choice of privatization procedures, the restriction of bidding competition imposed by the Treuhandanstalt's privatization strategy, and the empirical results of the privatization process in Eastern Germany.

The Treuhandanstalt's privatization policy is the subject of a controversial debate. At the heart of this controversy is the issue of whether the Treuhandanstalt should have rehabilitated the firms it holds before privatizing them. This study discusses the issue of *privatization versus rehabilitation* in a somewhat different light: the Treuhandanstalt grants to the buyers of firms extensive rehabilitation subsidies in the form of price rebates and negative selling prices. These rehabilitation subsidies are paid to achieve political and social goals in Eastern Germany. In view of an asymmetrical distribution of information, buyers are able to pocket some of these rehabilitation subsidies by misreporting the costs of rehabilitation investments (Chapter 7). The study therefore uses a game-theory model to discuss the issue of whether the funds might be better used to rehabilitate enterprises *before* they are privatized, or whether it makes more sense to pay rehabilitation subsidies to the buyer *following* privatization. The formal framework used to compare private- and public-sector rehabilitation regimes is not broad enough to cover all aspects of Eastern Germany's transformation process. The arguments in favor of a rehabilitation of firms by the Treuhandanstalt or by private buyers are therefore, by way of conclusion, discussed with an eye to the dynamic aspects of the privatization process in Eastern Germany (Chapter 8).

This study was originally completed in October of 1993 and submitted to the Johann Wolfgang Goethe Universität, Frankfurt/Main, as a doctoral dissertation. The data have been updated for the present book publication. To the extent that it was possible, the author has, in revising the manuscript, taken account of the literature on privatization in Eastern Germany that has appeared since October of 1993.

2   Why Privatization?

The question of ownership plays a key role in the transformation concepts of the transition countries in Central and Eastern Europe. This
issue marks the crossing point from reform to transformation. While
the reforms of the economic systems in Poland, Hungary and the Soviet
Union during the seventies and the eighties included the abandonment
of mandatory planning and the partial liberalization of prices,[1] the institutionalization of a regime of private property rights and the privatization of the state economic sector was ruled out until the break down of
the Berlin Wall.[2]

From an economic perspective, the close correlation between the issue
of ownership and the system question is by no means self-evident: the
ownership issue never played a central role in traditional microeconomics until the New Institutional Economics entered the picture
(Vickers/Yarrow 1988, 1). This can be attributed to the fact that the
prevailing paradigm of microeconomics, general equilibrium theory, is
indifferent toward different forms of ownership (Pareto 1910, 364).
Walrasian microeconomics shifted into the center of microeconomic
thinking the allocation of given initial endowments and production
factors to given ends. It can for that reason be interpreted as a "theory
of disposition" or a "theory of possession" (Riese 1990, 20) that systematically brackets out the role ownership plays in allocation (Riese
1990, 4, 22). Seen from this theoretical angle, the organizational principle of resource allocation is the constitutive feature of an economic
system, and not the issue of ownership. This is also true of the Freiburg
School's theory of comparative systems analysis, developed by Walter
Eucken. It conceives of systems as being differentiated in terms of
whether they set up plans centrally or decentrally (Eucken 1965, 78-79;
1975, 58-62), and the issue of ownership is logically subordinate to this
(Eucken 1975, 196). In conceptual terms, what is mirrored in the distinction between planned and market economies, is the organizational
principle of resource allocation as the system criterion, whereas the
issue of ownership defines the crucial difference between socialism
and capitalism (Riese 1991, 129; Bauer 1992, 297).

With the development of the various approaches of the New Institutional Economics, above all the theories of property rights, transaction
costs, and agency costs, neoclassical microeconomics was expanded to
include information costs and transaction costs, and thus opened up to
an analysis of institutional phenomena (Furubotn/Richter 1991; Williamson 1990, 71; Eggertsson 1991). The approaches of the New Institutional Economics are here supplemented by developments in game
theory made during the past two decades. Game theory has created a
formal apparatus that can be used in particular to examine the problem
of imperfect and asymmetrically distributed information in institutions
(Fudenberg/Tirole 1992). Seen in terms of these theories, the incentive
and sanction structure of different forms of ownership has a significant
influence on the economic behavior of individuals and economic institutions. Ownership has thus become a relevant category for explaining
economic activity.

This chapter will discuss the theoretical arguments in favor of the institutionalization of a regime of private ownership and the privatization of
the state economic sector. For analytical reasons, two factors are separated in discussing the issue of ownership: the question of *coherence*
and the question of *efficiency* of economic systems with private and
public regimes of ownership. Different theories are drawn upon here to
deal with these two issues: the issue of the coherence of economic systems cannot be settled within the Walrasian theoretical tradition,
which is indifferent toward the institutional foundations of an economic system. For this reason, János Kornai's theory of shortage has been
selected here as a starting point for the discussion of the systems problem; Kornai's theory is concerned with the question of the institutional conditions of the microeconomic coherence of economic systems.
The discussion then goes on to consider the role of ownership for the
coherence of reform and transformation strategies in the transition
countries (2.1).

The efficiency problem stands in the center of the historical debate on
economic accounting in socialism. While Friedrich Hayek and Ludwig
von Mises, two representatives of the Austrian School, disputed the
possibility of efficient allocation in an economic system whose means

of production have been nationalized, a number of socialist economists, using the tools of Walrasian equilibrium theory, have sought to prove that a socialist economy can achieve Pareto-optimal allocation. At the heart of this theoretical and ideological dispute is the question of whether, within the framework of a static theory that abstracts from all information and incentive problems, it is possible to deal meaningfully with the problem of ownership (2.2).

The theoretical framework of general equilibrium theory has been expanded to include a number of approaches that can be summarized under the heading of "New Institutional Economics." What is common to these approaches is that they extend neoclassical microeconomics to include information and transaction costs, thus opening the way to an analysis of institutional phenomena. They compare the comparative advantages of various institutional arrangements symmetrically, within a framework of market and bureaucracy failure. These approaches have, however, not developed a theory that can be applied irrespective of the framework of economic systems; as a rule they investigate individual institutional arrangements and rules under a given framework of order. These theories are therefore unable to contribute much to explaining the functional problems of planned economies, except for the general thesis that they violate the norm of efficiency compared to free markets. But they are suited to analyze the efficiency of different institutional rules and forms of ownership in the context of a market economy. This issue is of central significance for the privatization discussion: under the assumption that the institutional framework of a market economy is already given, the approaches can be used to analyze the efficiency of private and public forms of ownership. In historical terms, the institutionalization of a market-oriented framework has preceded privatization in the transformation processes in Central and Eastern Europe. And it is for that reason that findings on the potential returns of privatization may be expected from a comparative analysis of the efficiency of private and public forms of ownership (2.3).

2.1   Ownership and the Coherence of Economic Systems

In the reform discussion underway in the countries in transition, the issue of ownership has been highlighted by a study concerned with a macroeconomic problem: János Kornai's theory of shortage (Kornai 1980). Chronic shortage of resources has been a universal phenomenon of all Soviet-type economic systems. In contrast to neoclassical approaches, Kornai does not explain shortage as pent-up inflation due to an excessive supply of money at fixed prices (Cassel 1987); he instead assumes that the cause is to be found in the institutional structure underlying the economic system (Kornai 1980, 802; 1992, 262). This poses the question of the institutional conditions of the macroeconomic coherence of economic systems (2.1.1). The failure of market-socialist economic reforms that abandoned central mandatory planning and liberalized the administrative price system, while at the same time largely ruling out private ownership and the formation of private capital, can be explained against the background of this theory as a violation of the condition of coherence entailed by a hard budget constraint (2.1.2). This then makes it possible to infer the logical conditions for the transformation of a Soviet-type economic system (2.1.3).

2.1.1   Market Regimes and Ownership

The starting point of Kornai's theory of shortage is his description of the dichotomy of two market regimes, sellers markets with shortage and buyers markets with surplus (Kornai 1975, 231; 1980, 26; 1992, 243). Kornai's analysis of shortage starts out at the production level (Kornai 1980, 26-30; 1992, 262-280). He formulates the problem of production in different economic systems as a problem of linear programming under system-specific constraints (Kornai 1980, 23). He distinguishes three constraints: the resource constraint as a physical barrier of production, the demand constraint as a barrier to any potential sales of goods, and the budget constraint as a financial barrier posed by revenues and stocks of assets, which may not be overstepped by spending and debt (Kornai 1980, 23). As a physical constraint, the resource constraint is given by the environment of an economic system, while the two others are behavioral constraints determined by the institutions of an economic system. Kornai elevates the constraints of production to the level of a system criterion: while socialist economic systems produce at the limit imposed by the resource constraint ("resource-constrained systems"), production in capitalist economic systems is "demand-constrained" (Kornai 1980, 26).

The concept of the "soft budget constraint" (Kornai 1980, 299; 1986) assumes a key role in the explanation of shortage: the concept of a budget constraint as a secondary condition of the maximization of individual utility is borrowed from the microeconomic theory of households (Kornai 1986, 4) and applied to enterprises in socialist economic systems. The soft budget constraint determines the behavior of economic agents via their expectations for the future. While ex post the following identity holds for the flows and stocks of money in any economic system

Monetary assets (t_0) + monetary revenues =
monetary expenditures + monetary assets (t_1)

ex ante this identity is no longer given under the conditions of a soft budget constraint. The budget constraint is hard when the expectations of economic agents indicate to them that they will have to cover their expenses from their revenues and their stocks of assets. The higher the subjective probability that growing expenditures will be covered by external allowances, the softer the budget constraint (Kornai 1986, 4). In this sense the budget constraint can be defined as a postulate of the rational planning of economic agents (Kornai 1986, 4; 1980, 309).

The institutional conditions of a soft budget constraint are for Kornai soft prices influenced by firms, soft subsidies and allowances achieved by enterprises through bargaining, soft taxes that are not calculated as per clear-cut rules and hence can be influenced by the firms concerned, and soft loans that are not called in accordance with strict criteria (Kornai 1980, 302; 1986, 5). Kornai treats the cases of a perfectly hard budget constraint and a perfectly soft budget constraint as theoretical extreme cases. A budget constraint is perfectly soft if it poses no effective constraint to the behavior of a firm or any other economic agent. In classical, Soviet-type planned economies, enterprises are provided with a nearly soft budget constraint, whereas in the era of liberal capitalism in Great Britain and the USA in the last two centuries the budget constraint was close to hard (Kornai 1980, 311).

A soft budget constraint entails far-reaching consequences for the rational behavior of firms: under the behavioral hypothesis that management will be interested in expanding its enterprise (Kornai 1980, 23, 61), the demand of firms with a soft budget constraint is in principle unlimited, adjustments to changes in relative prices are not made, and the function of money is reduced to the role of a passive unit of account (Kornai 1980, 306; 1986, 9). The behavior of economic agents under a soft budget constraint entails a tendency to hoard goods, with "shortage breeds shortage" (Kornai 1992, 286).

While Kornai, in an earlier model, perceived no connection between an economic system's ownership regime and the phenomenon of chronic resource shortage (Kornai 1975, 301), the concept of the soft budget constraint shifts the issue of ownership into the center of the analysis. For Kornai, the phenomenon of the soft budget constraint results from the relationship between state and microorganization (Kornai 1980, 562). The state's paternalist behavior is the direct explanation for the soft budget constraint of economic agents. True, paternalism is a phenomenon universal to all modern societies (Kornai 1980, 566), but it is much more marked in socialist economic systems, because in them a direct relationship is constituted between state and enterprises via the regime of ownership:

"The social ownership of the means of production is accompanied by an active role for state power in the economy. (...) The central authorities take responsibility for the economic situation and, at the same time, they want to use every instrument in the armory which they deem useful" (Kornai 1980, 566; see also Kornai 1992, 495).

Kornai does not fully clarify the theoretical relevance of the soft budget constraint for explaining the phenomenon of shortage, and the issue

remains disputed. Paul Hare summarizes the criticism in the thesis that
the idea of the soft budget constraint explains both too much and too
little (Hare 1989, 72). Too much, because the model fails to consider
the institutional environment of enterprises, in particular the constraints
of the planning system, although it is claimed that the phenomenon of
shortage can be explained only with recourse to the planning process
itself (Soós 1984). Too little, because the phenomenon of the soft budget constraint, as Kornai himself emphasizes, also occurs in capitalist
market economies, without giving rise there to the system-specific phenomenon of shortage. The soft budget constraint can therefore explain
inefficiency, but not shortage (Gomulka 1986).

So there remains a gap in Kornai's explanation of the macroeconomic
disequilibrium of shortage with reference to the soft budget constraint.
Hajo Riese (Riese 1990; 1991) has attempted to close this theoretical
gap with reference to a monetary-Keynesian approach. In analogy to
Kornai, Riese distinguishes the market regimes of a sellers' market
with resource shortage in socialist economic systems and a buyers'
market with resource surpluses in capitalist economic systems (Riese
1990, 11). Riese traces the existence of buyers' markets as the prevailing market regime back to the monetary constitution of capitalist economic systems: the logical condition of buyers' markets is the contrived scarcity of money. In goods markets this contrived scarcity of money corresponds, as a complementary phenomenon, to the underemployment or excess supply of resources (Riese 1991, 132). For Riese,
the contrived scarcity of money in capitalist market economies rests on
the two conditions of a private credit supply and a state-sector regulation of the money supply. The private credit supply is conditioned on the
liquidity preference of the owner of assets. The owner of assets as
creditor temporarily transfers purchasing power to his debtor as a holder of assets, receiving in return a claim to interest on top of his claim
to repayment. The credit supply is restricted by the creditor's interest in
seeing his credit repaid and in realizing his claim to interest (Riese
1990, 24). The repayment of the credit, including interest, compels the
debtor to operate profitably, because the economic existence of his
enterprise depends on it (Riese 1991, 134; 1990, 83). The necessary
condition for realizing a claim to interest is government regulation of

the money supply, since it is this that guarantees that money remains tight, thus safeguarding the claim to interest of the owner of assets (Riese 1990, 74). For Riese, the institutionalization of a market-oriented monetary constitution is therefore linked to the question of ownership: it is the private formation of wealth and the private claim to interest that make up a market-type monetary constitution in the first place (Riese 1990, 74).

The corporate budget constraint described by Kornai at the microlevel presupposes for Riese a "universal budget constraint of the market system" (Riese 1991, 132) at the macrolevel, and this budget constraint is created by a monetary constitution and a monetary policy that guarantee that money will remain tight (Riese 1990, 9; 1991, 132). An economic system with mandatory planning will necessarily violate this budget constraint: the coherence of a planned economy is established via mandatory planning with quantitative output targets, all other allocation mechanisms being subordinate to it (Riese 1990, 32). Money and prices play a merely subordinate, passive role in a system with mandatory planning. The planning system supplies enterprises with the funds they require to meet their output targets (Kornai 1992, 131; Dembinski 1988). In other words, money is no longer tight. Instead of money, the economic agents hoard goods as a means of safeguarding their wealth (Riese 1990, 68). The consequence is a self-reproducing shortage of goods (Riese 1991, 132; Kornai 1980, 100). For Riese the soft budget constraint of enterprises then loses its relevance as a causal explanation of shortage, in his theory it is instead the necessary consequence of the primacy of mandatory planning (Riese 1990, 68).

Kornai's theory of shortage and the way in which it was expanded by Riese in a monetary-Keynesian theory lead to a distinction between two economic systems each of whose macroeconomic coherence is linked to an ownership regime: on the one hand the coherence of a decentral market economy is created through tight money at the macrolevel and a hard corporate budget constraint at the microlevel. The scarcity of money is in turn linked with a privately acquired claim to interest, while a hard corporate budget constraint is associated with private ownership of the means of production. The coherence of an

economic system with mandatory planning, on the other hand, presupposes at the macrolevel the primacy of quantitative output targets over
money supply, which in turn is not consonant with private control of
the supply of the credit. At the microlevel the primacy of mandatory
planning presupposes a soft corporate budget constraint. The two
macroeconomic disequilibria of resource shortage and resource surplus
(i.e. the underemployment of resources) correspond to the different
principles of order on which these economic systems are based.

2.1.2   The Incoherence of Market-socialist Reforms

Historically, the process of transformation in the Central and Eastern
Europe was preceded by failure to reform the economic systems. The
radical economic reforms introduced, for instance, in Czechoslovakia
in 1967, in Hungary in 1968 through the New Economic Mechanism,
in Poland in the 1980s, in the Soviet Union through Perestroika in the
Gorbachev era, and in China and the former Yugoslavia as well,
decentralized economic decision-making, at times going as far as to
abandon completely mandatory planning and liberalized the system of
price formation (Bauer 1987; Kosta 1984; Kornai 1992). But these reforms did rule out private property in the core areas of the economy
and continue to regulate the supply of money and credit provided to
enterprises via a monobanking system (Bauer 1991, 111). In these reform processes, the issue of ownership was taboo, as this would have
implied the abolition of the economic and political system (Bauer
1984, 70). These reformed economic systems may be designated as
market socialism because they sought to link public ownership of the
means of production and a state-run monetary and credit system with a
decentral allocation of resources through markets (Kornai 1990, 58).
The market-socialist reform projects have failed in the sense that they
have violated the coherence-condition of decentral coordination
through markets and are therefore unable to provide the foundation for
a permanent, institutionally stable economic system (Kornai 1992,
500). Tamás Bauer defined the coherence problem in the term "neither
plan nor market" (Bauer 1983, 310): the coherence of the economic
system is no longer brought about by means of mandatory output plans,

although, owing to the soft corporate budget constraint, it is not created by the market either (Bauer 1983, 310; 1980). What happens instead is that a consensual system of bureaucratic control is reorganized between state and enterprises (Antal 1979; Tardos 1980; Bauer 1976). This system of "vegetative control" (Bauer 1983, 311) safeguards the supply of enterprises and consumers alike by means of indirect instruments such as government orders and subsidies (Bauer 1983; 1987; Kornai 1986). What these systems have in common is that they - though they have succeeded in improving the supply of goods available to the population in the consumer goods markets - have not overcome the system-specific disequilibrium of shortage (Bauer 1991, 112; Lipton/Sachs 1990; Kornai 1992). The process of price liberalization saw, apart from shortage, the emergence of a phenomenon that occurred frequently, though not invariably (Bauer 1991, 107), and was largely unknown in the classical planning system: open inflation (Kornai 1992, 548; Bauer 1991, 112).

Seen in terms of the analysis conducted above, the market-socialist reforms failed due to a market-logical defect (Riese 1990, 46): the abandonment of mandatory planning and the liberalization of the price system created conditions necessary, but not sufficient, for the introduction of a decentral market system. At the microeconomic level, the condition for the coherence of decentral allocation was violated by the soft budget constraint of the state-owned business sector. As Kornai has shown in his analysis of shortage, marked by his specific experience of the Hungarian economic reform, the price system is unable to take on an allocative function as long as the enterprises are fitted out with a soft budget constraint (Kornai 1980). At the macroeconomic level, the constraint of tight money was violated, and it is this that constitutes the logical condition for the substitution of hoarding of resources by the formation of monetary wealth, and with it the transformation of the economy of shortage economy (Riese 1990, 49; Lipton/Sachs 1990, 89). Consequently, deregulation by abandoning mandatory planning and administrative price controls led to numerous undesired effects, such as reproduction and intensification of shortage (Kornai 1980, 486), pressure on wages, and inflation (Lipton/Sachs 1990, 106; Bauer 1991, 112). The reproduction of a vegetative system of bureaucratic control is the consequence, and not, as has often been assumed, the cause of the market defects. It was the condition necessary to create the coherence of market-socialist economic systems.

2.1.3   Ownership and Transformation

The market defects of the market-socialist economic systems led to a radicalization of the reform discussion in Central and Eastern European countries, until, finally, the system question itself was posed (Kornai 1986). According to the analysis conducted above, the coherence of an economic system with decentralized decision-making processes coordinated through markets requires at the macrolevel a monetary constraint created by a monetary constitution that ensures that money remains tight; what is required at the microlevel is a hard corporate budget constraint. Both conditions are bound up with the issue of ownership: the monetary constraint of tight money requires, aside from a monetary policy, formation of capital on a private basis, the microeconomic budget constraint calls for denationalization of the business sector:

> "In the absence of central planning, the financial system becomes the centerpiece of resource allocation. However, the financial system is essentially capitalist" (Hinds 1992).

In the transformation debate, both conditions of coherence are discussed at length under the concepts *macroeconomic stabilization* and privatization (Lipton/Sachs 1990; Kornai 1990). Apart from the choice of a transformation strategy and the sequencing of reform stages, one thing that these programs have in common is that their intent is on the one hand, at the macroeconomic level, to use a restrictive money supply and control of the process of credit to bring about a remonitarization of the economies concerned (Lipton/Sachs 1990; Kornai 1990; Nuti 1992; IMF/IBRD/OECD/EBRD 1991) and on the other hand, at the microeconomic level, to fit out enterprises with a hard budget constraint (Hinds 1992; Lipton/Sachs 1990, 115, 127; Kornai 1990, 57; Nuti 1991, 169). The salient points of the macroeconomic stabilization programs are the separation of the economic system's money supply from the creation of credit by institutionalizing a two-tier banking system, a restrictive interest policy and monetary policy, a control of the creation of credit by government banks, and limitation of effective demand by balancing public budgets (Kornai 1990, 172; Nuti 1991, 166; Hinds 1992, 122). The intention is for the state business sector to reach a hard budget constraint by means of administrative restraints and controls on the demand for investment goods, credit, and manpower (Kornai 1990, 60-80; Nuti 1991, 169; Lipton/Sachs 1990, 115-117). In other words, the conditions for a monetary constitution, which were called for by Riese and which guarantee that money remains tight, are set to be enforced.

The stability of these programs is under threat from two directions: the first stability problem arises due to the creation of credit by the commercial banks, which have as a rule developed from branch offices of the state monobank and are frequently interlinked through entangled ownership relations with their debtors. They can thus, in their roles as owners of capital, not clearly perceive themselves as creditors vis-à-vis the enterprises as their debtors (Hinds 1992, 122; Bauer 1991, 111). The second stability problem arises from the state-owned business sector itself; it is impossible to enforce any really hard budget constraint on it (Kornai 1990, 62; 1992, 495; Bauer 1991, 117). One important risk to stability is the practice, common among such enterprises, of providing one another with credit (Kornai 1990, 140). In both cases the intention is to substitute strong administrative controls for private ownership relations so as to limit risks to stability: aside from classical instruments of monetary policy such as high minimum reserve ratios and high interest rates (Nuti 1991, 167), the creation of credit by state-owned banks is also set to be restricted by central bank controls or controls exercised by other government institutions (Kornai 1990, 138; Lipton/Sachs 1990, 112). In the state business sector the demand for labor and wage levels are to be restrained by wage controls so as to prevent a wage-price spiral (Lipton/Sachs 1990, 115; Kornai 1990, 142-145).

In other words, two coherence problems have occurred in the transformation process, both of which are linked with the issue of ownership: the control of credit creation runs up against the problem that there is no sufficiently developed system of private capital formation, and the implementation of a hard corporate budget constraint is faced with the problem of public ownership. Unlike in the market-socialist economic systems, however, most countries in transition, by "remonetarizing" (Carrington 1992) their economies and decoupling their state business sectors from any direct access to public funds, have succeeded in transforming the market regime marked by sellers' markets with shortage into a market regime marked by buyers' markets with resource surpluses. The state business sector and the state credit system nevertheless continue to pose a threat to the coherence of the transformed economic systems. Numerous observers suspect that, in view of state-sector hegemony, the enterprises are not, like many state-owned firms in western industrial societies, subject to behavioral norms similar to those that are binding for private firms (Bauer 1991, 117; Kornai 1990, 59). Privatization is consequently necessary to create and safeguard the coherence of a market economy with decentralized decision-making processes.

2.2   Ownership and the Efficiency of Economic Systems

The question as to the possibility of efficient allocation in an economic system without private ownership of the means of production is at the heart of the debate triggered in 1920 by Ludwig von Mises on economic accounting in socialism (Mises 1920; 1922). Mises had denied any rationality to an economic system that abolishes private ownership of the means of production (Mises 1920, 104; 1922). According to his thesis, it is impossible to determine factor prices for capital without any trade in means of production, and without factor prices, in turn, it is impossible to evaluate and remunerate the contribution of individual production factors, so that rational economic accounting is impossible and money loses its function as a universal unit of account (Mises 1920). An efficient allocation of resources is consequently not possible in an economy without private means of production.

A number of socialist economists (Taylor 1938; Lerner 1937), including above all Oskar Lange in his famous article "On the economic
theory of socialism" (Lange 1938), responded to Mises' challenge by
seeking to solve within the framework of general equilibrium theory
the allocation problem that emerges when the means of production have been nationalized. Lange replaces the Walrasian auctioneer with a
central planning authority that uses trial and error to determine prices
for investment goods, while prices for consumer goods are set by the
market. The prices set by the planning authority are revised on the basis of observations of surpluses in supply and demand (Lange 1938,
280-282). Producers are forced to base their production decisions on
the prices set by the central authority as decision parameters (Lange
1938, 276). Corporate managers are also compelled to subject their
production decisions to two additional rules: first, the factor combination has to minimize average costs and ensure that the marginal productivity of all factors is equal, and, second, the output quantity must
be set in such a way that the marginal costs are equivalent to the price
of the product (Lange 1938, 273-275). It is then, in a state of equilibrium, possible for a socialist economy with nationalized means of production, just as it is for a capitalist economy, to achieve an allocation
that meets the efficiency criterion of the Pareto optimum. In other
words, Lange conceives of socialist planning as the simulation of a
general market equilibrium with perfect competition.

Yet Lange's solution deviates only in one crucial point from the Walrasian equilibrium model: his solution provides for trading at false
prices, i.e. before an equilibrium has been reached. The price revision
made by the planning authority is in this context something entirely
different from the Walrasian auctioneer's iteration process: it leads to
an iteration of completed allocation solutions, while in the Walrasian
model the allocative solution is reached only when the iteration is
complete (Richter 1992, 191; Riese 1990, 63; Lavoie 1988, 130). A
theoretical problem associated with general equilibrium theory, explaining the emergence of an equilibrium from an initial state of disequilibrium, thus becomes a practical problem in Lange's model (Lavoie
1988, 130). As is demonstrated by the so-called cobweb theorem, as
well as by more complex disequilibrium models (Hahn 1982; Hage-

mann/Kurz/Schäfer 1981), when trading is conducted at false prices, successive equilibria need not necessarily emerge; indeed, it is just as well possible for a disequilibrium to be reinforced in this way.[3] Later formalizations of Lange's model by Arrow and Hurwicz (Arrow/ Hurwicz 1960) and Malinvaud (Malinvaud 1967) circumvented this problem by permitting, in analogy to the *tâtonnement* process in Walras, transactions to take place only in a state of equilibrium, even when prices are set centrally (Richter 1992).

The question that arises beyond this logical problem is whether Lange's equilibrium solution constitutes a response to Mises' challenge of socialism. Lange can be accused of having made a categorial error[4]: as was demonstrated by Friedrich Wieser (Wieser 1899), Vilfredo Pareto (Pareto 1910, 364; 1897), and his pupil Barone (Barone 1935), general equilibrium theory is indifferent toward different institutions and economic systems. Also the existence of an equilibrium can thus be demonstrated logically by the formation of shadow prices for an economic system with nationalized means of production (Wagener 1979), but this proof is not relevant to an analysis of the ownership problem:

> *"If we posses all the relevant information, if we can start out from a given system of preferences, and if we command the complete knowledge of available means, the problem which remains is purely one of logic. (...) This, however, is emphatically not the problem which society faces"* (Hayek 1945, 77).

Hayek and Mises raise two fundamental objections to socialist economic systems which are not addressed by Lange in his model: the first objection refers to problems associated with information and incentives, the second aims at the dynamic adaptability of economic systems with nationalized means of production. Lange's model presupposes complete information, or, in modern terminology, the absence of transaction costs. The central planning authority must on the one hand be informed completely on the supply of and demand for all goods in order to be able to set equilibrium prices; on the other hand it must have knowledge of production technologies and available resources in order to enforce the rules according to which average costs can be minimized and to set optimal output volumes for corporate management (Lavoie 1988, 147). Hayek objects that the basic problem of any economic system lies in the fragmentation of economically relevant knowledge among numerous individuals (Hayek 1945, 520). The comparative disadvantages of a centrally planned economy as opposed to one coordinated decentrally through the market result from the problem that the economically pertinent knowledge is not available in its entirety for the central planning institutions. For Hayek this is not a question of process and storage capacities but one concerning the communication of knowledge. Like Herbert Simon after him (Simon 1972), Hayek assumes that economically relevant knowledge is idiosyncratic in character and cannot be articulated verbally or graphically, which consequently renders it inaccessible to processing by a central planning authority (Hayek 1945, 523-524). For Hayek it is here that the comparative advantage of individual plans and actions is decentrally coordinated by the price system: a decentral price system reduces the complex structure of means and ends governing the use of goods to the one single economically pertinent variable, information on the value of a good. It is in this way possible to communicate economically relevant information between individuals and to coordinate their actions, even if the knowledge behind the process remains distributed across numerous individuals (Hayek 1945, 528-529). Hayek does not assume that in a changing world this coordination will be perfect in the sense of a general equilibrium. But nonetheless, for Hayek the decentral coordinative performance of the price system is without doubt superior to central planning; he refers to it as an evolutionary "marvel" (Hayek 1945, 527).

For Hayek and Mises, price system efficiency is closely linked to the issue of incentives and competition (Mises 1936, 137; Hayek 1940, 197). Unlike the case of Lange's model, prices are here viewed by firms not as data but as strategic variables. While for Lange the issue of management's incentives to minimize costs remains an open one, for Hayek and Mises firms in an economic system with private ownership enter into competition for the discovery of cost-effective production techniques (Hayek 1940, 195-202). The driving force behind this com-

petitiveness is price competition, which, by definition, is ruled out in a
system with parametric prices (Hayek 1940, 196). For Hayek the market's competition mechanism generates in the first place the information that is presupposed in Lange and other models of equilibrium theory
(Hayek 1940, 196; Lavoie 1988, 123). The condition for this is in turn
a structure of incentives that is created by private ownership in the first
place. For Hayek and Mises, the ideal case is the one in which those
who make the pertinent production decisions also reap the returns and
bear the costs of their decisions (Hayek 1940, 188).

In other words, by interpreting the cost-minimizing factor combination
not as a statistical problem concerned in the rational choice between
given means but as a dynamic problem involving the discovery of new
production techniques, the Austrians linked the question of rational
price formation with the issue of competition and the incentives offered
by private ownership (Kirzner 1984). This points the way to the second
objection raised by the Austrians against Lange's equilibrium solution
of the allocation problem: Lange's equilibrium model assumes a static
world, while real economic systems are forced to solve the allocation
problem under dynamic, rapidly changing conditions of the economic
environment (Mises 1949, 244; Hayek 1948, 192). For Mises and
Hayek, the system question is not: what economic system is more apt
to reach a hypothetical equilibrium. It is rather: what economic system
is able to adjust more rapidly to disequilibria under the conditions of
incomplete information and uncertainty (Hayek 1948, 188). Mises and
Hayek thus base their argumentation on a decision problem different
from Lange's: while Lange, in the tradition of general equilibrium
theory, deals with the problem of economic decision-making as the
optimization of the choice between given means and given preferences,
the matter of concern to Hayek and Mises is the decision problem of
individuals in the face of uncertainty, with ends and means constantly
changing (Mises 1949, 100-104; Kirzner 1973, 26; Lavoie 1988, 78).
The dynamics of the capitalist economy results from the discovery of
new products and production techniques, motivated by the realization
of arbitrage profits. The search for new arbitrage opportunities is therefore invariably associated with disequilibria. Competition subjects these arbitrage profits to a process of constant erosion, and this results in a

trend toward equilibrium, though it in turn is disrupted by continuous discoveries of new products and production techniques[5]. A model which, like Lange's, calls on individuals to use prices as parameters must therefore, in the eyes of the Austrians, fail in coordinating actions and expectations under uncertainty (Richter 1992; 194).

The efficiency norms on which the debate on economic accounting in socialism are based are different ones: while Oskar Lange takes the Pareto optimum as his efficiency criterion, Hayek and Mises do not clearly define their efficiency norm (Murrell 1983, 94): For the Austrians, the primary criterion for the success of economic systems is not optimal allocation among given factor endowments with given preferences but the dynamic adaptability of an economic system with changing ends and means of the economic agents. Mises and Hayek then measure economic efficiency in terms of the coordination of individual plans under uncertainty and dynamic environmental conditions (Hayek 1945, 522-524; Lavoie 1988, 55). As opposed to the static efficiency concept of the Pareto optimum, their concept of efficiency is geared to the evolution of an economic system. Competition aims at the violation, not the realization, of a static equilibrium.

If the above-developed hypothesis is correct, that economic system with mandatory planning must necessarily violate the macrolevel budget constraint of tight money and the hard corporate budget constraint at the microlevel, the thesis postulated by Mises at the outset of the debate on economic accounting is validated: an economic system with central planning and state-owned means of production must abrogate the role of money as the universal indicator of scarcity. In an economic system whose coherence is created not by the tightness of money but by mandatory planning, the efficiency norms (Wagener 1979, 290-298) of a liberal economy are, in contrast to what Lange sought to prove with his socialism model, necessarily violated (Riese 1991, 130-133): the norm of static allocative efficiency is violated because in an economic system with quantitative planning and a soft corporate budget constraint prices have an accounting function, but no allocative function (Riese 1991, 131). Productive efficiency, too, in terms of H. Leibenstein's "X-efficiency" (Leibenstein 1966), must be low in an economic system whose coherence presupposes a soft corporate budget constraint (Kornai 1992, 293; 1986, 10; Riese 1991, 135).

Now, the static efficiency norms of equilibrium theory cannot be a yardstick for a comparative analysis of the efficiency of economic systems, because these norms are, of course, also violated in market economies with a regime of private ownership. In Hayek's sense, however, economic systems with central planning and a soft budget constraint give rise to lower levels of planning coordination on the part of economic agents and lower levels of dynamic efficiency, because in a system with in-kind quantitative planning, competition for the discovery of new products and production techniques is replaced by competition for state allocations of resources (Kornai 1986, 9; Gomulka 1986, 87). As an economic system with nationalized means of production and mandatory planning, socialism is consequently not impossible, though it does, owing to its functional logic, give rise to lower expectations of dynamic efficiency than economic systems with a private ownership regime and decentral coordination through markets:

> *"What can be verified empirically is no more than that societies which make use of all possible techniques of competition achieve this result in a much higher measure than others (...)"* (Hayek 1969, 250).

2.3   The Transaction Costs of Alternative Ownership Regimes

The equilibrium solution of the allocation problem in socialism, as developed by Oskar Lange, was not an adequate response to the challenge of Ludwig von Mises, because it systematically excluded the costs of coordinating economic decision-making. In their critique of Lange, on the other hand, Mises and Hayek emphasized the costs of coordination and decision-making through central planning. Yet this critique is based on a certain asymmetry: while the costs and problems of bureaucratic coordination are dealt with extensively, the coordination of economic decision-making through the price system in markets is addressed as a "marvel" (Hayek 1945, 527).

Since Oskar Lange, the neoclassical theoretical tradition has given rise to a good number of theories and approaches that deal with the costs of economic coordination, thus opening up microeconomics for an analysis of institutional problems. These approaches may be categorized under the term New Institutional Economics (Furubotn/Richter 1991; Eggertsson 1990; Williamson 1990). The most important areas addressed by the New Institutional Economics are the theories of property rights (Coase 1960; Demsetz 1967; 1964; Furubotn/Pejovich 1972), public choice,[6] transaction costs (Williamson 1975; 1985), and agency (Arrow 1986). These approaches differ from Walrasian microeconomics in their orientation in terms of contract theory. They deal symmetrically with the problem of coordinating economic decisions and activities, viewing it within the framework of failure of markets and bureaucracies (Richter 1992, 194). The New Institutionalist analysis focuses on the information and transaction costs involved in the conclusion of contracts (Williamson 1990, 61; Markl 1990, 2). In their most general form, transaction costs can be defined, with Kenneth Arrow, as the operating costs of economic systems (Arrow 1983, 43). These costs arise on the one hand from the expenses involved in the emergence, support, and change of institutions and on the other hand from the preparation, the conclusion, and the enforcement of contracts (Furubotn/Richter 1991, 8-9). Arrow distinguishes three sources of transaction costs: (1) the costs for the enforcement and the support of property rights (exclusion costs), (2) communication and information, and (3) disequilibria (Arrow 1983, 51). The difference between production costs and transaction costs is that production costs are contingent on the technologies deployed and the preferences of economic agents; these costs are the same in all economic systems. Transaction costs, on the other hand, are influenced by the organization of resource allocation, and thus by the institutions of an economic system (Arrow 1983, 51; Williamson 1985, 19). The distinction between production costs and transaction costs is of a purely heuristic nature; economic agents will minimize both production costs and transaction costs alike (Furubotn/Richter 1991, 8).

The concept of efficiency on which the New Institutional Economics bases its approaches in assessing institutional alternatives has not been fully clarified. Some representatives of property rights theory use a concept than can be described as "constrained maximation" (DeAlessi 1983; Demsetz 1969; Furubotn/Pejovich 1972). They generalize the concept of individual utility maximization and apply it to all problems of individual choice, i.e. including the choice between different institutions. Efficiency is in this case no longer measured in terms of a first-best optimum, but in terms of the given alternatives under consideration of all pertinent constraints and costs, including transaction costs (Demsetz 1969, 1):

> "(...) efficiency is being defined as constrained maximization. Efficiency conditions are seen as the properties of a determined (equilibrium) solution implied by a given theoretical construct. On this view, in a system solutions are always efficient if they meet the constraints that characterize it" (DeAlessi 1983, 69).

This approach can be criticized as tautological in that, depending on effective preferences and constraints, any institution can be defined as efficient (Eggertsson 1990, 20; Furubotn/Richter 1991, 13). The problem is that, unlike the case of the usual maximization problems, the choice between different institutions cannot be represented as a choice between given alternatives, since the space open to institutional alternatives is infinite and continues to develop over the course of time (Furubotn/Richter 1991, 14). This is the reason why there is no clear-cut concept of efficiency in the New Institutional Economics. Instead, its proponents as a rule assess pragmatically individual institutional alternatives with an eye to their comparative advantages (Williamson 1990, 48; Furubotn/Richter 1991, 14). This institutional comparison refers as a rule to a given basic institutional structure. In his famous analysis of the emergence of property rights, Harold Demsetz, for example, presupposes a society's preference for a private or public ownership regime as given (Demsetz 1974).

In order to limit the complexity of analysis, the New Institutionalist approaches are, in other words, forced to regard as given the greater part of a system of institutions and to investigate only individual institutional variables. As regards the individual subjects investigated, the New Institutional Economics has developed different lines of thought which, like the property rights approaches, examine individual variables of an economic system's institutional environment or, like transaction cost theory, examine individual arrangements within the given environment of an economic system (Davis/North 1971, 6; Williamson 1990, 64).

The approaches developed by the New Institutional Economics are drawn upon here to deal with two questions. The first question concerns the institutional alternative involved in coordination of economic activities through markets or bureaucracies (2.3.1). The second question is concerned with the comparative advantages of private and state-owned enterprises in supplying private (2.3.2) and public goods (2.3.3). The investigation of these two questions presupposes a free-market regime, i.e. free price formation, no mandatory planning, and safeguards for the freedom of contract. As regards the transformation of the Soviet-type economies, the issue is, in other words, the efficiency of state-owned and private property rights under a free-market framework, i.e. the potential returns of privatization.

2.3.1   Market Failure versus Bureaucratic Failure

The comparative advantages of alternative approaches to coordinating and organizing economic activity is the classical subject of transaction cost theory. Ronald Coase posed this question in his famous 1937 article in terms of the institutional alternatives involved in coordination of economic activities by markets or firms (Coase 1937). Coase sees the choice between the hierarchic coordination of economic activities in firms and decentral coordination through the price system in markets as stemming from the relative magnitude of the transaction costs incurred in each case. This explanation is open to the charge of tautology, if the concept of transaction costs is not operationalized (Alchian/Dem-

setz 1972, 783; Williamson 1985, 4; 1975, 4). The most differentiated
operationalization of the concept was developed by Oliver Williamson
(Williamson 1975; 1985). Williamson bases his theory on the behavioral assumptions of bounded rationality and opportunism. The assumption of bounded rationality is borrowed from Herbert Simon; it
proceeds from a limited cognitive capacity on the part of individuals,
i.e. what he assumes is a limited capacity to receive, process, and
communicate information (Simon 1967, XXIV; 1978). The assumption
of opportunism may be defined as "self-interest seeking with guile"
(Williamson 1975, 26) and it allows for uncooperative behavior on the
part of individuals, such as breach of contract. For Williamson the
problem of the organization of economic activities is a problem bound
up with the behavioral assumptions involved: in a world with perfect
rationality and without opportunism, the problem of the organization
and coordination of economic activities is, not unlike the case in
Hayek, trivial; central coordination through planning and decentral
coordination through markets lead to the same results (Williamson
1985, 57).

In a world with bounded rationality and opportunism, on the other
hand, the choice of the adequate form of coordination is conditioned on
specific transaction conditions: Williamson identifies as central variables for the choice of economic institutions uncertainty, frequency, and
asset-specificity. For Williamson, asset-specificity plays the key role in
explaining institutional arrangements: capital is asset-specific when it
is tied to the existence of a specific transaction relation and would lose
at least part of its value in a second best use. Asset specificity refers to
real capital and human capital alike. Under the assumption that uncertainty and the frequency or the duration of a transaction is given, the
deployment of asset-specific capital leads to a so-called "lock-in effect" (Williamson 1985, 53) between the parties to a transaction. Since,
in the case of bounded rationality and uncertainty, it is impossible to
enter into perfect contracts that contain a clear-cut agreement for every
possible state of the world, contracts, once concluded, must be adjusted
in any longer-term transaction relation. The problem with these adjustments is that once asset-specific investments have been made, there
is no more competition. The bargaining situation resembles a bilateral

monopoly, because the investor of asset-specific capital can realize the full returns on his investment only in the transaction relation with his bargaining partner, and the bargaining partner is unable to switch to another bidder when the investment concerned is asset-specific. The coordination of economic activities through the price system in markets is bound to fail in this situation. Depending on uncertainty, frequency, and the asset specificity of the capital employed, the contracting parties must develop governance structures adequate to the task of monitoring and adjusting imperfect contracts, and these structures must protect the capital employed under the constraints of bounded rationality and uncertainty against the risks posed by opportunistic behavior (Williamson 1985, 2).

In market economies there exist numerous institutional alternatives for coordinating economic activities. They can be arranged along a continuum marked on the one end by the classical paradigm of isolated barter in a market and on the other end by centralized hierarchic organization. Between these extremes there exist numerous mixed forms such as long-term supply agreements, franchising, cooperation agreements, etc. (Williamson 1985, 83). Williamson sees the rationale of the vertical integration of economic institutions in firms in the protection of asset-specific capital. Coordination of economic activities within a firm can defuse numerous problems of opportunistic behavior that arise when activities are coordinated through markets. As the integration of economic activities grows, however, the costs of bureaucratic decision-making and control increase: Williamson originally formulated the problem of bureaucratic failure as an information problem that, as organizations grow in size, leads to increasing losses of control and thus to growing costs stemming from opportunistic behavior (Williamson 1975, 20-40). This line of argument presupposes that, in organizational terms, firms extensively integrate all of their units. Organizational units can, however, also be integrated selectively. The integration within a firm is then restricted to the organizational elements and units which give rise to expectations of net returns when they are vertically integrated, while other elements are left in a state of disintegration. The flow of resources between the semiautonomous organizational units is then organized in the form of an internal capital market whose funds are allocated in terms of the expected return on investment. But if selective intervention is possible, i.e. an efficient combination of market-related and bureaucratic decision-making processes in firms, where is then the limit of bureaucratic coordination to be sought? To take up an old question posed by Lenin: why is aggregate production not concentrated in a "world trust" (Lenin 1929/1969, 11; Coase 1937, 394)?

Oliver Williamson, but also Oliver Hart and Sanford Grossmann in a model developed independently of Williamson (Grossmann/Hart 1986; Williamson 1985, 136), offer an answer to this question that is linked to the structure of ownership rights: when corporate units are integrated vertically under common ownership, the structure of incentives and sanctions that exists with separate ownership cannot be sustained. If, for example, integration is achieved by buying up an upstream company, the "residual right of control" (Grossmann/Hart 1986, 692) is transferred to the new owner. The change of ownership shifts the incentive structure: the manager of the integrated corporation is no longer its owner, and he consequently receives no residual income. The incentive structure of separate ownership rights cannot be simulated under the assumptions of bounded rationality and incomplete information: in an internal corporate accounting system, performance and misperformance cannot be attributed exactly, and are also open to manipulation. The manager of the integrated corporation has no long-term interest in safeguarding the firm's capital stock and can use disinvestment to raise corporate profits over the short run (Williamson 1985, 139), while the owner of the integrated corporation can manipulate internal corporate prices to lower the profits made by the integrated corporate unit (Grossmann/Hart 1986, 716). The assurance of a residual income is therefore not credible. It is thus only possible to agree on an incentive structure weaker than the one dominant in markets, and even this incentive structure can lead to high costs stemming from opportunistic behavior (Williamson 1985, 140). But if it is not possible for the management of an integrated corporation to appropriate a residual income, the management's incentive to invest personal effort in the corporation's productive efficiency will, ceteris paribus, be lower (Grossmann/Hart 1986, 716).

Apart from their incentive structure, vertical integration of corporations also - and this is presumably of even greater significance - alters their sanction structure: as compared with capital markets, corporations have privileged access to information on the risks and profit expectations of a corporate unit. This can on the one hand lead to a more efficient allocation of the capital employed, although on the other hand it can also entail an abrogation of the selection and sanction mechanisms of the market: while the persons concerned are forced to accept as accidental events the bankruptcy of a corporation or other extreme market events, internal corporate decisions require a rational justification (Williamson 1985, 151). The phenomenon of the soft budget constraint described by Kornai thus also occurs in major corporations and there, too, gives rise to a change in the rational behavior of the economic agents. This is basically an information problem: a corporation cannot commit itself to disregard the information provided by its organizational units. The privileged access to information enjoyed by bureaucratic organizations rules out the possibility of credibly threatening, and enforcing, ex post, the sanction mechanisms that obtain in markets. As compared with coordination of economic activities via markets, advantages associated with internal corporate auditing therefore weaken the sanction structure.

As compared with Hayek's thesis on the failure of planning, Williamson's transaction cost theory leads to a shift of emphasis:

> *"That markets are a 'marvel' is not disputed; to argue, however, that markets are the only marvel is detrimental to the study of economic organization"*
> (Williamson 1990, 67).

Williamson subjects the question of coordination to a symmetrical analysis within the framework of failure of markets and bureaucracies. In the presence of uncertainty and bounded rationality, coordination through markets fails for transactions that rely on asset-specific capital. Within vertically integrated organizations, on the other hand, asset-specific investments are easier to safeguard against the risks of opportunistic behavior, although this means that incentives will be smaller and sanctions weaker than would be the case with decentral coordination via markets. Thus as corporate size increases, the costs of bureaucratic coordination also rise. In the view of transaction cost theory, the evolutionary advantage of a market economy with a regime of private ownership is consequently not that central coordination of bureaucracies is replaced with decentral coordination through markets, but that it is possible to choose a more efficient mix between the two forms of coordination (Richter 1992, 195).

2.3.2   State Ownership versus Private Ownership

The substance and the structure of property rights, thus the underlying thesis of property rights theory, affect the allocation and the use of resources in specific and predictable ways (Furubotn/Pejovich 1972, 1139; Alchian 1987; DeAlessi 1980, 3). According to property rights theory, what is traded in markets is not physical resources but legal packages, or legal vectors (Demsetz 1974, 31; Coase 1978, 42; Wegehenkel 1981, 6). The sum of these rights may be designated as *property rights*. The term property rights is defined by Pejovich as "the socially and legally sanctioned behavioral relations between people who act in reference to the existence of scarce goods" (Pejovich 1982, 391; Furubotn/Pejovich 1972, 1139; Demsetz 1974, 31). As a special case of property rights, ownership, in the Roman legal tradition, includes the right of use (usus), the right to appropriate returns (usus fructus), and the right to alter and dispose of a good (abusus) (Furubotn/Pejovich 1972, 1140; Bromley 1989). Property rights are exclusive, i.e. they can entail the exclusion of third parties, though there are limitations on this: the scopes of action open to an owner are restricted by the social and legal norms of society (Furubotn/Pejovich 1972, 1140). The value of a good depends, ceteris paribus, on the package of rights associated with it (Furubotn/Pejovich 1972, 1139). The more precisely private property rights are defined and specialized, and the more intensive the social support they find (Demsetz 1964), the closer, according to property rights theory, is the relationship between individual utility and the returns and costs of an individual's decisions (DeAlessi 1980, 4). Consequently, the strength of an individual's incentives to take account of the social returns and costs of his decisions is directly proportionate to the unequivocalness with which private property rights are defined and enforced (DeAlessi 1980, 4). In the absence of transaction costs, thus the claim raised by the theorem named after Ronald Coase (Coase 1960), perfectly defined private property rights and freedom of contract are sufficient to ensure that all resources are evaluated at their opportunity costs and will be directed to their most productive use, independently of their initial allocation (Coase 1960; Furubotn/Pejovich 1972, 1143; DeAlessi 1980, 4).

In a world with positive transaction costs, it is not possible for all rights to be defined and specified, supported and traded (Demsetz 1964; 1974; DeAlessi 1980, 4). The property rights approaches also use positive transaction costs - the theory here overlaps with transaction cost theory - to explain the establishment and development of private firms. The property rights approaches see firms as a network of contracts (Alchian/Demsetz 1972, 783; Klein/Crawford/Alchian 1978, 326; DeAlessi 1982, 194). The concentration of control and decision-making rights in the hands of the owner-manager of a classical capitalist enterprise is explained with the solution of the control problem in team production (Alchian/Demsetz 1972; Klein/Crawford/Alchian 1978). The problem of the control and measurement of the contribution made by individual team members toward the aggregate product can, in the view of this approach, be solved by concentrating the right to the negotiation, monitoring, and control of contracts with one person who at the same time is given the right to appropriate the residual income (Alchian/Demsetz 1972, 783). The rights of control are assigned to the person who contributes the capital with the greatest asset specificity (DeAlessi 1982, 194; Grossmann/Hart 1986, 716), and whose contribution to the production process is most difficult to measure (Holmstrom/Tirole 1989, 73).

This theory proceeds on the assumption that rights of decision in the sense of the residual right to control and the right to appropriate residual income are united in one person. This ownership structure was characteristic of the classical capitalist firm, whose entrepreneur exercised both proprietary rights and control rights (Alchian/Demsetz 1972,

783). Now, in private firms the owners by no means always exercise themselves the residual right of control, instead often delegating it to a professional management. In the view of property rights theory, the separation of ownership and control leads to an "attenuation" of property rights (Furubotn/Pejovich 1972, 1149). The economic consequences of the separation of the rights of ownership and control have been discussed at length by the property rights approaches (Alchian 1969; Manne 1965; Furubotn/Pejovich 1972) and, in a more formal framework, by principal-agent theories (Jensen/Meckling 1976; Fama/Jensen 1983; Holmstrom/Tirole 1989; Vickers/Yarrow 1988). One finding that has emerged from this debate is that the scopes of discretionary action open to management are restricted by competition in the labor markets for managers, in the capital markets in which management performance is rated, in product markets, and through various internal control mechanisms. None of these markets and control mechanisms functions perfectly, and so management is left with some scope of discretionary action. The costs stemming from the separation of proprietary and decision-making rights are counterbalanced by returns stemming on the one hand from portfolio diversification and a greater degree of owner freedom to consume his wealth and on the other hand from the specialized qualifications of professional managers.[7] The crucial consideration for property rights theory is that this attenuation of property rights does not stem from legal restraints, but results voluntarily from the utility-maximizing behavior of owners. As long as owners voluntarily delegate their rights of decision to a professional management, it must, in the view of property rights theory, be expected that returns will exceed costs (Furubotn/Pejovich 1972, 1149-1150).

The structure of property rights in state-owned enterprises differs from property rights in private firms in terms of one central aspect: they cannot be transferred by the citizen as owner (DeAlessi 1980, 27). The nontransferability of publicly owned enterprises thus, in the view of the property rights approaches, leads to a situation in which expected returns of management decisions cannot be capitalized and the incentives to monitor management are consequently low (Picot/Kaulmann 1985, 964):

> *"Because property rights in the specialized assets*
> *of political enterprises are effectively nontrans-*
> *ferable, specialization in their ownership is ruled*
> *out. This inhibits the capitalization of future conse-*
> *quences into current transfer prices and reduces the*
> *incentive of owners to monitor managers"*
> (DeAlessi 1982, 205).

Furthermore, the individual owner's costs in monitoring the operations
of a publicly owned enterprise are prohibitively high (DeAlessi 1982,
205). The political agents to whom control of publicly-owned enterprises is delegated are not personally affected by returns and losses, and
they also pursue interests other than the realization of profits (DeAlessi
1982, 199).

Like Kornai, the property rights approaches make use of the soft budget constraint argument to explain the behavior of state-owned enterprises. State-owned enterprises are not exposed to the same competition as private firms, and access to public funds makes it possible for
them to survive for long periods, even when they make sizable losses
(DeAlessi 1982, 205-206). The scopes of discretionary action open to
the agents in charge of managing and controlling public enterprises are,
in the view of property rights approaches, thus substantially larger than
those of agents in private firms (DeAlessi 1980, 27; 1982, 206). The
costs they face in consuming nonpecuniary goods and reducing their
investment of effort are lower than in private firms (DeAlessi 1982,
207). The response of state-owned enterprises to market signals is consequently very much weaker than in private firms, and Leibenstein's X-
efficiency is lower (DeAlessi 1982, 206). The hypothesis of a lower
internal efficiency of state-owned enterprises as compared with private
firms has been verified empirically by several representatives of
property rights theory (DeAlessi 1980; Vickers/Yarrow 1988, 39-43;
Picot/Kaulmann 1985).

2.3.3   Private versus Public Goods

The theoretical hypotheses and the empirical findings of property rights theory thus lead to the conclusion that the incentive and sanction structure of private firms as opposed to public enterprises leads to a lower X-efficiency in Leibenstein's sense of the term. This does not yet answer the question of whether private property rights also give rise to higher allocative efficiency. Welfare economics since Pigou has been of the opinion that markets with perfect competition can achieve Pareto-optimal allocation only when no external effects occur (Pigou 1952). External effects may be defined as goods (or bads) which are caused by an economic agent without consideration of their impacts on the utility or production functions of other economic agents *and* for which no market can be formed (Weimann 1991, 19; Arrow 1978). The consequence drawn by welfare economics on the occurrence of externalities that cannot be internalized through markets is that the state should, in one form or another, intervene, e.g. by taxing or subsidizing their source, so as to heighten the efficiency of resources allocation (Pigou 1952; Baumol 1952). This view has been challenged by property rights theory (Buchanan/Strubblebine 1962; Demsetz 1964), in particular by Coase's famous essay, *The Problem of Social Cost* (Coase 1960). In the absence of transaction costs, thus the theorem named after Coase, a clear-cut definition and assignment of property rights is sufficient to internalize external effects through voluntary bargaining on compensation and to achieve Pareto-efficient allocation. The way in which property rights are assigned in personal terms is irrelevant for the efficiency of allocation (Coase 1960).

This claim of Coase's triggered a lengthy and controversial debate (Cooter 1991; Veljanowski 1982; Arrow 1978; Farrell 1987). Coase succeeded with the aid of his rigorous line of argumentation in demonstrating the reciprocity of the problem of internalizing external effects, thus putting to the question the apparently self-evident truth of the causative principle on which, for example, the so-called Pigou taxes are based (Weimann 1991, 27). It is, however, not possible to draw from the Coase theorem any conclusions on the comparative advantages of central and decentral, of public and private coordination where external

effects are concerned. Coase explicitly assumes a world without transaction costs. Under this assumption - this is the central result of the
above-discussed socialism debate between Lange and the Austrians -
public and private institutions can alike achieve a Pareto-efficient result. So what Coase demonstrated was no more than the fact that in the
absence of transaction costs a decentrally negotiated solution can reach
the same result that can be reached by the state through central allocation (Farrell 1987, 116). The most important outcome of the debate
stimulated by Coase is probably that it drew attention to the central
significance of transaction and information costs for the internalization
of external effects (Feess-Dörr 1991, 333). But what advantages result
for public and private coordination when external effects occur and
transaction costs are taken into account?

Game theory has been used to subject the Coase theorem to a rigorous
examination with regard to the problem of incomplete information
(Farrell 1987; Myerson/Satterthwaite 1983; Rob 1989). The point of
departure for Coase's claim that external effects can be internalized
through bargaining consists of examples based on bilateral bargaining,
such, for instance, as the case of a farmer who has suffered losses at the
hands of a cattle-rancher. In a world without transaction costs and with
complete information, it can be shown with the means of game theory
that, given rational behavior in keeping with the Coase theorem, a
strategic bargaining equilibrium will emerge between two parties, and
that this equilibrium also meets the Pareto-criterion (Weimann 1991,
37; Eggertsson 1990, 105; Feess-Dörr 1991, 330). But the existence of
a negotiated settlement presupposes that each side is perfectly informed
on the other side's payoffs. If this restrictive assumption is abandoned,
there is no reason why bargaining should arrive at an efficient result.
This assumption is restrictive in that the advantages of a decentral economic regime are, as Hayek has emphasized, precisely that information
is private (Farrell 1987, 116). Private information on utility functions
is, however, deployed strategically in bilateral bargaining: for instance,
an injured party will exaggerate her losses in negotiations in which the
person who has caused the damage is forced to pay compensation; the
injured party will in this way seek to obtain higher compensation from
the person who caused the losses, while, conversely, the person re-

sponsible for causing the losses will indicate as lower the benefit she has derived from the losses so as to diminish the amount of compensation she will be forced to pay (Arrow 1978, 29; Farrell 1987, 117). The same problem occurs with the supply of public goods (Farrell 1987, 117). This leads to a situation in which, with private information in bilateral negotiations, a bargaining process may even be broken off when the negotiations promise positive returns (Arrow 1978, 28; Farrell 1987, 119-121). Roger Myerson and Mark Satterthwaite advanced the theorem, that in bilateral bargaining there is no bargaining mechanism which provides incentives to participate in bargaining and to reveal truthfully one's own benefits and costs, and which simultaneously leads to an ex post-efficient bargaining outcome (Myerson/Satterthwaite 1983). In bilateral bargaining, in other words, an efficient solution need not emerge when the fact of incomplete information is taken into account. This holds true for the supply of private and public goods alike (Linhardt/Radner/Satterthwaite 1989, 16).

When the assumption of bilateral monopoly is abandoned, the picture changes: as the number of market participants increases, the negotiated solution for the supply of private goods converges toward the efficient outcome, even under the assumption of private information on the utility functions of the parties to the negotiations (Gresik/Satterthwaite 1989). This can be attributed to the fact that with an increasing number of market participants the risk grows that parties making false indications on the utility of a good will not be awarded the good. As Rafael Rob has shown, the reverse case holds when the supply of public goods is concerned: the greater the number of market participants, the stronger the individual incentives to achieve an information rent by providing false information on the utility (or disutility) of a good. The probability of an efficient bargaining solution therefore sinks as the number of market participants declines (Rob 1989; Weimann 1991, 43).

In other words, when information and transaction costs are taken into account, the discussion of the Coase theorem in terms of game theory leads to the conclusion that, when public goods are concerned and external effects are to be internalized, the efficiency of private bargaining in markets will decline when the number of market participants increa-

ses. It cannot be concluded from the failure of private negotiated settlements alone that government intervention is expedient. Government
intervention must not only be more efficient than private negotiated
settlements, the returns stemming from the internalization of an external effect or the supply of public goods must be greater than the costs
(Demsetz 1964, 12; Coase 1960). If the latter condition is given,
though, it is possible to proceed from the assumption that, transaction
costs considered, government intervention in the internalization of external effects and the supply of public goods generally entails comparative advantages vis-à-vis private negotiated settlements:

> *"It can be claimed without any particular courage*
> *that in most cases a tax-based solution will be su-*
> *perior to one based on bargaining, because most*
> *externality problems cannot be approximated using*
> *the situation of a bilateral monopoly, and the tran-*
> *saction costs rise as the number of persons affected*
> *increase. The economic justification of the causati-*
> *ve principle (...) thus does not consist in considera-*
> *tions of justice, which, at least as it is understood in*
> *the neoclassical context, may not constitute a com-*
> *ponent of positive economic theory; it instead con-*
> *sists in the lower transaction costs associated with*
> *it"* (Feess-Dörr 1991, 332-333; see also Farrell
> 1987, 122; Weimann 1991, 44).

It does, of course, not follow from the advantages of government intervention and regulation relative to private bargaining solutions in the
face of externalities and in the supply of public goods that state-owned
enterprises likewise possess efficiency advantages in the supply of
public goods. When they are regulated by government, public goods
can also be supplied by private firms. But the regulation and monitoring of public goods supplied by private firms frequently entails high
transaction costs. Only if the costs stemming from the conclusion and
the enforcement of a contract on the supply of public goods (or the internalization of external effects) are higher than the costs entailed by

the government supplying such goods do advantages result for state-owned enterprises relative to private firms (DeAlessi 1982, 200).

2.4   Conclusions

This chapter has discussed two issues: the significance of ownership for the *coherence* and *efficiency* of economic systems. The discussion of the issue of coherence led to the conclusion that decentral economic systems that coordinate economic activities through markets rely at the macrolevel on a monetary constraint of the economic system which guarantees the scarcity of money, while depending at the microlevel on a hard budget constraint on the part of economic agents. Both conditions can be met only with private ownership: apart from government regulation of the money supply, the first condition presupposes private wealth formation and a private supply of credit. The second condition is closely linked to the existence of private ownership: theoretical arguments no less than empirical findings indicate that it is easier to enforce a hard budget constraint on the business sector under private ownership than under public ownership. Conversely, an economic system with central quantitative planning is forced to violate both the monetary constraints and the hard budget constraint of enterprises. The coherence of these economic systems is created by mandatory planning, and it logically presupposes the other allocative mechanisms. Market-socialist economic systems that have sought to link decentral allocation via markets with a public regime of ownership were bound to fail because they have violated the conditions of coherence of both decentral market economies and central economic planning.

The efficiency issue can be dealt with in the context of various theories and efficiency concepts. As Oskar Lange, but also the classics of equilibrium theory, have demonstrated, it is, in a world with complete information and without transaction costs, logically possible to achieve a static equilibrium meeting the efficiency norm of the Pareto optimum both through decentral allocation via markets and through central planning. In a dynamic world with uncertainty and incomplete information, on the other hand, the advantage of decentral allocation through the price system emerges from the communication of knowledge that is fragmented and accessible to no one in its totality, as Friedrich A. Hayek and Ludwig von Mises were first to demonstrate. Economic systems with central economic planning give rise to expectations of poorer planning coordination and a lower level of dynamic efficiency in Hayek's sense, because these economic systems dispense with the price system as a mechanism of allocation and are unable to make use of competition as a technique of discovery in the same measure as market economies with a private ownership regime.

The approaches of the New Institutional Economics supplement the view of Hayek and Mises by analyzing the problem of allocation and coordination within the framework of the failure of markets and bureaucracies. From the perspective of the New Institutional Economics, two central arguments speak in favor of the efficiency of market economies with private ownership: transaction cost theory sees the evolutionary advantage of market economies in the fact that they, depending on their comparative efficiency advantages, can combine decentral coordination through the price system in markets with a great variety of forms of bureaucratic coordination, the vertically integrated firm being only one of many possibilities. In the view of property rights theory, the advantage of private ownership regimes as compared with public ones is to be found in the higher intensity of incentives and the harder budget constraint associated with private firms. Excluding externalities and the supply of public goods, the conclusion that emerges in a free-market framework is that

> "(...) the evidence on comparative performance indicates that the weaknesses of public sector monitoring are so serious, and so pervasive, that a general presumption in favor of private ownership is justified" (Yarrow 1986, 332).

The issue of the internalization of external effects and the supply of public goods was unable to be addressed in any length here.[8] The discussion of the Coase theorem did, however, lead to the conclusion that, when transaction costs are taken into account, external effects can

be internalized more efficiently through government intervention than
through private bargaining. As Oliver Williamson has pointed out, the
issue of ownership also remains problematical in market economies,
when external effects are taken into consideration:

> *"Transaction costs economics maintains that whe-
> ther or whether not property rights can be (1) well-
> defined and, once defined, can be (2) understood by
> and (3) effectively enforced by the courts they are
> all problematic. Indeed, problematic property rights
> invite the appearance of nonmarket modes of orga-
> nization that have the purpose and effect of provi-
> ding contractual integrity for transactions that are
> 'deficient' in any or all of these property rights re-
> spects"* (Williamson 1990, 66).

3   Transaction Costs of Privatization

There are two arguments that speak in favor of privatizing the SOEs in
the transforming economies: first, the enforcement of a hard budget
constraint as a central condition for the coherence of a market economy. Second, efficiency gains may be expected from privatization of
the state economic sector due to the incentive and sanction structure of
private ownership - to the extent that no external effects occur. The
issue of ownership, the last chapter concluded, can be discussed meaningfully only in a world with transaction costs. While the transaction
costs of private and public ownership regimes have been dealt with at
length in the economic discussion, the transaction costs of privatization
itself have not yet been analyzed. In the privatization discussion, these
costs have thus far either been completely neglected (Sachs 1991;
Lipton/Sachs 1991; Vaubel 1992) or given merely marginal consideration in ad hoc arguments (Kornai 1991). It is frequently assumed in the
privatization debate that it is free to transform ownership regimes and

that the primary distribution of property rights can be neutral for allocative efficiency:

> *"The Coase Theorem tells us that allocative efficiency does not depend on how property rights are initially distributed. This means that, from the economic point of view, it does not matter how firms are privatized - whether they are sold or given a away to whom. (...) The Coase Theorem assumes zero transaction costs. In the case of property rights over capital this simplification does not seem exorbitant"* (Vaubel 1992, 112).

The present study, in contrast, proceeds from the hypothesis that privatization entails nontrivial transaction costs under the behavioral assumptions of bounded rationality and opportunism and that the initial distribution of property rights affects the allocative efficiency of an economic system (3.1). The efficiency effects of different privatization procedures are contingent on the economic and institutional conditions existing in the countries concerned. Limited stocks of wealth and sparse economic competence on the part of buyers are identified as the relevant scarce factors for privatization (3.2). The main section of this chapter investigates the comparative efficiency effects of different privatization procedures under the given behavioral assumptions (3.3). The allocative efficiency of privatization depends on bidding competition. The choice of the privatization procedure has an impact on the degree of bidding competition (3.4). The final section summarizes the most important conclusions drawn from the investigation of the transaction costs of different privatization procedures (3.5).

3.1   Assumptions and Working Hypothesis

Essentially, the transaction costs approach bases its theoretical edifice on three assumptions: the asset specificity of capital and the two behavioral axioms of bounded rationality and opportunism (Williamson 1985). As regards privatization, the behavioral assumption of bounded rationality is here expanded by one aspect: individual rationality is not only bounded, it is also unequally distributed. Kenneth Arrow pointed out that the behavioral assumption of perfect rationality in traditional microeconomics does not adequately describe economic activity (Arrow 1991). Individual rationality, Arrow notes, is not only bounded in Simon's sense, it is also unevenly distributed over individuals (Arrow 1991). It is precisely the unequal distribution of abilities over individuals that give rise to the returns of economic transactions:

> *"The lesson is that the rationality hypothesis is by itself weak. To make it useful, the researcher is tempted into some strong assumptions. In particular, the homogeneity assumption seems to me to be especially dangerous. It denies the fundamental assumption of the economy, that it is built on gains from trading arising from individual differences"* (Arrow 1991, 202).

If economic abilities of individuals are developed differently, the goal of privatization can consist not merely in reorganizing the incentive structure of the economic system, but must also include a more efficient allocation of *economic competence* (Pelikan 1992). The term economic competence refers not only to cognitive skills and the human capital acquired through investment in individual qualifications; it also means those intuitive and speculative skills that representatives of the Austrian School have emphatically described as the sociological type of the entrepreneur (Mises 1949; Schumpeter 1954; Kirzner 1973).

The economic competence of agents is pertinent above all in connection with the asset specificity of the firms to be privatized. The capital of firms is by definition of high asset specificity: the rationale behind the vertical integration of economic activities in firms is protection of asset-specific investments in real and human capital (Williamson 1985). Firms are hence not homogeneous goods. Their capital is tied to specific transaction relations and uses. As a complement to the idiosyncratic character of the capital employed, corporate management therefore also requires specific levels of managerial competence. The owner need not himself posses these skills, he can just as well delegate the running of the firm to a professional management. As will be demonstrated below, however, the delegation of rights of disposition itself causes high transaction costs.[1]

Let us assume that the necessary legal and institutional conditions of privatization are given - a private ownership regime with freedom of trade, a market-based monetary and fiscal system. In a world with unbounded rationality and without transaction costs, the transfer of property rights to private individuals or institutions would involve no costs and the choice between different privatization procedures would be irrelevant. The highest bidder would at the same time also be the best owner. Here, on the other hand, the analysis of different privatization procedures is based on the hypothesis that privatization gives rise to nontrivial transaction costs in the presence of asset specificity of capital and economic competence that is both bounded and unequally distributed over individuals. The level of these transaction costs depends on the privatization procedures decided upon.

The efficiency criterion of a privatization procedures is minimization of transaction costs before and after public ownership has been transferred into private hands. In principle the transaction costs of privatization can be categorized in two different groups: first, the costs of the *transfer of property rights* themselves, i.e. all costs associated with information, bargaining, and monitoring that result both ex ante and ex post from the conclusion of contracts on the transfer of public property rights to private individuals. These costs can be prohibitively high, thus precluding any privatization of public property, even though a private individual may have a more productive use for an enterprise than the state. The level of these costs affects the scale and the pace of privatization.

Secondly, the costs of the *reallocation* of property rights that have already been privatized. Reallocation of property rights would not even be cost-free in a world without transaction costs. Following Harold Demsetz, the costs of the reallocation of property rights can also be designated as "realignment costs" (Demsetz 1966). In view of positive reallocation costs, the initial distribution of property rights through privatization is not neutral in terms of allocative efficiency:

> *"Given variety in demand and abilities, it is un-*
> *likely that a correct initial assignment of rights will*
> *eliminate all recontracting, but it may be possible*
> *to reduce costs significantly"* (Demsetz 1966, 66).

The efficiency of privatization procedures can thus be measured in terms the level of the costs of transferring state property rights to private persons and reallocating the property rights after privatization. The latter depends on how property rights are assigned through privatization, i.e. how efficient the allocation of property rights is under the assumption of unequally distributed individual competences and possibilities. The level of transaction costs can never be measured absolutely, although it can be analyzed comparatively with regard to the institutional alternatives involved in privatization under the given constraints of transformation processes.

3.2   Constraints and Scarce Factors Affecting Privatization

The transition countries in Central and Eastern Europe are subject to institutional constraints other than those obtaining for privatization programs in well established market economies (i.e. UK and Chile), affecting the scarcity of factors relevant for privatization. Due to a lack of a well established market environment and the appropriate institutions above all there are three scarce factors that affect the privatization of state owned enterprises: the limited supply of capital (3.2.1), the limited supply of economic competence (3.2.2), and the limited organizational and personal capabilities of privatization agencies (3.2.3).

3.2.1   Capital Supply

The limited supply of capital in the transition countries is seen by many authors as the chief constraint of privatization. The demand for a cost-free transfer of property rights is often derived from the limited savings of private households (Aleksashenko/Grigoriev 1991; Lewandowski/Szomburg 1989; Sachs 1991; Sinn/Sinn 1991; Sinn 1991). National saving is relatively low in the transforming economies: Jeffrey Sachs estimated for Poland, for example, the savings balances of the private households at 10 billion US $, while he estimates the capitalized value of the 500 biggest enterprises alone at 25 billion US $ (Sachs 1991, 7). In the former Soviet Union, the population's savings amounted to 297 billion rubles; the book value of the capital of enterprises is indicated as 1,880 billion rubles (Aleksashenko/Grigoriev 1991). Even though the book values of Soviet enterprises are apt to be a poor indicator for their market value, the savings of private households in the transition countries are doubtless lower than the market value of the state business sector.

Privatization is competing with other uses for scarce capital. But privatization of firms constitutes a burden on the capital market only when privatization revenues are used to fund additional consumption (Dluhosch 1991, 417). If the state, by cutting the public budget deficit, redirects privatization revenues into the capital market, privatization is neutral for capital markets (Dluhosch 1991, 417; Sinn/Sinn 1991, 105; Vuylsteke 1988, 16). What occurs then is merely an exchange of assets between the state and the private households. The use of privatization revenues for additional spending, on the other hand, has the same effects on the capital market as the funding of government spending through borrowing (Kornai 1991, 7; Kawalec 1989, 244): The capital employed for privatization is withdrawn from other uses, driving up, ceteris paribus, the interest rates in the capital market (Sinn/Sinn 1991, 104-110; Dluhosch 1991, 417). An increased rate of interest in the capital market in turn leads to rising opportunity costs in the purchase of state-owned enterprises. The consequence is falling prices and a decline in the number of objects that can be privatized (Sinn/Sinn 1991, 105).

But the same effect also occurs when enterprises are transferred free of cost to the population: if the ownership deeds are again sold after the cost-free transfer and the revenues are used to finance additional consumption, the resulting burden on the capital market is the same as if the state had sold the enterprises and used the revenues to fund additional government spending (Dluhosch 1991, 417). In this case the cost-free transfer of ownership deeds likewise leads to higher interest rates in the capital market and tends to crowd out investment.

Theoretically, the burden on the capital market caused by privatization is easier to limit when the state sells deeds of ownership, because in this case the use to which the revenues are put is subject to government control. This, however, presupposes that the state, despite the high social and political burdens associated with the transformation process, will refrain from using privatization revenues to finance additional government spending. One other factor that must be taken into consideration is that capital requirements are not restricted to the privatization of the state business sector, but must above all be seen in connection with subsequent rehabilitation-related investments. To this extent, the low capital supply in the transition countries constitutes an important constraint of privatization and the subsequent rehabilitation of the firms affected.

The shortage of capital in the transforming economies can be mitigated by an influx of foreign capital. While the national capital supply in the transition countries is, due to the limited stocks of assets owned by private households, unable to respond elastically to a rise in the demand for capital, a need for additional capital triggered by the privatization and rehabilitation of the state business sector in the transition countries could, theoretically, be met through capital imports. As long as the returns expected in the transforming economies are, adjusted for risk, higher than those offered by alternative investments abroad, rising interest rates should, theoretically, trigger an influx of international capital (Dluhosch 1991, 419). In fact, however, the transaction costs for the influx of international capital in the transition countries, with the exception of Eastern Germany, are very high: great uncertainty about the institutional and economic framework, currency risks, different languages and cultures lead to high transaction costs for foreign direct investment, but also for other investments of money and capital in the transforming economies. The influx of international capital is therefore apt to be limited even when high real interest rates are on offer. With the exception of Eastern Germany, which was integrated into the Western German capital market by the economic and monetary union,[2] the high macrolevel capital requirements for privatization and rehabilitation of the state business sector in the transition countries are not matched by an elastic supply of capital.

The constraint posed by the limited financial resources available to the individual buyer is the microeconomic side of the constraint posed by the inelastic supply of capital at the macroeconomic level. The public ownership regime in the transition countries has restricted the possibility of forming major wealth to a limited number of members of the nomenclature and the shadow economy. The financial endowment of potential buyers of firms in the transition countries is therefore seen as low. In the absence of transaction costs, the financial endowment of individual buyers would be irrelevant. It would be possible to mobilize any amount of capital desired in the national and international credit markets to purchase firms, if the expected returns of privatized firms were higher than the returns on alternative capital investments (Modigliani/Miller 1958). Under the assumption of bounded rationality and opportunism, however, nontrivial costs are incurred for the monitoring and control of credit relations (Jensen/Meckling 1976; Williamson 1988; Schmidt 1981). The lower the equity ratio, the higher the borrower's incentive to raise the investment risk once a contract has been signed, since the costs stemming from failure of the investment project are in this case borne by the lender, while any potential returns accrue to the borrower (Jensen/Meckling 1976, 334-337; Schmidt 1981, 206). The possibility of using the right of lean on tangible assets to protect lender interests against borrower opportunism declines in relation to the asset specificity of the capital invested (Williamson 1988, 580-581). The most important means of limiting the lender's risk is *credit rationing* (Baltensperger/Devinney 1985). Since the information on the risks of an investment are asymmetrically distributed between borrower and lender (Schmidt 1988), price fails as a credit allocation mechanism: as the interest rate rises, average borrower "quality" declines ("adverse selection"), and thus, the lender's returns will decline as the interest rate rises (Akerlof 1970; Baltensperger/Devinney

1985; Stiglitz/Weiss 1981). Credit rationing, on the other hand, curtails the incentive for opportunistic borrower behavior and lowers the risk of default facing the lender.

With credit rationing, the volume of outside financing is limited by the quotient of available equity capital and the minimum equity ratio. As uncertainty increases, the lender's risk rises, raising, ceteris paribus, the borrower's equity ratio (Baltensperger/Devinney 1985). In view of the high level of uncertainty over the given economic and institutional framework and the value of a firm's asset-specific capital, the required equity ratio is apt to be considerably higher in transforming economies than in western market economies (Sinn/Sinn 1991). Low bidder equity capital resources therefore constitute an important constraint of privatization and subsequent rehabilitation of enterprises in the transition countries.

3.2.2   Limited Economic Competence

The objective of privatization is an efficient allocation of property rights, i.e. the property rights to firms are to be transferred to those individuals and institutions who have the most productive use for them. Under the above-developed assumption of rationality that is bounded and unequally distributed across individuals, the economic competence of bidders is a scarce factor of privatization (Pelikan 1992, 46). It is here assumed that the demands for economic competence on the part of the bidder rise as asset specificity and size of the firm concerned increase. Eugene Fama and Michael Jensen have described this link in terms of the complexity of firms (Fama/Jensen 1983, 305). An economic organization is complex when the specific information pertinent to the decisions made by the organization are not concentrated in one agent or a limited number of agents, but are distributed over a large number of agents. The complexity of firms depends on the size of the organization and the specificity of its economic activities (Fama/Jensen 1983, 305). The number of bidders in possession of sufficient economic competence to run a firm decreases, ceteris paribus, as its complexity increases (Pelikan 1991). While the owner can delegate the control rights to the firm to a professional management, the expense and effort involved in controlling management also rise as a firm grows in complexity.[3] Under the conditions of high asset specificity and high uncertainty, the scarce economic skills of bidders therefore constitute an important bottleneck to privatization (Kornai 1991, 17-18).

The two constraints of limited bidder competence and financial resources may reinforce one another. Bidders with high levels of economic competence may run up against the constraint of insufficient financial resources, while bidders with adequate financial resources may face the constraint posed by insufficient economic competence. This constraint can be eased by financing via credit or equity, although it cannot be abrogated: the transaction costs of credit-based financing increase as the equity ratio decreases and the asset specificity of the capital increases (Jensen/Meckling 1976, 313-319; Williamson 1988, 579), thus making it impossible to fall short of a given equity ratio. Under the conditions of limited information and high uncertainty in transforming economies, equity financing in turn gives rise to particularly high transaction costs.

3.2.3   Limited Capabilities of Privatization Agencies

In well established market economies even the largest privatization programs cover some dozens or a maximum some hundred enterprises. In contrast to this, some thousand or tenthousand enterprises are assigned for privatization in the transition countries. The task or privatization is usually delegated to one or more public institutions, i.e. privatization agencies. These agencies have to deal with complex tasks like restructuring and valuation of enterprises before privatization, information and advertisement, carrying out privatization procedures, negotiating and contracting, contract control, etc. The financial and personal resources of privatization agencies are limited. Given bounded rationality, the organizational and personal capabilities of the privatization agencies are scarce factors that limit the pace and allocative efficiency of privatization processes.

3.3   Efficiency of Alternative Privatization Procedures

Given a world with nontrivial transaction costs, the allocative impera-
tive of privatization can be described in the following manner: Transfer
the ownership rights of state owned enterprises in such a way to the
private sector that under consideration of the limited capabilities of the
privatization agencies the two scarce factors capital and economic
competence are used efficiently. The efficiency of privatization procedures cannot be evaluated in absolute terms; it must instead be assessed
with regard to the relevant institutional alternatives. This section compares the most important privatization procedures practiced in the
countries in transition. The examination of these procedures proceeds
from the following assumptions:

(1) In privatization the state pursues the goal of an efficient allocation
    of property rights. Other goals, for example the maximization of
    state revenues by means of privatization, are subordinate to the
    goal of an efficient allocation of property rights.

(2) The state's property rights are administrated by a central govern-
    ment agency, be it a specific ministry as in Poland or be it a gov-
    ernment property agency such as the "Treuhandanstalt" in Eastern
    Germany and the "State Property Agency" in Hungary. This
    authority is the privatization agent. Privatization is organized cen-
    trally within this agency.

(3) Enterprises are not homogeneous goods. Under the assumption of
    bounded rationality, limited financial resources on the part of bid-
    ders, and uncertainty, the most important distinguishing features
    are the degree of asset specificity of capital and firm size.

A number of privatization procedures are being discussed and practiced
in the transforming economies. The most important alternative is the
allocation of property rights through *sale* or *cost-free distribution*. The
sales procedures may be differentiated in terms of the way in which the
transaction is formalized and standardized. On the one side of the
spectrum is the sale of firms through informal bargaining between the
privatization agency and one or more bidders. Multiple allocative cri-

teria can be used and complex contracts concluded when firms are sold through informal bargaining (3.3.1). A special case of privatization through *informal bargaining* is represented by *management-buyouts* (MBO) and *-buyins* (MBI); here the privatization agency either defers part of the price or provides other credits at preferential terms (3.3.2). As opposed to informal bargaining, privatization by *auction* standardizes the transaction and as a rule accepts only price as an auction parameter (3.3.3). The public privatization of *company shares* on the *stock exchange* is a mass transaction that by its nature dictates a standardization of allocation. In addition, privatization through the stock exchange logically presupposes a separation of the rights of ownership and control (3.3.4). The most important procedure of transferring firms free of charge is the distribution of *vouchers* to the population; the vouchers can then be used to purchase company shares. Like privatization on the stock exchange, voucher allocation enforces a standardization of the transaction and a separation of the rights of ownership and control (3.3.5). Unlike the other privatization procedures, *restitution* is based not on the allocation of property rights but on a legal claim raised by former owners (3.3.6). (See Fig. 3.1)

Fig. 3.1: Privatization Procedures

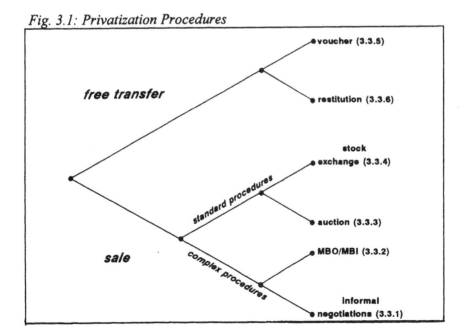

These procedures may be understood as Weberian ideal types that have been selected here for considerations of a functional nature. Privatization in the transition countries is of course not restricted to these procedures; it frequently occurs that different procedures are combined to privatize a firm.

3.3.1   Privatization through Informal Bargaining

The reallocation of property rights through bargaining conducted by the state with one or more interested parties is the most flexible and probably also the most frequent procedure used in privatizing firms. As a rule the bidder approaches the privatization agency. Frequently negotiations are conducted with one bidder only. The price is for the most part one of several allocative criteria. Other allocative criteria may include the bidder's reputation, his rehabilitation concept, and the volume of investment and employment planned by him.[4] The practical significance of this privatization procedure is inversely proportional to the skepticism with which it is viewed by many economists:

> *"(...) there are multiple criteria by which the winning buyer is determined. The Treuhandanstalt therefore has considerable allocative power - both in establishing these other criteria and in deciding how much weight to give fairly incommensurable goals. To invest the agency with such power is first of all contrary to the underlying philosophy of privatization: that allocative decisions will be made more efficiently through private competition than by the state agencies. It also opens the door to the risk of bureaucratic corruption and regulatory capture"*
> (Maskin 1992, 118).

The logic of this line of argument results from the behavioral assumptions of traditional microeconomics. If perfect bidder rationality is assumed, the bidder with the highest reserve price[5] will also have the most productive use for a firm. Under the assumption of bidder competition, the most efficient allocation of property rights is consequently achieved when these rights are allotted to the bidder who submits the highest offer. The use of multiple allocative criteria in informal privatization procedures therefore only opens up discretionary scopes of action that impair the allocative efficiency of privatization.

From the standpoint of transaction cost theory, the assumptions on which this line of argument is based are problematical. If the assumption of perfect bidder rationality is replaced with the more realistic assumption of bounded and unequally distributed rationality, the efficiency hypothesis cannot be sustained in this form. The difference between standard methods of allocation and informal sales procedures consists as a rule in the quality and structure of the information processed. In standardized procedures, only one type of information is pertinent, the price. In informal sales procedures, on the other hand, multidimensional information is exchanged; this information, which can be taken into account in a decision on allocation, may be with and without price character. As János Kornai pointed out, in most economic transactions a variety of information is processed, which can be classified as monetary flows, information with and without price character (Kornai 1975, 54-62). He assumes in contrast to traditional microeconomics that prices mirror only in an indirect and multiply refracted manner all information that is pertinent to an economic agent appraising a good (Kornai 1975, 68). In most of the economic decisions they make, economic agents therefore process not only information with price character but also information without price character. A "multiplication" of information is performed in order to heighten the quality of the decision to be made (Kornai 1975, 62).

Bidder valuation of firms is dependent on a great variety of information, ranging from the technical features of capital assets and products and employee qualification to complex assumptions on the development of demand in the relevant markets, etc. Under the assumption that individual rationality is bounded and unequally distributed over individuals, the highest bidder need not necessarily have the most productive use for an enterprise. Apart from the bidder's subjective order of preferences, his bid mirrors only indirectly the information he has processed on the enterprise concerned and his expectations as regards future developments. It is possible for a bidder with a lower level of economic competence to offer a higher price than a competitor who, though he has a more productive use for the firm, bases his bid on more information and more rational expectations concerning the risks and returns on his investment.

If the strict rationality assumptions of traditional microeconomics are abandoned, the processing of multidimensional information and multiple allocation criteria in informal bargaining is thus not a disadvantage but an advantage vis-à-vis standardized privatization procedures. The privatization agency need not base its allocation decision solely on the price of the highest bid. It can take into account a great variety of information, such as the reputation of a bidder, the plausibility of his rehabilitation concept, the planned volume of employment and investment, etc. If the privatization agency is interested exclusively in maximizing its privatization revenues, this information is irrelevant. If, however, the privatization agency, as is assumed here, pursues the goal of efficiently allocating state owned enterprises, it *can*, by taking multidimensional information into account, achieve a higher level of allocative efficiency than would be possible with standardized privatization procedures. Processing complex information without price character and making use of multiple allocation criteria do not make it necessary for a hyperrational state to establish reserve prices for buyers that are more exact than those of the bidders themselves. All the state needs to do is to form judgments ranking individual bidders or bidder groups. Informal bargaining can in this sense be seen as a complex communication process in which different signals and information with and without price character are exchanged. Under the assumption of bounded rationality, a signal not given need not necessarily lead to an efficient allocation of property rights. There is thus also no compelling reason why the bidder with the most efficient use should win. As opposed to standard procedures that consider only information with price character, however, informational efficiency can be heightened by processing multidimensional information, thus increasing the rationality of allocation (Vuylsteke 1988, 17). The efficiency of privatization decisions in this case depends not least on the economic competence of the agents in charge of allocation.

Aside from a higher level of informational efficiency, informal privatization procedures, as opposed to standardized procedures, are distinguished by two further advantages: first, the *bid package* can be specified flexibly in the bargaining process (Hax 1992, 145). The corporate structure of the enterprises in the countries in transition is as a rule not competitive. The privatization agencies are thus confronted with the alternative of either the divestiture of the firms and redefining their corporate structure in viable terms before they are privatized or addressing the issue of deconcentration in the bargaining process itself. The second option has the advantage that the agency then has additional information on the bidder's utilization concept, which makes it possible to reduce considerably the costs involved in divestiture (Hax 1992, 146). Standardized privatization procedures, on the other hand, presuppose an offer of viable enterprises, so that in this case the privatization agencies themselves will have to come to grips with the issue of deconcentration.

Second, informal privatization procedures facilitate the conclusion of *complex contracts*. As opposed to standard contracts, which provide for a clear-cut agreement and clearly define performance (Williamson 1985, 69), complex contracts are not completed fully, either in terms of time or in terms of subject matter (Williamson 1985). Complex contracts are intended to make possible flexible adjustments to contingent events that are unable to be anticipated fully when a contract is signed. They are incomplete and constitute a longer-term bilateral contractual relationship. The problem of complex contracts is that, given all contractual adjustments, the situation after a contract has been completed is one of bilateral monopoly which exposes both parties to the risk of opportunistic behavior. In contrast to the paradigm of isolated exchange, the pair-by-pair identity of the contracting parties is relevant for complex contracts (Williamson 1985, 62). At first glance the contracts concluded for privatization are not complex contracts. In practice, however, privatization contracts frequently contain agreements that constitute a complex contractual relationship between privatization agency and buyers: the Treuhandanstalt in Eastern Germany, for example, reaches agreement with nearly all its buyers on employment and investment guarantees tailored to the firm's altered business conditions.[6] The privatization agency often agrees to assume certain obligations, for instance for the clean-up of unregulated ecological burdens or the funding of social plans, or it is sometimes willing to agree to conditional buyer payments.

Two rational justifications can be advanced for the conclusion of complex contracts for the purpose of privatization: the first is to internalize external effects. This is true in particular of subsidies granted by the Treuhandanstalt for rehabilitation investments which are external for the investor but internal for the state.[7] Second, in view of risk propensities different for the state and the buyer, it is possible to reach a more efficient risk distribution if the state agrees to take on liability commitments and to accept conditional payments: under the specific conditions of system transformation in the Central and Eastern European countries, the degree of uncertainty is naturally high. The buyer will therefore demand a risk premium which is deductible from the purchase price. Many firms will not be sold if bidders are risk-averse. Under the assumption that the state is risk-neutral, while the buyer side is risk-averse, the state can increase its revenues and boost allocative efficiency by "trading in risk" (Maskin 1992, 130; McAfee/ McMillian 1987, 716-719). Risk-sharing between state and buyers reduces the uncertainty for the buyer side, and in this way more firms can be sold off at higher prices.

One possibility of risk-sharing is for the state to assume a share of *liability*. In this case the state does not sell the entire legal vector of a firm, but retains ownership of the rights that entail special risks. The assumption by the Treuhandanstalt of liability commitments for the clean-up of unregulated ecological burdens is one example. On the other hand, the state can also reserve rights to certain assets that give rise to expectations of returns that may be high, though they are currently not predictable - e.g. ex post valuation of properties after a number of years have elapsed. In reaching agreement on complex contracts on liability commitments, conditional payments, etc., a contractual problem arises only if all possible environmental states have not been anticipated fully and no water-tight agreement on conditional payments is reached in the contract. This, however, tends more to be the rule. Also, the information on existing states of the economic environment is as a rule distributed asymmetrically. This case entails a high risk of opportunistic behavior. The buyer may, for instance, provide false information on a firm's relevant environmental conditions as a means of getting around employment and investment commitments or increasing the costs required to clean up old ecological burdens by adding new ones to them or by conducting so-called "luxury clean-ups". In the sense of transaction cost theory, complex contractual relationships must be safeguarded against the risks of opportunistic behavior by means of agreements on incentives for cooperative behavior that go beyond accepted social norms (Williamson 1985). Chapter 7 examines at length the transaction costs for this kind of complex privatization contract using the example of agreements made by the Treuhandanstalt on employment and investment commitments. Complex contracts are of significance for the choice of a privatization procedure in that they presuppose an informal bargaining process. Two points of some importance to the conclusion of complex contracts are the identity of the contracting party and verification of the credibility of the commitments he has made so as to limit the risks of opportunistic behavior. It is therefore not possible to conclude such contracts through standardized procedures that contain only price information bearing on the allocation decision.

The three advantages of informal privatization procedures - the processing of multidimensional information, the flexible configuration of the packages offered, and the conclusion of complex contracts - are faced with two disadvantages: first, in informal bargaining bidding competition is for the most part restricted. The effort and expense involved in bargaining grow in proportion to the number of bidders involved. In informal bargaining the privatization agencies therefore as a rule negotiate with one bidder only or with a limited number of bidders. The costs of this competitive restraint are dealt with in detail in Chapter 3.4.

Second, the processing of complex information and the use of multiple allocation criteria lower the transparency of the transaction. The scopes of discretionary action open to the state agencies in charge of privatization rise, ceteris paribus, as the bargaining process increases in complexity. These principal-agent problems arising from the room for discretionary maneuver involved in informal privatization procedures themselves give rise to high transaction costs involved in controlling and monitoring the agents in charge of privatization. Incentive schemes cannot be used to limit these costs, because the privatization agency, as principle, is not in possession of adequate information about the value of its firms and is thus also unable to assess the privatization revenues it should realize.[8]

3.3.2   Management-buyout and -buyin

Management-buyout (MBO) and -buyin (MBI) are as a rule concluded through informal bargaining. The reason for this is the complex contracts required by this privatization procedure. To this extent, MBO and MBI are a special case of privatization by informal bargaining.

Two central constraints of privatization were identified above as scarce economic competence and capital. MBO can be characterized as a privatization strategy that eases the capital constraint faced by individuals with especially high levels of economic competence. The constraint posed by capital endowments can be eased, for instance, through price abatements, deferment of payments, credits granted at special terms, government credit guarantees, and the like. In cases of MBOs and MBIs, the credits or liability commitments given by the state often involve not only the purchase of a firm but also the funding of rehabilitation investments.

In management buyouts and buyins the state's position is formally that of a lender who demands of management an equity ratio for a given volume of credit that is lower than that demanded by lenders in the capital markets, i.e.

$$(3.1) \qquad K = \frac{E}{\alpha} > K^* = \frac{E}{\alpha^*}, \qquad \text{with } 0 \leq \alpha \leq 1$$

where K and K^* denote the overall capital available to the managers either from their own capital resources or from the state or the credit markets, E stands for their equity capital, and α and α^* represent the equity ratio demanded by the state or the credit markets. The lower the managers' equity ratio, the higher the incentives for an opportunistic increase of the risk ("moral hazard"), since in this case the state bears the risk, while the returns stemming from the risk accrue to the managers-owners.

MBO- and MBI-procedures give rise to complex contractual relationships between the state and managers. A distinction must be made between the ex ante and ex post risks involved in MBOs: the ex ante risk consists in the asymmetrical distribution of information on the value of the asset-specific capital concerned. When firms are sold to outside buyers, the information is as a rule distributed asymmetrically between privatization agency and buyer, i.e. privatization agency and buyer are equally poorly informed on the firm's value. In management buyouts, on the other hand, management naturally has information of better quality than that available to the privatization agency, the seller. In bilateral bargaining with asymmetrical distribution of information, the buyer side will therefore, regardless of the state's bargaining strategy, appropriate the lion's share of the net returns of the transaction.

Once a contract has been signed, the problem still remains that the managers-owners may opportunistically step up the risk involved in the investments they make. There exists a complex contractual relationship between the state as lender and the managers-owners. The risk of opportunistic behavior can, however, be restricted by making allowance for multidimensional information prior to and during the process in which control and monitoring structures are institutionalized once the contract has been concluded. Measures of this kind may include consideration of management reputation and the quality of the business concepts etc. presented before signing, and by including, once the contract has been signed, provisions covering representation of government agencies in the firm's supervisory board, prolongation of credit, regular reporting requirements, etc.

It is generally only rational for the state to assume credit risks higher than those acceptable to the credit markets, if the state's risk preference is higher than that of private banks and/or the state derives other advantages from assuming a higher risk. The latter is, for instance, the case when the state is faced with very high transaction costs in managing and monitoring enterprises, and these costs can be reduced by accelerating privatization. The differential between the equity ratio demanded by the state and the private capital markets ($\alpha^* - \alpha > 0$) is geared to the level of these advantages.

Limitation of the risk of opportunistic behavior also requires the state to demand an equity ratio from management. The asset constraint can in this way be eased by MBO- and MBI-procedures, but it cannot be abrogated. The maximum firm size appropriate for MBO and MBI is contingent on the financial resources available to management and the risks presented by opportunistic behavior; this approach is as a rule apt to prove adequate only for smaller and medium-size enterprises.

3.3.3   Privatization by Auction

Determination of a selling price is one of the core problems of privatizing state-owned enterprises. Firms are not homogeneous goods for which there is a fixed market price. The problem of pricing is bound up with incomplete information on a firm's value. The privatization agency is unfamiliar with the reserve price that a bidder is prepared to pay for an object. Because of the numerous problems associated with appraising firms, the privatization agency often is unable to form a reserve price of its own, i.e. the lowest price at which it is prepared to sell the object.

Auctions represent a procedure for establishing the price of goods for which there is no standard price (McAfee/McMillian 1987, 701). At auctions the price is set not by bargaining between sellers and buyers

but by bids made by market participants. At auctions the rule is that
one seller faces a number of bidders. The allocative criterion of auctions is as a rule the price of the highest bid.[9] To this extent auctions
are a standard allocation procedure that admits price as the only pertinent information.

Having been examined in depth theoretically, and proven their efficiency in practice, auction procedures have often been proposed as a
means of privatizing the state industrial sector in the transition countries:

> *"Privatizing productive assets in formerly central-*
> *ized economies is a task to which auctions seems*
> *especially well-suited"* (Maskin 1992, 115; see also
> Siebert 1992, 99-102).

The *economic theory of auctions* looks into the efficiency and the income effects of different auction procedures with an eye to the specific
environmental conditions of auctions (McAfee/McMillian 1987; Mil-
grom/Weber 1982; Riley/Samuelson 1981; Maskin/Riley 1985). Like
traditional microeconomics, auction theory bases its models on the behavioral assumption of perfect rationality, though it does give considerable attention to imperfect and asymmetrically distributed information and different risk preferences. This makes possible a formally rigorous analysis of the efficiency and earning effects of different auction
procedures, although the postulates thus won cannot simply be transferred to a world with bounded rationality on the part of economic
agents. This discussion will start out with the most important findings
of auction theory and then examine the comparative advantages and
disadvantages in the light of less rigorous behavioral assumptions.

Auction theory distinguishes four standard auction procedures, the
English auction, the *Dutch auction*, the *first-price sealed-bid auction*,
and the *second-price sealed-bid auction* (McAfee/McMillian 1987):
the *English auction* uses a public bidding procedure to successively
raise the price until only one bidder remains. The most important feature of the *English auction* is that each bidder is at any time familiar

with the height of the current bid. In contrast, the *Dutch auction* starts out with a maximum price that is then successively lowered by the auctioneer until one of the bidders accepts the price offered. In a *first-price sealed-bid auction* the bidders simultaneously submit nonpublic bids, and the highest bid is accepted. In contrast to the *English auction*, the bidders cannot observe the competing bids and are permitted to submit one bid only. The outcomes of the *Dutch* and *first-price sealed-bid auctions* are identical (McAfee/McMillian 1987, 706; Vickrey 1961). The *second-price sealed-bid auction*[10] is likewise won by the highest bidder, though this auction accepts only the price offered by the second highest bidder (McAfee/McMillian 1987, 702; Maskin 1992, 116). Under the laboratory conditions of risk neutrality and bidder symmetry[11] and independence of the valuation placed on the object by one bidder from that placed on it by another bidder, all four auctions arrive *on the average* at the same results (McAfee/McMillian 1987, 710).

In the face of different bidder *risk preferences*, the *English auction* and the *second-price sealed-bid auction* reach a Pareto-efficient allocation result, while the *first-price sealed-bid auction* and the *Dutch auction* do not: whereas in the *English auction* and the *second-price sealed-bid auction* a bidder cannot improve his position by submitting a bid that diverges from his reserve price, he can obtain a rent in the *Dutch auction* and the *first-price sealed-bid auction* by submitting a bid lower than his reserve price. The level of his "shading"[12] will depend on his assumption as to the bids made by the other bidders and on his risk preference. The higher his risk, the higher, ceteris paribus, will be the discrepancy between his bid and his reserve price. It is therefore possible for a bidder to win whose reserve price is lower than that of a rival bidder, but who has, owing to a lower risk preference, submitted a bid higher than that of a rival bidder with a higher reserve price and a higher risk preference. The allocative outcome of the *Dutch auction* and the *first-price sealed-bid auction* is consequently Pareto-inefficient when the bidders' risk preferences differ (Maskin 1985, 121; McAfee/McMillian 1987, 718).

The different auction procedures also vary in terms of their *informational efficiency*. Auction theory distinguishes between *private and common values* held by bidders (Maskin 1985, 124-130; McAfee/ McMillian 1987, 722). A value is private when a bidder's appraisal of an object is statistically perfectly independent of the appraisal made by other bidders. According to Hayek, the advantage of allocation through markets is to be found precisely in the communication of knowledge by the price system, which is spread across numerous individuals and accessible to no one in its totality (Hayek 1945, 519). A bidder's valuation of an object is therefore as a rule dependent on the way it is appraised by other market participants. Auction theory speaks in this case of common values. The question is whether, given common values, price formation through auctions reaches the informational efficiency attributed by Hayek to allocation through markets.

The value assigned to a firm by a bidder at an auction can be interpreted as a private bidder's *signal* on the firm's earning power, and this is pertinent to the firm's value for other bidders. A bidder's current reserve price is in such a case not geared solely to his own signal, it also takes note of the signals of other bidders (Maskin 1985, 123). An auction is efficient when the bid made by the bidder with the highest reserve price wins, the signals of other bidders having been taken into account. By definition, the two *sealed-bid auctions* and the *Dutch auction* preclude the bidders from observing the bids made by other bidders before they have submitted their own bid, thus making it impossible for them to consider these signals in forming their reserve price. The *English auction* differs from other auctions in that it offers bidders an additional piece of information: the remaining bidders can observe the price at which other bidders quit the auction. The bidders eliminated from the auction in this way reveal the private value which the firm has for them. Because of this informational feature, the *English auction*, given common values, will generally yield higher earnings than the *sealed-bid auctions* and the *Dutch auction* (McAfee/ McMillian 1987, 722; Milgrom/Weber 1985). Under the assumption of common values, auction theorists also rate the allocative efficiency of the *English auction* higher than that of other auction procedures, although, despite the common values, it need not necessarily lead to a Pareto-efficient outcome (Maskin 1985, 124-130; McAfee/McMillian 1987, 722). This is due to the fact that a bidder whose information is more important for another bidder's bid than it is for his own has no incentive to reveal this information in the bidding process. When common values are involved, it is sometimes easier for him to win an auction if he submits a lower bid than if he reveals pertinent information to his rival bidders by submitting a higher bid (Maskin 1985, 128; McAfee/ McMillian 1987, 722-723). The allocative outcome is in this case not Pareto-optimal.

The discussion within auction theory on common bidder values points to the central weakness of auction procedures: they can process only price information in their allocative decisions. This is a disadvantage especially when the assumption of perfect bidder rationality is abandoned. As was discussed at length in the section on informal sales procedures, if bidder rationality is bounded, it is impossible to sustain the assumption that the bidder with the highest reserve price will at the same time also have the most productive use for a firm. This shifts the problem in terms of the way it is seen in auction theory models: allocative efficiency then no longer depends on whether a mechanism is found that creates incentives for a bidder to offer, truthfully, his reserve price; it depends instead on whether, in comparison with situations limited to price information, it is possible to heighten the rationality of the allocative decision by taking account of multidimensional information. The discussion on common values adds a further aspect to this issue: what is at stake is the multiplication of information not merely vis-à-vis the allocator but also vis-à-vis rival bidders. Of the standard auctions it is the *English auction* alone that offers bidders immediate information on the highest bid of rival bidders as they are eliminated. Under the assumption of bounded rationality, this information is of limited relevance for a bidding process. The information behind a rival bidder's offer is not revealed to the other bidders. The time available is not sufficient to process the information provided by the elimination of other bidders. In an informal bargaining process, on the other hand, the privatization agency can force the bidders, e.g. by requiring them to present business plans and rehabilitation concepts, to reveal part of the information that has led to the formation of their reserve price. The privatization agency can in turn make part of this information available to other bidders. The better the bidders are informed, the higher are the revenues and the allocative efficiency of a sales procedure (McAfee/McMillian 1987, 722; Milgrom/Weber 1982). In a bargaining process the bidders will of course reveal to the privatization agency only part of the relevant information, and will strategically distort this information. This is especially true of the case discussed above in which a piece of information was of greater relevance to a rival bidder than it was for the bidder himself. There are, however, limits on the way in which information can be distorted in bidding competition, in that a bidder's chances of winning decline as information is more and more distorted. Informal privatization procedures thus increase the diversity of pertinent information not only for the allocator but for the bidders as well.

The significance of auctions for the privatization of firms is limited by an additional problem: auction procedures depend on competition. Owing to the asset-specificity of the capital of enterprises and the limited competence and financial resources of potential buyers, bidding competition is frequently low, in particular when the matter at hand is to privatize larger-size enterprises. The implications of limited bidding competition for the earning power and allocative efficiency of standard auctions, and the susceptibility of such auctions to bidder collusion, have been investigated extensively by auction theory: The revenues of auctions decline as the number of bidders decreases. In the presence of perfect bidding competition (McAfee/McMillian 1987, 711) the difference between the highest and second highest bids converges toward zero, the selling price thus reaching the highest possible value. All returns from the transaction will accrue to the seller (McAfee/McMillian 1987, 711; Holt 1979). If there is only one bidder, the auction is transformed into a bilateral monopoly, the selling price being identical with the reserve price set by the seller (McAfee/ McMillian 1987, 713). In this case, the seller can realize a higher price in bilateral negotiations.[13] The earning efficiency of auctions declines as the number of bidders decreases - though this is not necessarily true for allocative efficiency - as long as the bidder for whom the good has the highest value wins the auction (McAfee/McMillian 1987, 711).

The earning efficiency of auction procedures presupposes noncooperative bidder behavior. The bidders can, however, also form a cartel and
collude to reduce the price. The lower the number of bidders, the lower
will be the transaction costs required to form a cartel. The *English
auction* and the *second-bid auction* are particularly susceptible to collusion: with the *second-bid auction* the buyer cartel can decide that the
bidder with the highest reserve price for the item will submit a serious
bid, while all of the other cartel members submit bids below their reserve price. The winner's additional rent is then shared with the other
members of the cartel, without their having any incentive to bid higher
(Maskin 1985, 123). On the other hand, the sealed-bid auction offers
the individual cartel member an incentive to behave noncooperatively
and to bid somewhat higher than the highest price agreed upon, thus
obtaining a rent equivalent to the difference between his bid and his
reserve price (Maskin 1985, 123). Cartels are thus more apt to collapse
in sealed-bid auctions. According to the Folk theorem in game theory, a
cooperative outcome is possible here only in the case of infinitely reiterated games (i.e. auctions) (McAfee/McMillian 1987, 724). Collusion
impairs the earning efficiency of auctions, without, however, necessarily affecting their allocative efficiency: as long as the cartel reallocates
the good in favor of the bidder for whom the good has the highest value
(and a strategy of this kind is the dominant one), allocative efficiency is
not adversely affected (Maskin 1985, 123).

To summarize: The comparative advantage of auction procedures is
that they, bidding competition being given, are able to determine a
price for nonhomogeneous goods like firms without any comprehensive
valuation process. The simplicity of allocation is at the same time the
reason for the disadvantage of auction procedures: while allocation can
be simplified by restricting the information available to information on
price, it is in this case not possible to take into account multidimensional information that would permit inferences to be drawn on the efficiency of the use to which firms are to be put. In addition, auctions
depend on bidding competition. Under the assumption of uncertainty
and bounded rationality, the allocative efficiency of auctions thus decreases inversely to the size and complexity of the firms concerned.
The hypothesis was advanced above that as the asset specificity of

capital and the size of the firm concerned increase, the demands placed on buyer economic competence and financial resources will also rise. When the firms are highly complex, there is therefore neither sufficient bidding competition to guarantee the earning efficiency of auction procedures nor is it possible, under the assumption of bounded rationality, to reach a high level of allocative efficiency. Auction procedures therefore represent a good method for selling off small and medium-size firms; this is true for cases in which it is not possible to raise allocative efficiency essentially by taking account of multidimensional information and sufficient bidding competition is given. On the other hand, the lower the level of bidding competition and the higher the demand placed on buyer economic competence, the greater are the comparative advantages offered by informal privatization procedures as compared with auction procedures.

3.3.4   Sale of Company Shares on the Stock Exchange

The sale of complete enterprises through informal bargaining or auction procedures is limited by the constraint of restricted buyer financial resources. This constraint can be eased by selling enterprise shares publicly on the stock exchange. The individual shares can be purchased for reasonable sums and resold in a secondary market without incurring high transaction costs. Trading in company shares also makes it possible for the share-owners to diversify their portfolios, thus contributing to a more efficient allocation of risks.

Public trading in company shares on the stock exchange does, however, logically presuppose a separation of ownership and control, or more precisely, separation of the rights of ownership and decision. This separation alters the character of ownership, and whereas the sociological type of the entrepreneur unites the functions of decision-management and risk-taking in one person, now these functions are distributed across different groups. The problem of separating ownership and control was addressed by Adam Smith in the Wealth of Nations[14] and since the 1936 study of Adolph Berle and Gardiner Means (Berle/Means 1932) it has become a classical topos of the theory of the firm. Joseph Schumpeter even suspected that the separation of the rights of ownership and control would in the end abrogate capitalism:

> *"Mere stockholders of course have ceased to count*
> *at all - quite independently of the clipping of their*
> *share by a regulating and taxing state. Thus the*
> *modern corporation, although the product of the*
> *capitalist process, socializes the bourgeois mind; it*
> *relentlessly narrows the scope of capitalist motiva-*
> *tion; - not only that, it will eventually kill its roots"*
> (Schumpeter 1954, 156).

The arguments advanced in this discussion are also shaping the privatization debate in the transition countries: while the adherents of an *entrepreneur capitalism* warn of the danger that a broad dispersion of property rights could prevent the emergence of any genuine owners capable of efficiently managing their firms, i.e. that the goal of privatization might thus be missed (Kornai 1991, 39; Bauer 1992; Schmieding 1992), other authors emphasize the advantages of risk diversification and the easing of the capital constraint that can be achieved by anonymously trading company shares in capital markets (Lewandowski/ Szomburg 1989; Sachs 1991; Sinn/Sinn 1991; Vaubel 1992). Using the perspective of the New Institutional Economics, it is possible to distinguish returns and costs in the separation of the rights of ownership and decision. The returns are specialization profits that result from an efficient allocation of the two scarce factors of capital and economic competence (Fama/Jensen 1983a, 306; 1983b). While in a classical capitalist enterprise the equity capital is bound to the person of the entrepreneur (Alchian/Demsetz 1972, 783), the separation of the rights of ownership and decision affords the possibility of diversifying portfolios. In the view of portfolio theory (Fama/Jensen 1983a, 305; 1983b, 329), diversification can be used to reach a more efficient allocation of risks (Arrow 1964, 31). Also, when the rights of control and ownership have been separated, a firm's growth is no longer restrained by the entrepreneur's equity ratio (Jensen/Meckling 1976, 326-328). Finally, there emerge in this way additional degrees of freedom for the consumption of the capital gains involved, which in turn raises the utility of capital

(Fama 1983, 331; Wienecki 1991, 403). On the other hand, the separation of the rights of control and decision also makes possible a more efficient allocation of economic competence: when, in publicly traded firms, the rights of ownership and decision are delegated to a professional management, the choice of decision-makers no longer depends on their financial resources, it is instead geared solely to their qualification. The scarce resource of economic competence can consequently be allocated more efficiently (Fama/Jensen 1983b, 306).

These specialization returns stemming from the separation of the rights of control and ownership contrast with the costs stemming from the diminished incentives of a management that has no ownership rights in the firm. The lower management's share of the firm's capital, the lower, ceteris paribus, will be its incentives to run the firm in the sense of its owners (Jensen/Meckling 1976). Michael Jensen and William Meckling define as agency costs the costs that arise when owners delegate control rights over a firm to its management (Jensen/Meckling 1976, 308). The agency costs consist of monitoring costs incurred by the principal or his agent ("bonding costs") and the loss of the residual income ("residual loss") that results from delegation of control rights to management (Jensen/Meckling 1976, 308). In a wider sense, agency costs can also be designated as transaction costs (Jensen/Meckling 1976, 308; Williamson 1988, 572; 1990, 67).

The level of the agency costs and the discretionary latitudes open to management are contingent on the competition in three markets: the capital market, including the market for corporate takeovers (1); the product market (2); and the labor market for managers (3):

The main argument of disciplining management is based on the efficiency of *capital markets* (Furubotn/Pejovich 1972, 1150; Alchian/ Demsetz 1972, 788; Picot/Kaulmann 1985; Kaulmann 1987). The advantage of separating the rights of control and decision is that, unlike the case of unincorporated firms, the company shares can be sold in a secondary market with low transaction costs. The property rights are allocated anonymously, the personal configuration being irrelevant, although current trading in company shares does provide a control potential: the expected company earnings are evaluated on a day-to-day basis, and hence the market price of company shares reflects expectations on the capitalized value of current management decisions (Pejovich 1976, 15; Furubotn/Pejovich 1972, 1150; Alchian/ Demsetz 1972, 788). The market value of the company shares constitutes a two-fold constraint on the discretionary behavior of management: first, as the market value of company shares declines, the costs of external financing rise, which in turn restricts the scopes of action open to management (Picot/Michaelis 1984). Second, if the value of company shares is impaired by discretionary management behavior, the incentives to replace the current management will grow. Management can be replaced either by the current owners (Furubotn/Pejovich 1972, 1150; Demsetz/Lehn 1985) or by new owners in connection with a takeover (Manne 1965).

A number of theoretical and empirical arguments have been advanced against the efficiency of control of management by the capital markets: first, doubts have been expressed as to whether owners effectively exercise their control function. If corporate ownership is widely dispersed, the control of management has the character of a public good: the costs of control are borne by each shareholder himself, while the earnings stemming from such control benefit all shareholders alike. Individual free-rider behavior is therefore rational even when it would be possible to raise considerably the earnings of shareholders as a group by stepping up the efforts invested in control (Vickers/Yarrow 1988, 13; Alchian 1969, 501; Alchian/Demsetz 1972, 788).

Second, control by takeover entails high transaction costs and risks. Grossmann and Hart have shown that free-rider behavior on the part of shareholders who expect a takeover to increase the value of their shares can cause a takeover bid to fail (Grossmann/Hart 1980). Empirical studies, too, have found only weak correlations between low corporate profitability and the probability of takeovers, while noting a negative correlation between company size and the frequency of takeovers (Singh 1975).

Competition in *product markets* likewise restrains management's discretionary behavior. The latitudes open to management are limited by a "bankruptcy constraint" (Vickers/Yarrow 1988, 24-26) in that the elimination of an firm from the market impairs management's earnings and the value of its human capital. If competition were perfect, management's discretionary latitudes would shrink to zero in that any divergence from the profit-maximizing norm would squeeze the company out of the market (Pejovich 1976, 10; Fama 1983a, 289; Kaulmann 1987, 75; Picot/Kaulmann 1985, 960). Perfect competition, however, is an idealized assumption. Depending on the intensity of competition, real markets allow a more or less high level of "X-inefficiency" (Leibenstein 1966). The discretionary latitudes open to management, and thus the agency costs of the separation of ownership and control, are consequently conditioned by the competition in the company's product markets (Vickers/Yarrow 1988, 26).

Finally, competition in the *labor market for managers* restricts management's discretionary behavior (Alchian/Demsetz 1972, 788; Alchian 1969; Furubotn/Pejovich 1972, 1150-1152). The value of the human capital of a manager, and thus the manager's current and future income flows, depends on how the firm's owners or control organs evaluate a managers behavior (Alchian 1969, 504). A firm's management is not a monolithic block; there is instead both internal and external competition for management posts (Fama 1983a, 289; Alchian 1969, 504). This competition governs management control from the bottom to the top, because the lower levels of management have an incentive to signalize management's discretionary behavior to the firm's owners (Kaulmann 1987, 80; Picot/Kaulmann 1985, 961). To the extent that management refrains from playing endgames, i.e. to the extent that incentives for cooperation are not removed by a manager's intention to leave the firm, the labor market for managers constitutes, in the view of the property rights literature, an effective constraint against discretionary behavior (Furubotn/Pejovich 1972, 1154; Alchian 1969, 504).

Under the assumptions of bounded rationality and opportunism, none of these markets operates perfectly, and thus the separation of owner-

ship and control gives rise to nontrivial transaction costs (Jensen/
Meckling 1976, 328; Pejovich 1976, 16). These transaction costs must
be weighed against the earnings stemming from an easing of the asset
constraint on the expansion of enterprises and the specialization gains
of management and risk-bearers.

The separation of the rights of decision and control also give rise to
high transaction costs stemming from the primary allocation of company shares on the stock exchange: public trading in company shares
presupposes extensive knowledge if investor risk is to be limited
(Schmidt 1981, 201). One condition for the issue of company shares on
the stock exchange is evidence of the profitability, or at least the high
profitability potential of the firm concerned (Vuylsteke 1988, 13).
Firms that wish to issue shares on the stock exchange are therefore
obliged to provide extensive control and information services such as
the establishment of control organs, balance statements, independent
audits, advertising, and promotion (Vuylsteke 1988). These information and control services have a fixed-cost share, and thus as company
size increases, the costs involved in issuing stock will decline (Schmidt
1981, 203). Proof of financial standing is especially expensive in
transition countries, because the transformation of their institutional
and economic framework has led to depreciation of part of their asset-
specific capital, and old accounting data is not an adequate basis for
forecasting a firm's future success. In order to create confidence in
valuations of existing firms, the companies are obliged to have audits
performed by internationally reputable auditing organizations (Apáthy
1991; Sachs 1991).

A new issue of stock also gives rise to high costs in western countries
with developed capital markets. In their study on the British privatization program, John Vickers and George Yarrow indicate a figure, depending on company particulars, of between 2.8 and 11.2 percent of
privatization revenues for advertising, promotion, intermediary fees,
etc. (Vickers/ Yarrow 1988, 181). The costs for new issues on the stock
exchange are estimated for Great Britain at an average of 4.5 percent of
privatization revenues (Vickers/Yarrow 1988, 183). These expenses are
considerably higher in transition countries: for five major corporations

in Poland which were privatized via the stock exchange, Jeffrey Sachs calculated costs for company valuation, investment bank fees and bonus payments amounting to 25 percent of company value (Sachs 1991, 8). Even the primary allocation of company shares gives rise to nontrivial transaction costs. Two different price-setting procedures are used for the primary allocation of stock: the most frequent one is a public offer for sale at a fixed price. Oversubscribed shares are allocated on the basis of a specific rationing scheme (e.g. in favor of small investors), undersubscribed shares remain with the state. Middlemen are often put under an obligation to take on undersubscribed stock, and receive a risk premium for doing so (Vickers/Yarrow 1988, 173-176). This allocation procedure necessarily leads to mismatches: if the fixed price is too low, the state loses revenues and the buyers are able to pocket a rent. The shares issued in connection with the British privatization program were on the average fourfold oversubscribed, prices rose an average of 18.4 percent on the day of the issue (Vickers/Yarrow 1988, 177). When shares of the Hungarian travel corporation Ibusz were privatized on the Vienna stock exchange, the shares were 23-fold oversubscribed, and they were subject to sharp course fluctuations following the issue (Apáthy 1991, 20). When the issue price is too high, the state is unable to privatize all of the shares. Misallocation due to non-market-clearing issue prices is a particular problem when the company's stock has not yet been traded on the stock exchange. It is therefore easier to reach a market-clearing price when company shares are offered step by step in a number of tranches (Vickers/Yarrow 1988, 171).

Another primary allocation procedure is to auction off company shares ("*tender offer*"). The state sets a minimum price and calls on buyers to submit bids. The shares are sold to the highest bidders at the price at which demand and supply are in equilibrium. Undersubscribed shares are sold to bidders at the minimum price (Vuylsteke 1988, 112; Vickers/Yarrow 1988, 173). Middlemen are often put under an obligation to purchase undersubscribed shares. The risk of bidder collusion is low due to a wide dispersion of the shares (Vickers/Yarrow 1988, 173). The allocative and earning efficiency of this procedure is naturally higher; the British privatization program saw fluctuations of mostly less than one percent on the day of issue (Vickers/Yarrow 1988). The disadvantage of this tender-offer procedure is its complexity for investors. The fixed-price procedure is more attractive particularly for small investors. If the intention is to broadly disperse the shares and to accelerate privatization with the help of discount prices, the fixed-price procedure is for this reason preferable (Vuylsteke 1988, 113).

Compared with informal privatization procedures, but with auction procedures as well, privatization on the stock exchange is time-consuming and cost-intensive. Only viable enterprises with a good financial standing can be traded. In the large-scale privatization programs in Great Britain and Chile, the firms concerned were first rehabilitated and restructured (Smith 1991, 12). In the transition countries, only a small proportion of the enterprises concerned is viable.[15] The transaction costs involved in splitting up and rehabilitating large-size enterprises are, however, especially high under the specific conditions encountered in the transition countries. Even the problems involved in applying for a listing could doom to failure the privatization of a major share of the state business sector on the stock exchange (Sachs 1991).

One matter, however, that is of great significance is the issue of the impact that the separation the of rights of control and decision have on the allocative efficiency under the specific conditions prevalent in the transition countries. In the western industrialized nations, corporations whose shares are traded on the stock exchange represent the latest stage in the development of property rights. Even in countries with developed capital markets, they make up only a comparatively small share of productive capital. Privatization of the state business sector via the stock exchange turned this development upside down, placing the broad dispersion of company shares at the beginning of the development of private property rights. It must be expected that a shift will occur in the equilibrium between the costs and earnings linked with the separation of the rights of control and decision under the specific conditions of system transformation: the uncertainty as to the capitalized value of the firms concerned is much too high to give rise to expectations of any efficient control of corporate management via the capital markets. There are no viable business data available that could provide information on which predictions of future earnings could be based (Apáthy 1991). The transformation of the economic and institutional framework conditions has led to a depreciation of a share of asset-specific capital, and thus past operating statements cannot provide the basis for forecasts of a firm's future. In view of the high level of uncertainty on the value of firms, it is unlikely that the information available in the capital markets can be communicated efficiently. Competition in the product markets in the transition countries is underdeveloped. The ability of firms to file for bankruptcy is often restricted by legal, but also political, framework conditions, so that in particular many large firms continue to operate under the conditions of a soft budget constraint. The principal-agent costs of publicly traded corporations will therefore be far higher than in western countries with developed capital markets. In privatization on the stock exchange, the advantage involved in an easing of the asset constraint is counteracted by very high transaction costs of primary allocation and the management and control of privatized enterprises.

3.3.5   Voucher Schemes

In the transition countries, a cost-free distribution of vouchers is practiced as a means of overcoming the capital constraint and accelerating privatization. The cost-free distribution of vouchers to the population was proposed for the privatization of large enterprises in the Czech and Slovak republics by the former finance minister and current prime minister Václav Klaus and his former deputy Dusan Tríska (Tríska 1990), in Poland by the later privatization minister Janusz Lewandowski and by Jan Szomburg (Lewandowski/Szomburg 1989), in Hungary by Karol Attila Soós and Márton Tardos (Bauer 1992, 297) and in Russia by Anatoly Tchubais and Maxim Boycko (Boycko/Shleifer/ Vishny 1995). Different procedures are to be used for the allocation of company shares:

In the Czech Republic and Slovakia vouchers were used to purchase at auctions shares of large firms for which no restitution claims have been filed and for which there will no prospective private buyers from abroad (Charap/Dyba/Kupka 1992, 16-20). Every Czech citizen over 18 years of age was entitled to purchase the vouchers for a symbolic price of 100 Kcs (some 33 US $) per 1000 investment points and 35 Kcs for a book of vouchers (Charap/Dyba/Kupka 1992, 17). The state catalogues the companies to be privatized and sets a reserve price for the shares based on a valuation. The participants in an auction can decide on the basis of the investment points they have acquired how many shares they wish to purchase. But the shares are not allocated when, as in the case of the Walrasian auction process, a market-clearing equilibrium is reached between supply and demand; they are in this case rationed on the basis of specific schemes: if aggregate demand is lower than or equal to supply, all bidders win. The remaining shares are then offered at a lower price in subsequent stages of the auction process. When aggregate demand is more than 25 percent above supply, the vouchers are returned to the investors and the shares are offered for sale at the next stage at a higher price. When demand is less than 25 percent above supply, the individual bidders are the first to be served, while the demand of investment funds can be reduced by as much as 20 percent. Citizens can participate individually in auctions or transfer their shares to investment funds, receiving in return shares of the fund (Charap/Dyba/Kupka 1992, 17). Russia and some other republics of the former Soviet Union combined voucher-schemes with management- and employee-buyouts. The bulk of the enterprise shares was transferred to the management and the employees against vouchers and cash with huge price preferences. In contrast to the Czech model, the privatization through vouchers led in Russia to a take-over of control by the enterprise insiders (Boycko/Shleifer/Vishny 1995).

In Poland the population can purchase company shares not via auction but through holdings in intermediary investment funds. These investment funds can in turn acquire, at auctions, shares in state-owned enterprises. An action program going back to the Bielecki Government (Delhaes 1992) provides for the establishment of between five and twenty intermediary investment funds, each of which can acquire by auction 33 percent of a firm's shares, with 27 percent of the shares being distributed over the remaining investment funds. In addition, the principal shareholder established in this way is given the voting rights for 30 percent of the shares that remain government property and are earmarked to provide, at a later point of time, the financial base of the country's social insurance fund (Delhaes 1992, 62). A model similar to that in Poland is also scheduled to be tested in Albania (Åslund/ Sjöberg 1992, 141-143).

Apart from distributive arguments,[16] the most important argument in favor of privatization by voucher is acceleration of the privatization process. The intention in privatizing large enterprises is to abrogate both the microeconomic constraint entailed by the limited financial resources available to individual buyers and the macroeconomic constraint posed by low levels of saving (Lewandowski/Szomburg 1989, 264). Whether the issue of vouchers will in fact lead to an acceleration of the privatization process is also a disputed issue: like the case of privatization via the stock exchange, preparations for auctioning off company shares via vouchers is time-consuming and cost-intensive. But the main objection to privatization by voucher is that the abrogation of the asset constraint is bought at the expense of an inefficient reallocation of property rights.

Like privatization on the stock exchange, the distribution of investment vouchers logically presupposes the separation of the rights of ownership and decision. Compared with privatization on the stock exchange, property rights are even more widely dispersed when this method is used. The costs of information on the firm concerned and control of the management in charge of decision-making are prohibitively high for the individual entrepreneur. The rights of control and decision must be delegated to agents. Privatization by voucher gives rise to three groups of agents who can take over the entrepreneur's rights of decision and control: first, individual shareholders who, by consolidating relatively small shares of capital, can gain, either directly or indirectly, control over investment funds. Second, the management of investment funds either set up by government or developed privately can gain control of large portions of the productive capital of entire economies. Third, and finally, the more widely dispersed the shares are, the easier it is for the management of the firms to protect themselves against replacement and control by the owners.

In their classical study on the agency problem, Michael Jensen and William Meckling pointed out that when the agent's capital share declines, the incentives for discretionary behavior will, ceteris paribus, rise (Jensen/Meckling 1976, 315-318). In developed western industrialized economies, it is possible to restrict this discretionary behavior when capital-, product-, and labor-markets for managers operate efficiently. With privatization by voucher, the agents hold infinitely small proprietary interests, while the efficiency of control mechanisms of capital markets has not yet developed: the informational efficiency of capital markets in which the property rights to a majority of large firms are allocated to a great variety of small and poorly informed shareholders must be seen as very low. Government creation or private development of intermediary investment funds does not solve the problem, it merely shifts it: the question is how the management of investment funds is to be controlled. The discretionary behavior open to agents, be they intermediary investment funds or the management of the firms themselves, are therefore very large. The actual goal of privatization, to increase the intensity of the incentives of decision-making management and reallocate economic competence, may thus be missed when property rights are increasingly dispersed through privatization by voucher:

> "The central point is that the voucher scheme does not solve the problem it is intended to solve, as it does not turn voucher holders into genuine private owners. (...) the sense of privatization is to replace government officials as principals, in relation to managers of large firms as agents, by genuine private owners. Thousands of small shareholders in a former socialist country cannot play that role" (Bauer 1992, 297-298; see also Kornai 1991, 39).

3.3.6   Restitution

There is today a far-reaching consensus among the public of the transition countries that the expropriation of productive assets under socialist regimes was not legitimate (Kornai 1991, 8). Once the Communist

parties had been toppled, a number of governments therefore decided
to return at least part of the expropriated firms to the former owners or
their heirs (Charap/Dyba/Kupka 1992, 15; Delhaes 1992, 61; Kiss
1991). Restitution is for the most part justified with ethical motives
(see Chapter 4), though efficiency arguments are sometimes also cited:
the expectation is that restitution of firms to their former owners and
their families will restore close personal ties to property, thus ensuring
that the uses to which it is put will be particularly productive and en-
courage a revival of entrepreneurial traditions. Under the assumption of
nontrivial transaction costs it can, however, be demonstrated that restitution gives rise to particularly high costs stemming from the assignment and reallocation of property rights.

Restitution requires a protracted process involving the definition and
assignment of property rights. Both the scope and state of the property
and the identity of the former owners has as a rule changed since the
property was expropriated (Sinn/Sinn 1991, 77). Firms were merged,
old production facilities closed down while new equipment was acquired, new plant built while the old was disposed of, etc. Many company divisions and properties were resold several times over, so that it
is now conceivable that various legitimate claims will be lodged
(Sinn/Sinn 1991, 77-78). In cases of expropriations that go back more
than forty years, the beneficiaries of restitution are as a rule no longer
the former owners but their heirs and communities of heirs. Restitution
must reconstruct completely the former ownership relations and decide
in favor of one of a number of competing legal claims. In a state ruled
by law, the guarantee of protection against arbitrary legal procedures
requires that all individuals have a complete right of appeal. If it proves
impossible for all of those concerned to reach an agreement, a final
decision on the ownership relations in question has to be made by the
highest appeals court. Another difficulty facing the reconstruction of
ownership relations is that title registers that can be used to define
clearly property ownership in western societies were not kept on a reli-
able basis, and often destroyed, falsified, or blackened out, in the
transition countries (Sinn/Sinn 1991, 76-81).

In a state governed by the rule of law, the final personal restitution, taking account of all claims lodged, takes not years but decades (Wissenschaftlicher Beirat beim Bundesministerium für Wirtschaft 1991, 9-11). But firms cannot be resold until the ownership issue has been decided finally, and any changes made in such enterprises are subject to numerous restrictions. The economic incentives to invest capital in firms whose ownership deeds are unclear are low. Restitution therefore not only retards privatization, it also jeopardizes any productive use and further development of the firms concerned until the issue of ownership has been settled finally (Wissenschaftlicher Beirat beim Bundesministerium für Wirtschaft 1991, 9-13). According to property rights theories, the value of a resource is dependent on the definition and security of the property rights to it (Furubotn/Pejovich 1992, 1139). Restitution subjects property rights to numerous constraints until the issue of ownership has been settled finally, while at the same time also increasing legal uncertainty, thus leading, ceteris paribus, to a decline in the value of such firms.

The allocative criterion of restitution is not economic competence and the financial resources of the beneficiaries but a legal claim extending back to the period prior to expropriation. In all transition countries, the significant waves of expropriation took place decades ago, most expropriations having been made during the immediate postwar period. It is not only the firms but also the owners' human capital that has changed since then. The former owners are as a rule no longer apt to be in a position to take on the rights of decision for enterprises restored to them. In cases of expropriations effected decades ago, restitution leads to a random selection of owners and not to an efficient reallocation of property rights (Sinn/Sinn 1991, 77; Kornai 1991, 8). In most cases it is therefore necessary to resell the ownership or decision-making rights. In cases of restitution, however, the costs involved in reallocating property rights are especially high: property rights are often transferred not to one individual but to several claimants. These persons must then reach agreement on the use of their property.

Seen in relation to other privatization procedures, the allocative efficiency of restitution has, in every respect, a number of comparative drawbacks: the definition and personal assignment of property rights is more time-consuming and entails higher transaction costs than any other privatization procedure, and this high level of allocative effort does not lead to an efficient assignment of property rights, which gives rise to very high reallocation costs.

3.4   Privatization with Limited Buyer Competition

Competition of buyers is more the exception than the rule in the privatization processes of the transition countries. Analytically, it is possible to distinguish two causes for restricted buyer competition in privatization processes: first, the idiosyncratic character of the firm as a good restricts the number of buyers. With increasing asset specificity of capital and company size, the demands placed on the economic competence and financial resources of a bidder grow. The number of bidders involved in the privatization of complete enterprises therefore decreases as the complexity of the enterprise increases. The privatization agencies and governments in the transition countries can of course use a number of measures to influence the extent of bidding competition; these include information and promotion, reduction of restrictions on foreign direct investment, and above all deconcentration of the enterprises concerned. But deconcentration reaches its limits in the high transaction costs with which the state is confronted in identifying and creating viable corporate entities. It must on the whole be expected that there will be only a low level of bidding competition in the privatization of large firms that formerly formed part of the key industries of the Central and Eastern European countries.

Second, buyer competition is affected by the choice of a privatization procedure. When company shares are privatized which can be traded publicly in a secondary market, there will generally be bidding competition. But this presupposes the separation of the rights of ownership and control, which in turn gives rise to high transaction costs involved in the control and primary allocation of such firms. If privatization is restricted to the sale of complete enterprises because of the high transaction costs involved in the separation of the rights of ownership and decision, then the only alternatives are informal bargaining and auction procedures. Under the assumption of bounded rationality, informal negotiated agreements can reach a higher level of informational efficiency than formal bidding procedures. The reverse side of this procedure is, however, that, precisely because of the complexity of the information to be processed, bargaining is as a rule conducted with only one bidder or a limited number of bidders (Härtel et al. 1992, 21). One of the central arguments against selecting informal bargaining procedures for privatization is therefore the restriction of bidding competition they involve (Siebert 1992, 99; Maskin 1992, 117). Any premature commitment to one bidder on the part of the privatization agency emphatically undercuts the agency's bargaining position (Härtel et al. 1992, 21-22). In a bilateral monopoly the bidder can then strategically weaken the privatization agency's bargaining position by playing for time (Härtel et al. 1992, 22; Siebert 1992, 99). The demand is often made that competitive bidding procedures should be given preference over informal bargaining solutions as a means of avoiding this competitive restraint (Maskin 1992, 116; Siebert 1992, 99).

The present study, on the other hand, advances the thesis that the case of a bilateral monopoly is not even given when a privatization agency bargains with only one bidder. Even in bilateral bargaining, the bidder is faced with the risk that a further bidder may enter the bargaining process at a later point of time. The threat of bidding competition alone is sufficient to affect a bidder's behavior. This argument was developed in a different context by Joseph Schumpeter:

> "(...) competition of the kind we now have in mind acts not only when in being but also when it is merely an ever-present threat. It disciplines before it attacks. The business feels himself to be in a competitive situation even if he is alone in his field (...). In many cases, though not in all, this will in the long run enforce behavior very similar to the perfectly competitive pattern." (Schumpeter 1942/ 1954, 85).

The theory of "contestable markets" developed by William Baumol, John Panzer, and Robert Willig (Baumol/Panzer/Willig 1992) is of course based on a similar notion: in a market where costs of entry and exit are zero, monopolists and oligopolists will, given elastic demand, adapt their behavior to the conditions of perfect competition (Baumol 1992, 1-15).

Competitive restraint is here examined using the procedures of game theory. The argument is developed in two steps: the first step presents the outcomes of bargaining in a bilateral monopoly. The sequential bargaining model is then expanded to include the chance that a further bidder might join the negotiations at a later point of time. The intention is to use this model to analyze Schumpeter's idea that competition can also be effective as a threat. The analysis will show that merely the threat that a further bidder may enter the bargaining will cause the outcomes of bilateral bargaining to converge toward the competitive solution; this amounts to a refutation of one of the central arguments against the use of informal bargaining procedures.

A number of simplified assumptions must be made before it is possible to employ the procedures of game theory to examine the existence and the outcomes of strategic bargaining equilibria in a bilateral monopoly: both parties must have solved for themselves the problem of valuation. The bargaining space is limited by the reserves prices of seller and buyer alike. The privatization agency's reserve price p_{pa} is the cutoff point below which the agency would be worse off if it sold the object. Conversely, bidder reserve price p_b denotes the upper limit above which the bidder would be worse off to purchase the object. The individual reserve prices are the points of conflict in the bargaining. The difference between the bidder's reserve price and the seller's reserve price is the net return of the transaction π ($\pi = p_b - p_{pa}$). Both parties behave rationally, i.e. the privatization agency will neither submit nor accept an offer below its reserve price, while the bidder in turn will neither submit nor accept an offer above his reserve price. Consequently, a transaction will take place only if the bargaining results in positive net returns ($p_b \geq p_{pa}$). Finally, it is assumed in the name of simplicity that complete information is given, i.e. the valuation is known to each party. The author has elsewhere analyzed the outcomes that result in the presence of imperfect and asymmetrical information on the part of the contracting parties (Brücker 1995, 144-152; see also Myerson/Satterthwaite 1993; Ausubel/Deneckere 1989). This simplification does, however, appear permissible for the examination of different outcomes in a bilateral monopoly, latent bidding competition being given.

Traditional microeconomics regards the outcome of bilateral bargaining as indeterminate (Harsanyi 1956, 144; 1990, 190; Eggertsson 1990, 109). Since Edgeworth it has placed only two rationality-related demands on the outcome of bilateral bargaining: first, neither of the parties may accept an outcome that would place it in a position worse than that which could have been achieved without bargaining (*individual rationality* or *participation constraint*). Second, the outcome must meet the criterion of Pareto optimality, i.e. no other outcome is possible that would improve the position of the one party without weakening the other party's position (*common rationality*) (Harsanyi 1956, 144; 1990, 190). These postulates are met in an Edgeworth box with two bargaining parties when the outcome lies within the lens of the two curves of indifference of initial financial endowment (individual rationality) and along the contract curve of Pareto-optimal distributions (common rationality), i.e. in the "core" of the Edgewood box. In other words, traditional microeconomics defines the limit of any efficient outcomes, but does so without making any propositions on the distribution of the net returns in bilateral bargaining.

Game theory, on the other hand, seeks to define unambiguously the outcomes of bilateral bargaining. Under the assumption that each party is familiar with the other party's reserve price, the so-called *Nash equilibrium* (Nash 1950; 1953) provides a clear-cut outcome based on rational expectations of the actions of the other party. What is behind the Nash equilibrium is the following intuition: to the extent that both players have the same strategic possibilities and the same bargaining power, no player will accept an outcome that places him in a worse position than his counterpart. The net returns of the bargaining will hence be divided equally between two players (Harsanyi 1990, 191).

Formally, the bargaining solution maximizes the so-called Nash product (Harsanyi 1990, 192; Holler/Illing 1993),

$$(3.2) \qquad \pi = \left(u_{pa} - c_{pa}\right)\left(u_b - c_b\right) \quad \text{with } u_{pa}, \, u_b \in F \text{ and } u \geq c,$$

where u designates the utility of the bargaining solution for each player, c each player's conflict point, F the space defined by possible bargaining solutions, and π the net return of the transaction. The Nash product reaches its maximum when the net returns of bargaining are divided equally between the two players. The Nash solution fulfills the Pareto criterion, i.e. no player can benefit from a different outcome without disadvantaging the other player (Harsanyi 1990, 191).

The Nash equilibrium is based on rational expectations of the behavior of the other players: no player can improve his position by deviating from his equilibrium strategy, provided that the other player also plays his equilibrium strategy.[17] The Nash equilibrium is to this extent not a strong equilibrium in *dominant* strategies, which, regardless of the strategy selected by the other player, must invariably be the best strategy; it is instead a weak equilibrium which depends on rational expectations of other players' behavior.

The Nash solution can also be modeled as a sequential bargaining process in which it is always the same player who has to make the next concession and whose last bid contains a lower Nash product than the bid made by his fellow-player (Zeuthen 1930; Harsanyi 1956). This behavior can also be the result of a rational player's calculation: a player whose last bid contains a Nash product lower than that of his counterpart takes a greater risk that the bargaining process may be terminated, leaving him only his conflict payoff (Harsanyi 1956, 149). The outcome of this sequential bargaining process converges toward the Nash solution, i.e. in a bargaining equilibrium both players receive the same share of the net returns of the transaction (Harsanyi 1956; 1990).

The Nash equilibrium is a statical equilibrium, it disregards duration and costs of the bargaining process. Under dynamic conditions, it may be assumed that the bargaining parties would prefer an earlier result to a later one. The length of the bargaining process entails costs. In privatizing enterprises in transition countries, these costs are unequally distributed between the privatization agency and the bidder: while the privatization agency is forced to bear both its firms' current losses and the risk of a possible capital loss in the form of a lower selling price, the bidder is faced only with the opportunity costs of lost profits and the risk, that the firm in question may rise in value. The political pressure to waste no time in privatizing the state-owned business sector additionally increases the costs incurred by the privatization agency in the bargaining process. In other words, the time preferences of privatization agency and bidders will tend to differ owing to the high transaction costs involved in running and controlling the state business sector. In a bilateral monopoly the bidder can thus improve his strategic position and force down the price by protracting the negotiations.

The effects of different time preferences on the outcome of bilateral bargaining were first analyzed in a paper by Ståhl (Ståhl 1972) dealing with a sequential bargaining process with a finite time horizon. Rubinstein (Rubinstein 1982; Fudenberg/Tirole 1992; Holler/Illing 1993; Sutton 1986) later expanded this model to include games with an infinite time horizon, and then generalized the results. In a Ståhl-Rubinstein game, a pie set to be divided up between two players diminishes in size from bargaining period to bargaining period. In our case the pie is the potential net return of privatization defined as the differential of the privatization agency's reserve price and the bidder's reserve price. Per definition it is set at one ($\pi = p_b - p_{pa} = 1$).The Ståhl-Rubinstein game models a sequential bargaining process in which both players submit reciprocal bids. In period $t = 0$, for instance, the bidder proposes dividing up the pie in such a way that he receives share x and the privatization agency is left with share 1-x. If the privatization agency accepts the bid, the payoff that results is π ($\pi = \pi_b, \pi_{pa} = x, 1-x$). If it rejects the outcome, it can in subsequent period $t = 1$ submit an offer itself (y, 1-y), which may in turn be accepted or rejected by the bidder, etc. The bargaining process has no time limits, but the pie to be distributed becomes smaller over the course of time. The costs of each bargaining period are denoted by the individual discount factor δ_i ($0 = \leq \delta_i \leq 1$) of each player i[18] at which the payoffs ($\pi = \pi_{pa}$, π_b) are discounted.

The utility functions of the privatization agency and the bidder are then

$$(3.3a) \qquad U_{pa} = \delta_{pa}^t P_{pa} \qquad and\ 0 \leq \delta_{pa} \leq 1,\ \delta_{pa} \leq \delta_b\ ;$$

$$(3.3b) \qquad {}_b = \delta_b^t P_b \qquad and\ 0 \leq \delta_b \leq 1,\ \delta_b \leq \delta_{pa}$$

Privatization agency and bidder are indifferent both toward a bid made by another player at time t and the realization of their own proposal in subsequent period t+1, if

$$(3.4a) \qquad \delta_{pa}^t(1-x) = \delta_{pa}^{t+1} y \quad resp. \quad 1-x = \delta_{pa} y\ ;$$

$$(3.4b) \qquad {}_b^t(1-y) = \delta_b^{t+1} x \quad resp. \quad 1-y = \delta_b x.$$

Transformation of these conditions of indifference in the bargaining equilibrium results in optimal bids x* and y*:

$$(3.5) \qquad x* = \frac{1-\delta_{pa}}{1-\delta_{pa}\delta} \quad and \quad y* = \frac{1-\delta_b}{1-\delta_{pa}\delta}\ .$$

Both parties will accept this solution in the first period, because their position cannot be improved by a new bid in the subsequent period. The bargaining solution described here with optimal strategies x* and y* represents a *subgame-perfect Nash equilibrium* (Selten 1975), i.e. no player can improve his position in any subgame (here: in any bargaining period) by making an offer in a subsequent period, if the other player plays his equilibrium strategy, too (Holler/Illing 1993, 18, 255).

Fig. 3.2: Payoffs in the Rubinstein-Game

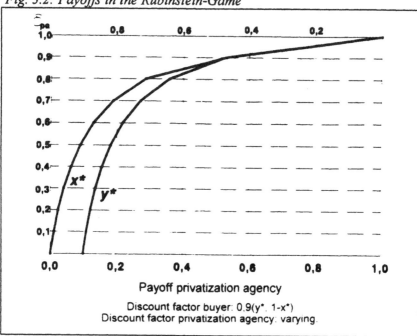

Payoff privatization agency

Discount factor buyer: 0,9(y*, 1-x*)
Discount factor privatization agency: varying.

The subgame-perfect equilibrium of the Ståhl-Rubinstein game benefits the player with the greater patience or with the lower time preference: If $\delta_{pa} = 0$, threats made by the privatization agency will have no force, so that the bidder, when it is his turn, can secure the entire pie for himself. If both discount factors are equally great ($\delta_{pa} = \delta_b = \delta$), the payoffs that result for the first player are $x^* = 1/(1+\delta)$ and $1-x^* = \delta/(1-\delta)$. It is thus advantageous to submit the first bid. If discount factors δ approximate to 1, the solution of the Ståhl-Rubinstein game converges toward the Nash solution.[19]

Bilateral monopoly and imperfect bidding competition constitute the two extreme cases in the privatization of state-owned enterprises in the transforming economies. While the privatization agency in many cases bargains with only one bidder, a further bidder can joint the bargaining process at a later point of time. This is the normal case in privatization via informal bargaining. There is latent bidding competition. The question is how this latent bidding competition will affect the bargaining strategies of both parties. Does latent competition "discipline before it attacks" (Schumpeter)?

The situation of latent bidding competition is represented by an extension of the Ståhl-Rubinstein game: in analogy to the Ståhl-Rubinstein game, privatization agency and bidder submit reciprocal bids in a sequential bargaining process. The privatization agency's reserve price is set at zero ($p_{pa} = 0$) and the bidder's reserve price at one ($p_b = 1$), so that, as in the Ståhl-Rubinstein game, the net returns are normalized as one. In the task of privatization, the privatization agency is under substantially more time pressure than the bidder ($\delta_{pa} < \delta_b$), so that the bidder, in the bargaining equilibrium of bilateral monopoly, is able to secure for himself the greater share of the net returns ($\pi > 1/2$). Unlike the case in the Ståhl-Rubinstein game, however, a further bidder can join the bargaining process in the subsequent bargaining period. It is assumed for the sake of simplicity that the offer submitted or accepted by the new bidder in the subsequent period is equivalent to the bidder's reserve price ($x_{b2} = 1$). Probability p that a further bidder will enter in the subsequent period is common knowledge of the privatization agency and the bidder.

The structure of the ensuing bargaining period is represented in Fig. 3.3: in initial period $t = 0$, the case of a bilateral monopoly is still given, though in subsequent period $t = 1$, q is the probability that a further bidder will appear. When, under the new bargaining conditions in period $t = 0$, it is the bidder's move, the privatization agency can either accept the payoff of his bid 1-x or in the subsequent period, with a probability of q, realize payoff 1, with a counterprobability of 1-q that no further bidder will appear, and it must make the old bidder a counteroffer. When it is the privatization agency's turn, the bidder can either accept the payoff of the privatization agency's offer of 1-y or, with a probability of 1-q, submit a bid x of his own. But probability q is the likelihood that he will realize a payoff of 0 because the privatization agency has sold to another bidder (Sutton 1986). (See Fig. 3.3.)

Figure 3.3: Rubinstein-Game with Latent Bidding Competition

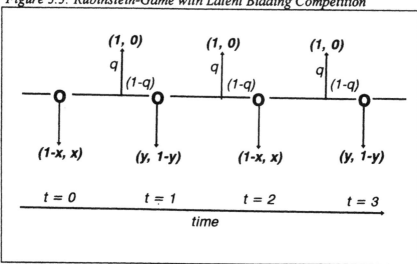

Under the new bargaining conditions, privatization agency and bidder are then indifferent toward a bid submitted by the other party and the expected benefit in the subsequent period, if

(3.6a)
$$\delta^t_{pa}(1-x) = (1-q)\delta^{t+1}_{pa}y + q\delta^{t+1}_{pa}1$$
$$resp. \quad 1-x = (1-q)\delta_{pa}y + q\delta_{pa}$$

(3.6b)
$$\delta^t_b(1-y) = (1-q)\delta^{t+1}_b x + q\delta_b 0$$
$$resp. \quad 1-y = (1-q)\delta_b x$$

Simultaneous solution of the equations of indifference then results in the equilibrium bids x* and y* of the bidder and the privatization agency in the case of latent bidding competition:

(3.7a)
$$x^* = \frac{1-(1-q)\delta_{pa} - q\delta_{pa}1}{1-(1-q)^2\delta_{pa}\delta_b};$$

(3.7b)
$$y^* = \frac{1-(1-q)\delta_b + (1-q)q\delta_{pa}\delta_b 1}{1-(1-q)^2\delta_{pa}\delta_b}.$$

The consequences of the altered competitive conditions in the privatization process with the modified Rubinstein game can best be demonstrated using an arithmetic example: Fig. 3.4 shows the outcomes of the modified Rubinstein game for the privatization agency's discount factor δ_{pa} of 0.8 and the bidder's discount factor δ_b of 0.9. In a bargaining equilibrium, the outcome for a probability of $q = 0$ that a further bidder will appear, i.e. in the case of a complete bilateral monopoly, is a payoff for the privatization agency of 0.286 when it is the bidder's move, and 0.357 when it is the privatization agency's move. Even at a probability of 10 percent that a new bidder will appear, the privatization agency's share increases to 0.52 when it is the bidder's move, and 0.611 when it is the agency's move; the figures are 0.696 and 0.805 when the probability is 0.3. Consequently, even at low probabilities for the appearance of a new bidder, outcomes emerge that are similar to those that would occur if the bidder were already involved in the bargaining process. (See Fig. 3.4.)

Figure 3.4: Payoffs in the Rubinstein-Game with Latent Bidding Competition

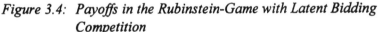
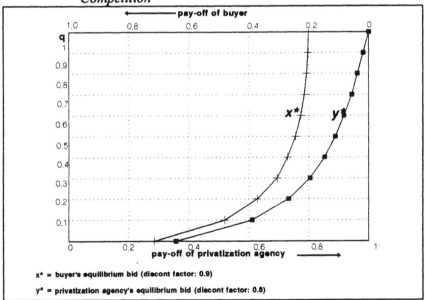

Schumpeter's hypothesis is thus supported by the modification of the Rubinstein game developed here: even the low risk that a competitor may enter the game is sufficient to approximate the bidder's rational bargaining strategy in bilateral negotiations to a bargaining situation with competition. In other words, competition develops its effects even when its is only present in the latent form of a threat.

For the privatization strategies in transforming economies, this result therefore leads to the conclusion that no grave competitive disadvantages are incurred by the privatization agency when it engages in bilateral bargaining, as long as the bargaining process is open. The easier it is for a further bidder to join the bargaining process with a bid of his own, and the higher the risk of competition for the existing bidders, the more strongly the outcome of bilateral bargaining - with given specificity of the assets of the firm to be privatized - will approach competitive conditions. One central argument against the use of informal sales procedures can thus be refuted.

Figure 3.5: Comparative Features of Privatization Procedures

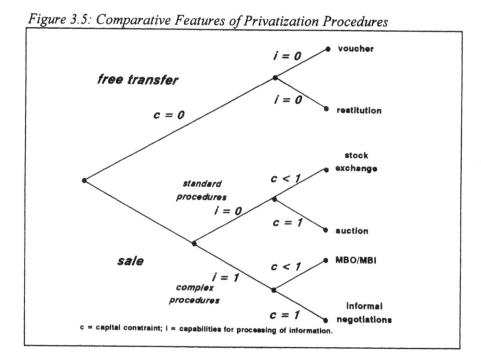

3.5   Conclusions: allocative effects of privatization procedures

The comparative evaluation of the efficiency of alternative privatization procedures was based here on the behavioral assumption of bounded and unequally distributed competence and the constraint of limited financial endowment. Fig. 3.5 summarizes the features of the privatization procedures discussed here with an eye to these two constraints. Under the assumption of bounded rationality, privatization through informal bargaining has a greater level of informational efficiency than the other privatization procedures, in that it also makes it possible to take account of information without price character ($i = 0$).

Auction procedures do simplify allocation, but they can consider no more than price information and thus, under the assumption of bounded and unequally distributed rationality, achieve only a low level of informational efficiency ($i = 0$).

The privatization of complete enterprises by means of informal bargaining or auction procedures is faced with the problem of the constraint posed by the limited financial endowment of buyers and, at the macroeconomic level, the limited capital supply: in view of bank credit rationing, these presuppose a bidder equity ratio adequate to finance the purchase and to rehabilitate the firm ($c = 1$). Although this constraint can be eased somewhat by management buyouts and buyins, it cannot be set aside ($c < 1$). The rationale of privatizing company shares on the stock exchange or auctioning them off against vouchers distributed free of cost stems from the goal of easing or setting aside the financial constraint facing bidders. Theoretically, a broad dispersion of company shares on the stock exchange can mobilize more capital for privatization, in that this permits even bidders with limited financial resources to participate ($c < 1$). Privatization by means of vouchers completely sets aside the financial constraint of the individual buyer on the microeconomic level ($c = 0$). At the macroeconomic level, however, the problems posed by the limited supply of capital and a crowding-out of investment remain if the shareholders sell their shares and use their returns to finance additional consumption. When privatization is effected through vouchers and the stock exchange, the easing of the microeconomic financial constraint is bought at the price of separating the rights of ownership and decision. The separation of these rights makes it possible to trade shares in a secondary market with low transaction costs. The valuation of firms and appraisal of management decisions in developed capital markets represent the control potential required to restrict the discretionary scope open to management. The expectation here is that the informational efficiency of capital markets is for the time being low in transforming economies, and that a broad distribution of property rights gives rise to very high principal-agent costs. The informational efficiency of a procedure that places small shares in the hands of anonymous buyers is of course low ($i = 0$). What results is consequently a tradeoff between the low level of allocative efficiency of a privatization of company shares in the form of vouchers or via the stock exchange and the low demands placed on the financial endowment of bidders. Whether an easing of the financial constraint will also accelerate privatization remains to be seen: preparations for public trading in company shares is both cost-intensive and time-intensive for the firms concerned. Moreover, when the financial constraint is eased, it is eased only for the purchase of firms, not for their rehabilitation.

Restitution is as a rule justified on ethical grounds, and not on grounds of efficiency. Placing allocation on a purely legal footing gives rise to high transaction costs involved in assigning and defining property rights. Economic competence and financial endowment do not constitute allocation criteria, and the informational efficiency of this procedure is therefore low ($c = 0$, $i = 0$). (See Fig 3.5; Table 3.1.)

The choice of an adequate privatization procedure is contingent on the nature of the firms in question. The asset specificity of capital and firm size were named above as discriminatory factors. Growing company size and factor specificity of capital are linked with increases in the demands placed on bidder competence and capital endowment. While auction procedures make it possible to reach high levels of allocative efficiency for small firms with low asset specificity, the demands placed on the informational efficiency of the privatization procedure grow in proportion to firm complexity. The comparative advantages of informal privatization procedure gain in significance with growing company complexity.

Table 3.1: Allocative Effects of Privatization Procedures

	informal bargaining	MBO/MBI	auction	stock ex-change	vouchers	restitution
allocative criterion	multiple criteria, competence	multiple criteria, competence	price	price/ rationing	price/ rationing	legal claim
contract type	complex	complex	standard	standard	standard	standard
buyer competence	high	high	indeter-mined	irrelevant	irrelevant	indeter-mined
demand on individual capital endowment	high	medium	high	low	zero	zero
costs of primary allocation	low	low	low	high	high	high
agency costs	low	low	low	high	high	low
reallocation costs	high	high	high	low	low	very high

Privatization on the stock exchange and in the form of investment vouchers is suited only for larger firms because of the high fixed costs of information and shareholder control; the constraint posed by buyer equity capital applies in any case only for larger firms. There are, however, doubts as to whether the informational and control potentials of the newly developed capital markets are sufficient in the first place to ensure the benefits of private ownership when company shares are broadly dispersed.

4   Distributive and Welfare Effects of Privatization

The privatization of the state-owned business sector in the transition
countries affects not only allocative efficiency, it also influences the
distribution of income and wealth. The welfare effects of privatization
can therefore only be evaluated if the distribution of property rights
and privatization revenues is also taken into account. The goal of allocative efficiency is reached in the privatization of the state-owned
business sector only if the property rights are assigned to those individuals and institutions who have the most productive use for them. If
economic competence is a scarce factor and financial endowments are
unequally distributed, all that can be expected of an efficient privatization is an enforcement and reproduction of existing inequalities:

> *"Although the market and capitalist property have
> many useful qualities, above all the stimulation to
> efficient economic activity, fairness and equality
> are not among their virtues. They reward not only
> good work but good fortune, and they penalize not
> just bad work but ill-fortune. While they are useful
> to society as a whole by encouraging exploitation of
> good fortune and resistance to ill-fortune, they are
> not 'just'. I think, it is ethically paradoxical to mix
> slogans of fairness and equality into a program of
> capitalist privatization"* (Kornai 1991).

In other words, there is a trade-off between efficient allocation and a
just distribution of property rights. This chapter will first develop, following John Rawls' theory of justice, normative criteria required for an
evaluation of distributive and welfare effects in the transition countries
(4.1); it will then go on to discuss, with an eye to these normative criteria, the sale of state-owned property to privileged groups (4.2) and
the distributive and welfare effects of different privatization procedures
(4.3).

4.1　Norms of Justice and Privatization

The Pareto optimum is a criterion of efficiency, but not one of welfare, and it can for that reason not be used to evaluate institutional change in terms of welfare economics (Sen 1970, 22; Koopmanns 1957, 49; Hahn 1984, 45). The aim here is to evaluate the distributive and welfare effects of privatization on the basis of the ethical principles developed by John Rawls in his theory of justice (Rawls 1971). Rawls, in the tradition of the theories of social contract, bases his principles of justice on a fictive original position of equality in which, under a "veil of ignorance" (Rawls 1971, 136-142) as to their social status, their possessions, and their specific skills, but yet in a state of complete human knowledge, rational individuals came to an agreement on two fundamental principles of justice[1]:

(1) Each person is to have an equal right to the most extensive total system of equal basic liberties compatible with a similar system of liberty for all.

(2) Social and economic inequalities are to be arranged so that they are both: (a) to the greatest benefit of the least advantaged, consistent with the just savings principle, and (b) attached to offices and positions open to all under conditions of fair equality of opportunity (Rawls 1971, 302, 60).

The first principle, the so-called *principle of liberty*, defines a package of basic and libertarian human rights that apply equally to all people. The second principle, the so-called *principle of difference*, contains two ethical postulates: the postulate of *distributive justice* does not rule out an unequal distribution of social wealth, though it regards it as legitimate only when it increases the benefit of the least favored. The postulate of *procedural justice* requires free access to all social positions independently of origin or status, ethnic or religious differences (Höffe 1977, 17). The two principles of justice are not of equal rank; the principle of difference is ethically subordinate to the principle of liberty (Rawls 1971, 40-45). Liberty as the paramount human good enjoys absolute priority and may not be traded off against other goods. Claims to liberty may be restricted only by competing claims to liberty raised by others (Rawls 1971, 62-63). The strongest principle of distributive justice likewise has priority over the weakest principle of procedural justice (Rawls 1971, 89).

Rawls' theory of justice can be seen as a "constructive countermodel" (Höffe 1977, 18) to utilitarian ethics. The principle of difference in particular conflicts with the utilitarian principles aimed at the maximization of the sum total of society's benefits or the average benefit of the members of society (Rawls 1971, 161-166; 183-192). The content and justification of Rawls' principle of justice are by no means undisputed (Arrow 1977; Sen 1977; Buchanan 1972), but it will not be possible to conduct here a discussion on Rawls' grounding of his ethical principles (Reese-Schäfer/Schuon 1991; Habermas 1992; Rawls 1992). The discussion on the welfare and distributive effects of privatization are here based on Rawls' principles of justice, because they link the Enlightenment's understanding of liberty with the social norms of distributive justice and stop short of anticipating normatively the question of ownership: for Rawls it is neither, as with Friedrich von Hayek's political liberalism, private ownership of the means of production (Hayek 1944) nor, as with Karl Marx and Frederick Engels, the abrogation of wage labor, and with it the abolition of private property, that constitutes the necessary condition for the achievement of individual liberty (Marx/Engels 1848). Rawls assigns the question of ownership - as long as the freedom to choose an occupation and consumer sovereignty are not affected (Rawls 1971, 272-273) - not to the higher-ranking principle of liberty but to the ethically subordinate principle of difference. This avoids immunizing the question of ownership against economic arguments (Rawls 1971, 259-260; 280-281). Rawls assumes that his ethical principles can be fulfilled equally within different basic institutional structures, i.e. in both capitalist and socialist social systems:

> *"Throughout the choice between a private-property economy and socialism is left open; from the standpoint of the theory of justice alone, various basic structures would appear to satisfy its principles"* (Rawls 1971, 258).

On Rawls' principle of difference, two ethical postulates must be fulfilled in the process of privatization: first, the principle of *distributive
justice* requires that we should be able to reasonably expect of privatization and the choice of a privatization procedure that they will lead to
an improvement of the position of those who are least favored in a society, and that this improvement will go beyond any other possible distribution of property rights. In other words, an unequal distribution of
property rights through privatization is ethically justified only when the
gains of improving efficiency through privatization are so high that it
improves the position of less favored persons, be it in their role as employees, be it through a welfare-oriented redistribution of incomes,
more than would be the case without privatization or in the case that a
different privatization procedure had been chosen.

Second, the lower-ranking principle of *procedural justice* requires that
in the process of privatizing the state-owned business sector it must be
possible for all members of society to acquire state-owned enterprises.
As regards the financial endowments and individual competences of
individual members of society, the principle of procedural justice does
not, however, require all members of society to be accorded equal initial chances to acquire enterprises. In other words, the allocative criteria must be the same for all members of society, while this does not
hold for their initial endowments.

4.2   Privatization and Procedural Justice: The Problem of
"Nomenclature Privatization"

The question whether applying the principle of procedural justice in
the matter of privatization is also just in the social sense is frequently
debated in the transition countries. If the postulate of procedural justice
is met, it must be expected that specific social groups that have privileged economic competence and large financial resources will be favored by the reallocation of property rights. Seen from a sociological
angle, these are three social groups: the former nomenclature (1), the
so-called shadow economy (2), and foreign investors (3). The demand

has often been raised in public political discussions in the transition
countries that these groups be excluded from privatization:

> *"According to the conception of the liberals, those
> who have seats in the councils (...) should be the
> persons who have the financial means to purchase
> firms. This line has little to do with Polish realities.
> (...) No one (or as good as no one) was able to ac-
> cumulate from wages capital that that could have
> any significance in the process of privatization. Two
> groups could participate in this process: Polish citi-
> zens who have (with few exceptions) illegally ac-
> cumulated the means required, and capital-owning
> foreigners. Those, on the other hand (...), who,
> through their own hard work, bought off by the
> state with starvation wages, have created the assets
> to be privatized (...) stand - as a group - to lose part
> of their wealth to owners of capital from the states
> which, directly or indirectly, have contributed to
> our nation's loss of its independence, property, and
> autonomy"* (Dryll 1989, 3; Delhaes 1992).

The slogans "spontaneous privatization" and "nomenclature privatization" ("uwlaszczenie nomenklatury") are used in the controversial discussion of the transfer of property rights to members of the former *nomenclature*, which was made up of representatives of industry and the
political sphere (Bauer 1992; Staniszkis 1991; Levitas/Strzalkowski
1990). The distinction between procedural and distributive justice of
course has a heuristic character; these problems tend to become blurred
in the political debate. What is meant on the one hand by nomenclature
privatization is the appropriation of state-owned property by members
of the old political and economic elites, who exploit their personal
power and discriminate against other members of society to achieve
their ends, thus violating the principle of procedural justice. What is
implied on the other hand is also the legal acquisition of property rights
by members of the former nomenclature, who make use of their eco-

nomic competence and their financial resources to the same end; in other words, what is at issue here is a problem of distributive justice.

The members of the former nomenclature form a social group which, compared with other members of society, is privileged with regard to its economic competences and financial resources. In the transition countries, recent decades have, in comparison e.g. with the phase following the October Revolution in the Soviet Union, seen a growing professionalization and technocratization of the economic and bureaucratic elites (Konrad/Szelenyi 1981), and thus these elites, as compared with other social groups, and beside their privileged access to information and material resources, are marked on the average by higher levels of economic competence (Bauer 1992, 301). A number of sociologists and economists therefore see in this group - apart from the members of the shadow economy - the nucleus of a new middle class in the transition countries (Hankiss 1989; Bauer 1992, 299; Staniszkis 1991). Under the assumption of scarce resources unequally distributed across individuals, the (re)allocation of property rights in favor of members of the former nomenclature is entirely efficient. But this reallocation of property rights is regarded as unjust by broad segments of the population, because the acquisition of competence, information, and assets by members of the former nomenclature is not perceived as *legitimate*. The offices and posts in the administrative and economic bureaucracies of the transition countries were of course not filled in accordance with the principle of equal opportunity; they went instead to a political elite that was itself not democratically legitimated.

Yet if Rawls' principle of difference is applied consistently, it is not possible to exclude the former nomenclature from the reallocation of property rights either on the principle of distributive justice or on the principle of procedural justice: first, it must reasonably be expected that dispensing with the economic competence of the former economic and political elites would lead to an inefficient allocation of property rights, so that, depending on the degree of welfare-related redistribution, even the less favored would in this case be worse off, which would constitute a violation of the postulate of distributive justice.

Second, the principle of procedural justice requires that, in the sense of equal and fair opportunity, all posts and offices be open to all members of society, thus making it impossible to exclude any one specific group such as the members of the former nomenclature. The exclusion of specific groups from the privatization process would amount to a continuation of the politicization of economics in the sense that political criteria and loyalties would influence access to economic positions (Levitas/Strzalkowski 1990, 413). The societies of the transition countries are thus faced with the trade-off of either correcting politically the unjust distribution of wealth and offices by the *ancien régime*, thus violating the norms of justice of newly established democratic societies, or of enforcing the norms of fair and free access to all economic posts, thus reproducing the *ancien régime's* unjust distribution of wealth and offices.

Another question is whether the principle of procedural justice should be suspended in favor of the former nomenclature. This is sometimes called for as a means of accelerating privatization and increasing the efficiency of the economic system (Staniszkis 1991; Bauer 1992; Levitas/Strzalkowski 1990). The considerations that speak against suspending the principle of procedural justice include arguments of efficiency and justice: in the first place, neither are all members of the former nomenclature in possession of high levels of economic competence and great financial resources nor do they monopolize the competences and financial resources of an economy. If the members of the former nomenclature succeed in acquiring shares of state-owned assets as a result of their privileged access to posts and offices and excluding all other individuals and institutions from the (re)allocation of property rights, this situation would, ceteris paribus, lead to a more inefficient (re)allocation of property rights than would be the case if the access to privatization were both free and fair.

Second, suspension of procedural justice, in the sense of Rawls' principle of difference, could then only be justified if it augmented the ethically higher-ranking principle of distributive justice. But since the suspension of the principle of procedural justice would entail preferring a group that is privileged in any case and restricting the allocative efficiency of privatization, it cannot reasonably be expected.

The same arguments can, ceteris paribus, be applied to members of the *shadow economy*, In all transition countries a more or less sizable informal economic sector has developed that can be described as a nuance of gray along a scale ranging from black for pure criminality to white as perfect legality (Kornai 1992). The legal status and social acceptance of this economic sector differ between the transition countries. Like the members of the former nomenclature, the representatives of the informal economic sector have *on the average* higher levels of economic competence and greater financial resources than other social groups. Dispensing with these skills and financial resources in the process of privatization would entail losses in efficiency that cannot be justified by Rawls' postulates of procedural and distributive justice.

As compared with other groups, *foreign investors* are especially well endowed in financial terms. In view of the limited financial endowment of the economic agents in transforming economies, a reallocation of property rights in favor of foreign investors must consequently be expected, particularly when the concern is to privatize larger firms. In many transition countries warnings are therefore being voiced of a "national sellout" (Dryll 1992, 3; Kornai 1991; 1990), and the privatization statutes of many countries contain numerous restrictions on the purchase of enterprises by foreigners.

Limiting sales to domestic buyers reduces the inflow of capital from abroad, diminishing, ceteris paribus, the value of the firms concerned. The sale of firms involves an exchange of assets, and thus redistribution results only when the enterprises are sold below their capitalized value.[2] To the extent that the latter possibility can be ruled out, there is, neither in terms of efficiency nor as regards allocative considerations, no rational argument against the sale of firms to foreigners.

In summary, it can be said that application of Rawls' normative criteria provides no justification for excluding specific social groups from the privatization of state-owned enterprises. On the other hand, the principle of procedural justice must be applied consistently, without disadvantaging or privileging any one group. This is also true of groups that have, in the view generally held, not acquired their assets and competences legitimately, as in the case of the former nomenclature or the shadow economy. The exclusion of specific groups reduces, ceteris paribus, the allocative efficiency of privatization and the value of the firms to be privatized. This in turn changes for the worse the position of those disadvantaged in the privatization process, so that both the lexicographically higher-ranking principle of distributive justice and the lower-ranking principle of procedural justice are violated.

4.3   Distributive Effects of Different Privatization Techniques

It is possible to distinguish between *primary* and *secondary distributive effects* in the privatization of the state-owned business sector. The primary distributive effects result from the redistribution of state-held ownership deeds to private individuals and institutions, while the secondary distributive effects stem from the consequences of privatization for efficiency and employment. Privatization is based on the assumption of an increase of X-efficiency. Thus far, increases of X-efficiency have been linked with growing underemployment in transforming economies, and what results is therefore an unequal distribution of the returns of growing efficiency. These secondary distributive effects cannot be attributed to privatization alone, they must also be seen in connection with other institutional changes, such as the abolition of the system of mandatory planning, price deregulation, and the remonetarization of the economies concerned. The secondary distributive effects are presumably of greater significance than the primary effects, but they have nevertheless been left out of consideration here, because an analysis of these secondary effects would on the one hand run up against methodological problems and on the other hand go beyond the scope of this study. The study therefore restricts itself here to the primary distributive effects of *sale* (4.3.1) and *cost-free transfer* (4.3.2) of state-owned assets to private persons.

4.3.1   Sales Procedures

The sale of firms as a means of privatization first of all involves merely
an exchange of assets. The state's assets are decreased by the amount
of the returns expected from the privatized property deeds to the firms
concerned and increased by the amount of the revenues stemming from
the privatization. In a world with perfect bidding competition and
without transaction costs, the state, as the monopolist seller, would receive all net returns of the transaction, regardless of the sales procedure
chosen. The buyer pays his reserve price, which, under the assumption
of perfect rationality, is equivalent to the expected cash flow from the
firm's capital, including the expected capitalized value of investments
made for rehabilitation purposes (Sinn/Sinn 1991, 90). The state receives a rent in the amount of the difference between its and the
buyer's reserve price. Under the assumption that the state, through its
spending policy, will improve the position of those least favored in a
society, the reallocation of property rights will also improve the situation of those who are worst off.

If the assumption of perfect bidding competition is relaxed, the net returns of privatization are divided between the state and the buyers. In
the case of a *bilateral monopoly*, assuming perfect information on both
sides in a bargaining equilibrium, the net returns of the transaction are
divided equally between the two sides.[3] In the case of imperfect information, no equilibrium of rational expectations need result which
would at the same time give rise to a Pareto-optimal allocation of the
property rights concerned. The state is faced with the alternative of
either revealing truthfully its reserve price and accepting the possibility
that all of the returns of the transaction will fall to the buyer side, or
maximizing its privatization returns and accepting a non-Pareto-
optimal allocation of the property rights (Brücker 1995, 152). What
happens in the former case is that the reallocation proceeds in favor of
the buyer and at the expense of the state, and thus also of the less advantaged; in the second case the reduced allocative efficiency can also
impair the position of the less favored. In terms of Rawls' principle of
difference, it is impossible to come to an unambiguous theoretical decision on this conflict; this would require an empirically based hy-

pothesis on the relative magnitudes of the reallocative and efficiency effects involved.

With *auction procedures*, the buyer receives a rent in the amount of the difference between his reserve price and the second highest bid.[4] Like the case of multilateral bargaining, this buyer rent decreases as bidding competition increases.

The distributive and welfare effects of privatization through sales procedures are more difficult to assess in a world with bounded rationality, uncertainty, and nontrivial transaction costs. Under the conditions of system transformation, the economic data change much more rapidly and uncertainty is significantly greater than in developed western market economies. Growing uncertainty entails growing transaction costs (Williamson 1985). If both uncertainty and transaction costs are high, it is possible for above-average gains to be made; these are defined here as *arbitrage* (Kirzner 1973, 9-15; Wegehenkel 1981, 23). Arbitrage can be seen either as a premium for an investment made under high risk, and thus as factor income, or, in the sense of the Austrian School, as a rent accruing to investors as a result of their speculative intuition and fortunate circumstances (Wegehenkel 1981, 23). For the Austrian School, arbitrage has a socially useful function: it is the incentive to discover new investment opportunities. High arbitrage profits lead to imitation and are therefore subject to erosion in the course of time due to increasing market transparency and growing competitive pressure. The social costs of arbitrage are consequently limited (Wegehenkel 1981, 26).

Arbitrage is necessary and unavoidable in the process of privatizing the state-owned business sector in the transforming economies. It is especially at the beginning of the process that large arbitrage profits can be realized; these are eroded as market transparency grows. These profits benefit the groups that have privileged access to information and assets, and luck. Seen from an ethical angle, arbitrage is invariably linked with a redistribution of wealth from those who are worse off to those are better off. Seen from the angle of redistribution, and under the assumption of great uncertainty and bounded rationality, the overall outcome of privatization is thus substantially less advantaged: the buyers appropriate shares of state-owned assets as their arbitrage profits.

One way of restricting the redistributive effect due to arbitrage would be for the state, or a government fund, to retain a minority interest, which would be sold after the erosion of arbitrage profits had boosted prices. A minority interest of this kind would, however, dilute the buyer's property rights, and the smaller the interest held by the owner-manager, the lower, ceteris paribus, would be his incentives to use the firm productively (Jensen/Meckling 1976, 308). So there is a trade-off between the intensity of the incentive involved in transferring complete property rights and ensuring the public a share of arbitrage profits.

It was argued in Chapter 3 that it is possible, in the face of uncertainty and nontrivial transaction costs, to increase the allocative efficiency of privatization by agreeing on *complex contracts.*[5] The rationale of the conclusion of complex contracts is on the one hand to achieve, by *"trading in risk,"* a more efficient allocation given that preferences of risk differ between state and buyers, and on the other hand to ease the financial constraint of competent buyers. One additional possibility is to agree in complex contracts to an ex post valuation of properties and assets so as to ensure that the public receives a share of the arbitrage profits. To the degree that it is possible to use complex contracts to achieve a higher level of allocative efficiency, and thus also higher sales prices, these transactions are also justified in ethical terms: the outcome is a general increase in incomes, which, assuming a state policy of income redistribution, would also benefit the less advantaged. If, on the other hand, the goal of efficient allocation is not met and the buyers succeed in using opportunistic behavior to appropriate state-owned assets, the outcome will be a redistribution benefiting those who are better off and disadvantaging the less favored.

The redistributive effects of privatization linked with the sale of state-owned firms are justified in ethical terms if these effects also improve the position of the less advantaged. This can only be the case if, despite arbitrage profits of buyers, the revenues of privatization are higher than the capitalized value of expected earnings of the enterprises under state ownership.

4.3.2   Cost-free Transfer

As opposed to outright sale, the cost-free transfer of property rights does not entail an exchange of assets between the public and private sectors. What happens instead is that property rights are distributed by the public sector, i.e. by all individuals in society, in favor of those who stand to benefit from a cost-free transfer (Kornai 1991, 10). Cost-free transfer of property rights to the population would only be distributively neutral if the shares in each enterprise sold were to be assigned individually to each member of society (Dabrowski 1991, 320). Any allocation of this kind would, however, prove inefficient in that it would totally fragment shareholdings. Any other allocation of property rights would lead to a redistribution of wealth in favor of those who stand to benefit from a cost-free transfer.

It is possible to distinguish three procedures for allocating property rights free of cost, and each of them can be justified with specific ethical arguments: (i) cost-free transfer of investment vouchers, (ii) cost-free transfer of property rights to employees, and (iii) restitution.

(i) A cost-free transfer of *investment vouchers* to the population is justified with arguments stemming from radical egalitarianism. The constitutional promise of socialism is redeemed by transferring property rights to the population free of charge, thus in the end transforming state ownership of the means of production into true social ownership:

> *"Such an operation (the cost-free transfer of state-owned property - H.B.) could be called the expropriation of the state or privatization, but it is essentially a socialization of ownership through reprivatization; an actual transfer of real property rights to those who are the nominal owners by virtue of the constitution. Dispersed ownership or generalized*

private ownership are a more real form of sociali-
zation than formal declarations which differ bla-
tantly from reality" (Lewandowski/Szomburg
1989).

But what is to be expected of a cost-free transfer of investment vouchers to the population is not any sort of egalitarian allocation but a quick
redistribution of property rights. This redistribution is also the aim of
the proponents of voucher allocation; it is seen as a means of achieving
a concentration of capital, and with it functioning control rights. The
redistribution of shareholdings is selectively fostered at the institutional level by asking a symbolic price for the transfer of investment
vouchers as a means of excluding poorly informed and less interested
segments of the population from the allocation of property rights.

Viewed in terms of Rawls' normative criteria, the cost-free distribution
of investment vouchers fulfills the ethical postulate of procedural justice while not meeting the postulate of distributive justice. All members
of society have the same right to participate in voucher allocation, and
the allocation criteria are the same for all members of society. But, like
the case of sales procedures, the initial individual chances involved in
allocation by voucher are unequally distributed: individuals with adequate financial resources and privileged access to information are favored by an allocation of property rights through investment vouchers
(Bauer 1992, 297; Kornai 1991, 36-38). What must be expected following the voucher-based primary allocation of property rights is a reallocation of the shares and a concentration of property rights in the hands
of a small minority in possession of sufficient financial resources.
Since a broad dispersion of shares tends to erode the information available to the individual shareholder, and the shareholders will thus be
unable to manage their property rights efficiently, *higher* arbitrage
profits are more likely when the shares are resold than if the state sold
its property rights directly. A second distributive effect results from the
high agency costs of voucher allocation: the smaller the shares held by
the decision-makers, the higher, ceteris paribus, will be their incentives
to appropriate assets and economic returns of the firm to the detriment
of the other shareholders (Jensen/Meckling 1976, 308). A broad dis-

persion of company shares through voucher allocation therefore makes it possible for the existing management or owner groups with a comparatively low concentration of capital to amass great assets at the expense of the other shareholders.

Consequently, voucher privatization leads to expectations of greater redistributive effects in favor of those who are better off than would an outright sales technique. The principle of distributive justice is violated by voucher privatization in that following the primary allocation of the investment vouchers the expectation would be that the property would be reallocated in favor of those privileged in terms of their financial resources and access to information, and this would not be matched by any large gains in efficiency due to the high agency costs of the broad dispersion of the shareholdings. Those who are less advantaged would therefore be unable to profit from the efficiency gains of privatization.

(ii) While the cost-free transfer of property rights to company employees does lead to a broader dispersion of ownership than sales procedures, it does not allocate property rights equitably: this approach privileges employees vis-à-vis nonemployees, persons employed in capital-intensive firms as opposed to persons employed in less capital-intensive companies or the civil service (Hodjera 1991, 277; Kornai 1991, 23). Regarded in terms of distributive justice, this unequitable redistribution would be justified only if this type of reallocation at the same time also benefited the less advantaged. Theoretical and empirical arguments centering on the contradiction between the interests of employees as wage-earners and owners of capital have been cited to dispute the possibility of increasing the efficiency or productivity of firms whose ownership is transferred - be it outright or in the form of a *controlling interest* - to its employees, cannot be resold, and must remain with the company when such employees depart (Estrin 1991, 356-359; Kornai 1991, 21; Hodjera 1991, 277; Wieneki 1991, 403; Jasinski 1992, 177-179).

In several transition countries, employees can acquire cost-free, or purchase at preferred prices, minority interests which, due to their limited size of e.g. 10 to 20 percent, do not constitute relevant decision variables (Sachs 1991, 10). In terms of efficiency, most economists see no problems with an allocation of property rights of this sort (Kornai 1991, 23; Sachs 1991, 10). In terms of agency theory, declining capital interests lower the owner-manager's incentives, so that, ceteris paribus, the efficiency of firms will tend to decline as employee participation increases. But employee-held minority interests have no more than marginal implications for efficiency. In terms of allocation-related factors, a cost-free transfer of minority shareholdings to employees can be justified as a correction of the distributive effects associated with arbitrage (see above). The distributive justice of this type of allocation of property rights is, however, lower in this case than if a minority holding of the same amount were to remain with the state or in a government fund.

(iii) The call for *restitution* is based on two ethical arguments: in the first place, restitution is seen as a means of reparation of injustice done to owners by the expropriations conducted in the former East Bloc by restoring their property to them or to their heirs. Second, it is seen as a means of restoring the legal security of private property and providing property with a permanent sacrosanct status (Kornai 1991; Sinn/Sinn 1991).

Reallocation of property rights through restitution implies, as do other forms of cost-free transfer, a redistribution of public wealth in favor of those who were expropriated and their heirs. In terms of Rawls' principle of difference, compensation for wrong suffered might even be justified if those most disadvantaged by the injustice of state power in the countries at the former East Bloc stood to benefit most by such compensation. The great variety of injustice perpetrated in the countries of the former Eastern Bloc ranges from arbitrary and politically motivated executions, unwarranted imprisonment, and dismissals to restrictions on freedom of movement and access to vocational training (Kornai 1991, 9). Restitution would serve to compensate a specific social group for a specific injustice it has suffered. This group was not necessarily the group most disadvantaged by injustice in the transition countries:

> *"The sense (of justice on which restitution is based*
> *- H.B.) is, to be sure, quickly qualified when one*
> *considers that the loss of life, quality of life, free-*
> *dom, and income cannot be compensated for. An*
> *alternative model would thus have been to distrib-*
> *ute to all of the disadvantaged the entire wealth*
> *available when the old communist regime went*
> *down"* (Sinn/Sinn 1991, 73).

Nor is the second ethical argument in favor of restitution plausible. It is not possible to restore the legal security of ownership ex post via restitution, and ex ante the legal security of ownership is not increased but lowered by restitution. The legal security of ownership achieved by restitution is assured only when property rights can be assigned to persons and the judicial system has, through due process of law, decided on competing claims. But, for reasons of efficiency and in view of considerations of welfare, limitations on legal claims to property are likely, and they in turn will reduce the legal security of ownership and violate the principle of procedural justice.[6] Finally, restitution cannot guarantee for the unforeseeable future the legal security of the private ownership of the means of production. A more effective approach would be a constitutional guarantee of private ownership *and* stable economic development (Kornai 1991, 9).

All in all, restitution, accompanied as it is by high costs, lengthy procedures, and inefficiency of allocation, tends more to impair the welfare of the economies concerned,[7] thus disadvantaging even those who are least favored. Restitution can at times even violate the principle of distributive justice.

4.4   Conclusions

There is no more a perfectly just privatization procedure than there is a perfectly efficient one. It is only possible to discuss the relative justice of a privatization procedure in relation to the pertinent institutional alternatives. Basically, privatization involves expectations, direct or indirect, of a redistribution of public wealth to the benefit of the more advantaged members of a society. This redistribution can be justified ethically only if it at the same time increases the welfare of the least advantaged. This can in principle only be achieved if a welfare state redistributes a share of private capital gains in favor of the less favored members of society.

Comparative analysis of different privatization procedures shows that the redistributive effects linked with a cost-free transfer are *greater* than they are when property rights are sold outright. The sale of property rights amounts to a exchange of assets; there is a redistributive effect in favor of the buyers only when arbitrage profits are made. In view of the great uncertainty surrounding the institutional and economic framework and the value of the asset-specific capital of the firms involved, this is to be expected. Owing to unequal initial financial endowments and economic competence, three social groups with low levels of social acceptance will profit from this redistribution in the transition countries: the former nomenclature, the shadow economy, and foreign investors. Any restriction of the principle of procedural justice and any discrimination of these groups would, ceteris paribus, lower allocative efficiency, thus reducing the value of the firms concerned, which would also disadvantage the less favored members of society. It is therefore not justified against the background of Rawls' postulates of distributive and procedural justice.

Cost-free allocation of property rights improves the position of those who benefit from such transfers, and does so at the expense of the public at large. Even when property rights are broadly dispersed, e.g. through allocation of property rights by voucher, the expectation is that a swift reallocation and concentration of wealth will soon ensue. Since a broad dispersion of property rights leads, at least at the outset, to high agency costs, and since it is plausible to assume that the arbitrage profits stemming from reallocation are in this case higher than if the state were to sell property rights directly, there is reason to expect a greater reallocative effect. As far as restitution is concerned, the primary allocation of the property rights in itself entails a redistribution in favor of those who are as a rule better off. The redistributive effects of cost-free transfer would be justified only if this procedure, by heightening allocative efficiency, improved the welfare of society as a whole, thus favoring those who are less well off. But this is not to be expected. One conclusion concerning the welfare effects of different privatization procedures is therefore that the preferable approach is to combine different techniques both with an eye to allocative efficiency and with a view to the distributive justice associated with the cost-free transfer of property rights.

5   Transformation of the Legal and Economic Framework

Privatization has been preceded by the transformation of the most important institutions of the economic system in Eastern Germany. The mandatory planning system and the administrative price system were abandoned; the Western German legal system was introduced; monetary reform entailed the introduction of a market-oriented monetary constitution; and private property rights to Eastern German business enterprises were guaranteed by transforming the legal system. This chapter examines first the *transaction costs* that result from the establishment of private property rights and free trade (5.1) and second investigates the effects of the transformation of the economic system and the accession of the former GDR to the Federal Republic's economic and currency area on the *production costs* of Eastern German enterprises (5.2).

5.1   Transformation of the Legal System

The New Institutional Economics treats a society's legal order as a system of rules covered by the state's power potential and limiting the freedom of action of individuals (North 1981, 20-23; Posner 1977, 100; Wegehenkel 1981, 6-10). The institutionalization of a legal system is logically preceded by an exchange of property rights: the core of ownership, the right to exclude third parties, can be enforced only by the institutionalization of a legal system which defines protected property rights and delineates the boundary between *meum* and *teum* (Wegehenkel 1981, 12; Hayek 1977, 147). In the view of the New Institutional Economics, the legal system is a public good on which depends the level of the costs involved in the specification, negotiation, and enforcement of contracts on which economic exchange is based (North 1981, 24; Wegehenkel 1981, 8; Furubotn/Pejovich 1972, 1145). The efficiency criterion used by the New Institutional Economics to assess the rules of legal systems is the economization of transaction costs (North 1981, 24; Furubotn/Pejovich 1972; Wegehenkel 1981, 27). Theoretically, two classes of transaction costs can be distinguished in the transformation of economic and legal systems: the costs of the *primary allocation* of property rights and *current* transaction costs (Wegehenkel 1981, 13). The costs of primary allocation consist of the costs of *legal institutionalization*, i.e. the costs entailed in defining, specifying, and enforcing property rights, and the costs entailed in *assigning* property rights, which also include the costs of privatization. The transaction costs of the primary allocation of property rights are *sunk* costs which, once incurred, are no longer taken into account by economic agents in their calculations (Wegehenkel 1981, 13). The current transaction costs of an economic system, in the words of Kenneth Arrow "the operating costs of an economic system" (Arrow 1969, 48), are determined primarily by the choice of the rules constituting the economic and legal system and their enforcement. But under the assumption that the reallocation of property rights entails nontrivial transaction costs, these costs are also contingent on the assignment of property rights and thus on the choice of a privatization procedure.[1]

The constitutive rules of its economic and legal system were defined when Eastern Germany reached the fundamental decision to accede to the Western Germany's legal and economic system. The transformation of Eastern Germany's legal system can thus be characterized as a process entailing a rapid assimilation to and assumption of the Western German legal and economic system, a process that - with a few exceptions - was completed when Eastern Germany became part of the Federal Republic of Germany. During the interregnum of the Modrow Government (Suhr 1991), the legislative reverted to the prewar German legal system and abolished the legal institution of "socialist property",[2] with its primacy of "people's property" over cooperative and private forms of ownership, and formally transformed it into private property under civil law (Knüpfer 1990). Private and state-owned property were placed on equal legal footing by a law on the foundation and activities of private enterprises,[3] and company law was adapted to the laws of the Federal Republic.

Following the transition period represented by the Modrow Government, the de Maizière Government and the Federal Government pursued the goal of a rapid Eastern German accession to the Federal Republic of Germany and a takeover of Western Germany's legal institutions. There was to be a minimum of provisional arrangements and exemptions. The first stage was an accord on the economic, monetary, and social union of the two German states.[4] As the cornerstone of economic union, the Treaty between the GDR and the FRG defined the "social market economy as the shared economic order."[5] Aside from the modalities of the monetary union,[6] the Treaty regulated the adaptation of the GDR's economic order to the legal institutions of the Federal Republic of Germany: the Treaty contained provisions ensuring, among other things, that the first three books of the commercial code, the law on public limited companies, and the credit laws of the Federal Republic would apply in both countries as soon as it came into effect.[7] All laws and statutes that were inconsistent with the Treaty and might restrict private economic activity, private ownership, and the free movement of foreign exchange and capital were abolished or adapted to the laws of the Federal Republic.[8] Thus in agreeing to the Treaty on monetary union, the GDR took over all of the important legal institutions of the Federal Republic.

The property rights to Eastern Germany's state-owned business enterprises were transferred to a central institution, the Treuhandanstalt, and it was given the task of privatizing and managing its holdings. The Treuhandanstalt was given the property rights to all state owned enterprises (*Volkseigene Betriebe*), trusts (*Kombinate)*, and other economic entities entered in the registry of state owned enterprises, and the administrative and financial assets of the Ministry for State Security

(*Staatssicherheit*) and the Office for National Security (National People's Army).[9] Rail and postal facilities were transferred to the Special Fund of the Deutsche Reichsbahn[10] and to the German Post Office,[11] while the administrative and financial assets of the GDR' local and regional authorities went to the federal government and Eastern Germany's Länder and municipalities.[12] The property rights and deeds to the state-owned housing corporations were assigned to the municipalities.[13] The interface between private and state economic activity was thus defined along the lines existing in the Federal Republic.

The Treuhandanstalt's legal basis was the *Treuhandgesetz*, which was passed by the GDR parliament (*Volkskammer*) on July 17, 1990[14] and taken over, with some modifications, by the Federal Republic's legal system via the Unification Treaty.[15] The legislative here assigned to the Treuhandanstalt the task of *privatizing and competitively restructuring* the economic entities transferred to it, including their deconcentration and rehabilitation.[16] Noncompetitive enterprises were to be closed down and their assets utilized.[17]

This open formulation of the Treuhandanstalt's legal task has been criticized by various camps. While the one side called for a clear-cut priority for privatization and the exclusion of Treuhandanstalt rehabilitation activities (Maurer/Sander/Schmidt 1991, 45, Sachverständigenrat 1991, 14-17), the other side noted critically that no clear-cut priority is accorded to rehabilitation (Priewe 1991, 844). My view is that both sides overestimated the effects of the general intent of a law. A definition of legal intent by itself does not constitute an effective constraint on the actions of the relevant actors. A complex issue such as the priority of the privatization and rehabilitation activities of an institution like the Treuhandanstalt cannot be inferred from general legal intents.

The Treuhandanstalt was in János Kornai's sense the classic case of an institution fitted out with a *"soft budget constraint"* (Kornai 1980, 304; 1986). In financial terms, there were no effective constraints on the Treuhandanstalt's rehabilitation or privatization activities. On October 9, 1990, in a hard declaration of patronage by the German Finance Minister, the state agreed to assume responsibility for all liabilities of the Treuhandanstalt (BMF 1990a; BMF 1991b). The Treuhandanstalt was consequently not subject to bankruptcy regulations. In anticipation of its privatization revenues, the Treuhandanstalt was permitted to take on credit itself and to provide credit guaranties. Although the volume was limited by law, it was adjusted to the Treuhandanstalt's needs in the second half of 1990. Finally, a credit authorization framework totaling 25 billion DM was established for 1990 and 1991;[18] this line was expanded to 30 billion DM p.a. for the period between 1992 and 1994 (FAZ 1992a, 11). All in all, the Treuhandanstalt had an overall deficit of some 250 billion DM at the end of 1994.

The Treuhandanstalt's privatization task and its rights of free disposal were restricted by the fundamental policy decision to restore expropriated property to its former owners. The principle of restitution was included in the unification treaty after the federal government had brought massive pressure to bear (Sinn/Sinn 1991, 67); the principle was given constitutional status (Fieberg/Reichenbach 1992, XIII). The right to restitution can be claimed by all natural and legal persons who, following the foundation of the GDR, were expropriated directly or indirectly, by means of economic pressure,[19] and/or were, between January 30, 1933, and May 8, 1945, persecuted for reasons of race, religion, or ideology and in consequence lost their property.[20] The expropriations undertaken under the laws of the occupying powers between 1945 and 1949 - these were said to include some 70 percent of Eastern Germany's production potential that was expropriated (Sinn/Sinn 1991, 68) - were explicitly exempted from restitution.[21] These persons were, however, permitted under the most recent regulation to file claims for compensation.

The principle of restitution logically ruled out the privatization of property rights for which restitution claims had been filed - otherwise it would be impossible to file for restitution. The German law governing property - it had been amended a number of times - was marked by the contradiction that it aims on the one hand to uphold the principle or restitution, while on the other hand attempts were made, using numerous special regulations and exemptions, to avoid the restraints on free disposal implied by it. *On principle*, all expropriated assets must be restored to their rightful owners.[22] Those entitled to restitution also had a right to have their property deconcentrated.[23] Once an application for restitution had been filed with the proper authorities, the Treuhandanstalt or other government institutions were, de jure, faced with a *restraint of disposal*.[24] De facto, however, this restraint was abrogated by creating generous exemptions for economically deserving investments.[25] Investments that fell into this category included all investments that preserved or secured jobs, created housing capacity, or contributed to improving infrastructure[26] - in other words, just about any investment. At first not much was achieved using this approach, because the municipal and district authorities were unable to issue enough investment certifications. But a breakthrough was achieved by an amendment adopted in March of 1991 and giving the Treuhandanstalt itself the right to issue investment certifications.[27] The Treuhandanstalt, itself a party in its role of privatization agency, was in this way given the right to invalidate restitution claims. The principle of restitution over compensation had thus, in practice, been reversed.

In acceding to the Federal Republic, Eastern Germany had on the whole taken over a proven and functioning legal system, which made it possible to minimize the costs of defining and specifying property rights and rights of disposal. The move at the same time shored up expectations as to the stability of the new legal institutions, thus limiting the costs of enforcing property rights (Siebert/Schmieding/Nunnenkamp 1991, 9-11). This gave Eastern Germany an important advantage over other transition: the transaction costs for foreign direct investment and the purchase of enterprises were lowered, in particular for Western German investors.

Problems involving overlapping responsibilities had been avoided by transferring all privatization-relevant property rights to a central institution with a high level of autonomy and nearly inexhaustible resources. The Treuhandanstalt's independence and strength made it possible to rapidly organize and implement privatization processes, although this has at the same time increased the risk that this power could be abused. The German government consciously took on this risk in order on the one hand to accelerate privatization and on the other to avoid having to assume political responsibility for the activities and mistakes of the Treuhandanstalt.

Because of the protracted restitution process and the uncertainty involved in assigning property rights, the principle of restitution gave rise to high transaction costs for the primary allocation of these rights. In addition, the principle of restitution led to a legalization of privatization decisions and thus to inefficient allocation of property rights.[28] The de facto reversal of the legal principle of restitution over compensation was able to mitigate the negative economic consequences of restitution, but not to obviate them.

5.2   Transformation of the Economic System in Eastern Germany

In János Kornai's sense, the institutional changes have served to transform the central behavioral constraints of economic agents into those posed by a demand-constrained economic system instead of those typical of a resource-constrained system. Accession to the economic and currency area of the Federal Republic not only altered the pertinent behavioral constraints of economic actors, it also led to acute rises in relative prices and production costs (5.2.1). The rise in factor costs and the drop in producer prices following monetary union largely depreciated the existing production potential of Eastern German enterprises (5.2.2). On the other hand, high capital subsidies were used to lower the opportunity costs for private direct investment, thus creating an incentive for the privatization and capital-intensive rehabilitation of Eastern German enterprises (5.2.3).

5.2.1   The Transformation of an Economy of Shortage through the Monetary Union

As was discussed at length in Chapter 2, abolition of the system of mandatory planning and price deregulation do not in themselves constitute sufficient conditions to create the coherence of a market economy.[29] The economy of shortage described by János Kornai can only be transformed as a system when a monetary constitution guaranteeing the scarcity of money has been institutionalized in addition. Most of the transition countries succeeded, by institutionalizing a market-oriented monetary constitution and enforcing a restrictive demand regime, in transforming sellers markets into buyers markets, thus eliminating the phenomenon of chronic shortage (Sachs/Lipton 1990; Bauer 1992). The other aspect is that abolition of directive-based planning and the enforcement of a restrictive fiscal policy is necessarily linked with a drop in demand, and this has led to marked drops in production in all countries in the process of transformation.[30]

This transformation of the economic framework alters the behavioral constraints relevant to the business sector. The constraint posed by chronic resource shortages no longer holds for state-owned and private enterprises, and they are instead confronted for the first time with a hard demand constraint. This transformation of the pertinent behavioral constraints is also linked with a partial depreciation of capital stock: in Soviet-type economies, the capital stock of enterprises was developed with an eye to a resource-constrained economic system. In transition countries, a company's success is contingent on its ability to procure, hoard, and find substitutes for intermediate inputs. The vertical integration of such companies is much greater, since chronic resource shortage and uncertainty on supplies lead to transaction costs for obtaining intermediate inputs that are higher than in market economies (Ben-Ner/Neuberger 1988). Transformation of the economic framework largely depreciates investments in traditional supplier relations and the production of intermediate inputs. In the terminology of transaction cost theory, part of the asset-specific capital[31] that was invested under the specific conditions of planned economy has become obsolete due to the transformation of the economic system.

In Eastern Germany, too, the institutionalization of a market-oriented monetary constitution was the point of departure of the transformation process. Owing to the *political* decision (Hoffmann 1991, 13; Siebert 1992, 19; Priewe/Hickel 1991; Brücker 1990) to join Western Ger-

many's economic and currency area, the initial conditions for the transformation of Eastern Germany differ in five central points from those
facing the other transition countries: First, in taking over the Deutsche
Mark (DM) Eastern Germany was endowed with a key international
currency which, in contrast to the situation in the other transition
countries, need not first stabilize its function as a means of payment or
a store of value (Siebert 1992). Second, the Eastern German economy
was integrated into a highly developed economic area without any
exchange-rate buffer and exposed to Western German and world market competition in nearly all of its markets (Siebert 1990a; 1990b, 9;
Frankfurter Institut für Wirtschaftspolitische Forschung e.V. 1990;
Götz-Coenenberg 1990). Third, Eastern Germany's currency apprecia-
ted by setting the exchange rate of Mark of GDR to DM at 1 : 1 for all
flow variables[32],[33] while all of the other transition countries were forced to devalue their currencies. Fourth, the politically generated pressure aiming at adjusting living standards led to a jump in the factor
costs of labor. Fifth, and finally, system transformation has been accompanied by a large transfer of public funds from Western Germany
to Eastern Germany.

During the first phase of integration into the Western German economic and currency area, Eastern Germany experienced the worst drop in
production and employment ever seen in German economic history.[34]
Gross domestic product dropped by one third in the second against the
first semester of 1990, and GDP was 37 percent below its 1989 level in
1991.[35] Since 1992 the economy has been proceeding on a path of
growth between five and six per cent p.a., but, despite huge transfers
from Western Germany, in 1995 GDP was still some 15 per cent below
its 1989 level. Production of the manufacturing industries declined by
half immediately after monetary union, sank to around one third of its
1989 level in 1991, and reached only 40 per cent of its 1989 level in
1994. Employment in the primary labor market (excluding persons in
government-sponsored employment programs) dropped by 45 percent,
from 9,747 million to 5,386 million, between 1989 and 1992, and has
been stagnated afterwards. Due to annual transfers of some DM 200
billions from Western Germany the level of domestic demand is nearly
doubling the GDP. The share of gross investments accounts for some

60 per cent of GDP or some 35 per cent of domestic demand (see Table 5.1). Compared with the transformation processes in the other countries

Table 5.1: Key Economic Indicators for Eastern Germany

	1989[1]	1990[2]	1991[3]	1992[3]	1993[3]	1994[4]	1995[5]
GDP[6] DM Bn.	325.0	267.3	206.0	222.1	235.0	254.5	276.0
Index: 1989 = 100	100.0	82.2	63.4	68.3	72.3	78.3	84.9
GNP[6] DM Bn.	324.0	267.5	214.0	232.2	243.5	262.0	283.5
Index: 1989 = 100	100.0	82.3	65.9	71.5	75.0	80.9	87.5
Domestic Demand[6]							
DM Bn.	325.0	238.9	358.3	412.0	434.2	467.0	491.0
Index: 1989 = 100	100.0	73.5	110.2	126.8	133.6	143.6	151.1
Gross Investment[6]							
DM Bn.	57.8	65.2	92.1	117.7	134.2	156.0	176.5
Index: 1989 = 100	100.0	112.8	160.6	203.6	232.2	269.9	305.4
Index: 2nd. sem. 1990 = 100							
Industrial Production[7]	197.0	144.9	n.a.	n.a.	n.a.	n.a.	n.a.
Manufacturing Production[8]	n.a.	n.a.	66.6	62.4	65.8	76.4	n.a.
Working Population							
Thousands	9,747	8,820	7,321	6,463	6,273	6,300	6,375
of these in:							
Employment Schemes	0	3	183	388	260	280	280
Full-time Vocational							
Training Schemes	0	24	280	491	381	225	200
Short-time Working							
Schemes (full-time equiva-							
lent)	0	345	903	198	95	50	40
Employed in							
Primary Labor-Market	9,747	8,448	5,955	5,386	5,537	5,745	5,855
Memo: Unemployment	0	241	913	1,170	1,149	1,160	1,075

1 GDP, GNP and domestic demand: estimate of the DIW; labor-market data: Statistisches Bundesamt.
2 1st sem. 1990: estimate of the DIW; 2nd sem. 1990: Statistisches Bundesamt.
3 Preliminary accounts of Statistisches Bundesamt.
4 Estimate of Gemeinschaftsdiagnose (autumn 1994).
5 Forecast of the Gemeinschaftsdiagnose (autumn 1994).
6 Prices of 1991.
7 Industrial production according to the accounting system of the GDR (NMP).
8 Manufacturing production according to the accounting system of the FRG (SNA).

Sources: Statistisches Bundesamt 1994a; 1994b; Gemeinschaftsdiagnose 1994; DIW 1992c; own calculations.

in transition, the initial decline in production in Eastern Germany was severe, but, due to the huge transfer-payments from Western Germany, after the initial drop growth of output was also relative high (see Table 5.2).

Table 5.2: Decline in Gross Domestic Product and Industrial Pro-
duction in Central and Eastern Europe

	1989	1990	1991	1992	1993	1994	Σ 1988-1994
Eastern Germany GDP	2,4	-17,8	-22,9	7,3	6,3	8,5	-19,7
Industrial Production	1,7	-26,4	-54,0	-6,3	5,4	16,1	-60,5
Czech Republic GDP	2.4	0.8	-14.2	-7.1	-0.3	3.0	-15.5
Industrial Production	1.7	-3.3	-22.3	-10.6	-5.3	0.0	-35.3
Slovak Republic GDP	1.1	-3.8	-14.5	-7.0	-4.1	1.0	-25.1
Industrial Production	-0.7	-3.6	-17.6	-14.0	-10.6	-4.0	-41.8
Hungary GDP	0.7	-3.5	-11.9	-4,3	-2.3	1.0	-19.2
Industrial Production	-1.0	-9.6	-18.8	-9.7	4.0	n.a.	n.a.
Poland GDP	0.2	-11.6	-7.6	1.5	3.8	4.5	-9.9
Industrial Production	-1.4	-26.1	-11.9	3.9	5.6	n.a.	n.a.
Romania GDP	-5.8	-5.6	-12.9	-13.6	1.0	0.0	-9.9
Industrial Production	-5.3	-23.7	-22.8	-21.9	1.3	n.a.	n.a.
Bulgaria GDP	0.5	-9.1	-11.7	-5.6	-4.2	0.0	-27.0
Industrial Production	-1.4	-16.5	-22.4	-12.2	-7.0	-6.0	-51.0
Russia GDP	1.6	-4.0	-9.0	-19.0	-12.0	-12.0	-44.3
Industrial Production	1.4	-0.1	-8.0	-18.8	-16.0	n.a.	n.a.
Sources: EBRD 1994; ECE 1993; 1994; author's calculations.							

Analytically, it is possible - according to a study by George Akerlof and a team from Berkeley University (Akerlof et al. 1991) - to distinguish between two causes for the drop in production in Eastern Germany following economic and monetary union: first, the issue of a convertible currency and the integration into the world marked it entailed resulted, not unlike the case in other transition countries, in a *shift in demand* in favor of western products. This demand shift is the result of new choices open to buyers and can be traced back to numerous factors such as the curiosity to purchase goods otherwise not readily available and a change in buyer preferences or to comparative disadvantages of eastern goods as regards quality, poor organization of sales and marketing, marketing problems, etc. (Akerlof et al. 1991, 10) The low transaction costs encountered by western suppliers boosted this effect somewhat as compared with other Central and Eastern European countries.

The second reason for the drop in production is a *price-cost squeeze* (Akerlof et al. 1991, 12) on Eastern German enterprises. This is a result of the specific price and cost conditions following monetary union in Eastern Germany: while producer prices were determined by Western Germany's price levels, the predominant share of Eastern Germany's manufacturers were unable to cover their costs in view of rapidly rising factor costs and short-term factor productivities.[36]

5.3 The Effects of Price-cost Squeeze on Eastern German Enterprises

The hypothesis of a price-cost squeeze can be verified empirically. George Akerlof et al. simulated the effects of price and cost conditions on Eastern German enterprises with the aid of an input-output projection. The intention of this study is first to complement the findings of Akerlof et al. by documenting the empirical development of price and cost levels following monetary union (5.3.1) and then to compare the empirical losses of Treuhand enterprises with Akerlof's input-output projection (5.3.2).

5.3.1 The Rise in Factor Costs

When Eastern Germany joined Western Germany's economic and currency area, its labor costs soared. The decision to convert wages and salaries paid in GDR marks into DM at a rate on one to one was a political decision that set the level of hourly labor costs at around 39 per-

cent of the wage level in Western Germany.[37] According to information
of the Statistisches Bundesamt and according to estimates made by the
Deutsches Institut für Wirtschaftsforschung (DIW), gross monthly
wage and salary earnings[38] per person employed rose within two years
following monetary union from 1,544 DM to 3.704 DM *in nominal
terms* (DIW 1992c, 623). Payroll costs per man-hour increased from
11,54 DM to 25,84 DM (DIW 1992c, 632). This amounts to a rise of
gross earnings per employee following monetary union from 36.5 percent to 69 percent of the level in Western Germany by the end of 1992,
and a rise per man-hour from 39.5 percent to 73 percent of the level in
Western Germany (DIW 1992c, 628, 632; SVR 1992, 111). Man-hour
productivity rose in the same period from an initial level of 22.7 percent to roughly 45 percent of the level in Western Germany (DIW
1992c, 623). The productivity gains are in large part due to layoffs in
Eastern Germany. Of the 9.68 million persons employed in Eastern
Germany in 1989, only 5.13 million, or 53 percent, were still employed
in the primary labor market in 1992 (i.e. excluding job-creation programs and qualification measures).[39] Unit labor costs in Eastern Germany, based on a level of 174 percent of the Western German figure
immediately following monetary union, remained largely stable in the
last quarter of 1992, reaching, following some fluctuation, 164 percent
of the Western German level.[40] (See Table 5.3.)

While the factor costs for labor doubled within two years in Eastern
Germany compared with the level prior to monetary union, *producer
prices* in Eastern Germany dropped by some 40 percent due to Eastern
Germany's accession to the economic and currency area of the Federal
Republic, and have remained constant since then (SVR 1992, 99). Under the assumption of given technologies, these price and cost conditions were, following economic and monetary union, bound to lower
the 1989 production potential of Eastern German enterprises.

CHAPTER 5   129

Table 5.3: Development of Wages and Productivity in Eastern Gemany

	1990[1]				1991				1992			
Qrtr.	I[1]	II[1]	III	IV	I	II	III	IV	I	II	III	IV
(1)	1616	1678	1544	1734	1848	2167	2473	2855	2708	2985	3256	3704
(2)	41.0	40.1	36.5	40.1	45.5	49.0	55.3	55.6	62.9	65.4	67.9	68.9
(3)	10.74	11.03	11.54	13.55	15.04	18.20	21.54	22.62	19.05	21.67	24.71	25.85
(2)	43.5	40.3	39.5	41.8	56.3	62.7	69.8	65.4	68.6	71.1	74.4	73.2
(4)	10.66	11.73	12.14	15.80	14.40	17.57	21.57	24.55	19.60	22.24	27.01	26.96
(2)	37.9	36.8	22.7	28.3	27.7	32.3	37.5	41.8	35.8	38.9	45.0	44.7
(5)	114.8	109.5	174.0	147.7	203.3	194.1	186.1	156.4	191.6	182.7	165.3	163.7

(1) Gross incomes from wage labor per person employed and month (original prices in DM, at respective prices).

(2) Percentage of Western Germany figures.

(3) Gross incomes from wage labor per man-hour (original values in DM, at respective prices).

(4) Productivity (gross domestic product in DM per man-hour at current prices).

(5) Unit labor costs, percentage of Western German values (per man-hour).

1) Gross incomes from wage labor, GDR. 1st and 2nd quarters 1990 and all 1992 values; DIW estimate.

Sources: Author's calculations, based on DIW and Statistisches Bundesamt data on national accounts. Labor volume and productivity: DIW 1993, 64, 70; 1992c, 626, 632; gross income from wage labor up to 1991: Statistisches Bundesamt: Volkswirtschaftliche Gesamtrechnungen, Fachserie 18, series 3.

5.3.2 The Effects of the Price-cost Squeeze on the Profitability of Eastern German Enterprises

The effects of price and cost conditions on the profitability of Eastern German enterprises following economic and monetary union were simulated by George Akerlof et al. with an input-output projection (Akerlof et al. 1991, 12-23). Akerlof's projection is based on the assumption that the factor productivities of the capital stock of Eastern

German enterprises were constant in the short term (Akerlof et al. 1991, 10). To analyze the *cost structure* of Eastern German enterprises, the Akerlof study refers to the data of 116 GDR combines (*Kombinate*) that produced for western markets. To earn one DM in trade with the West, these enterprises had to spend an average of 3.73 GDR marks (Akerlof et al. 1991, 14; Filip-Köhn/Ludwig 1990). If we consider the abolition of the old system of levies and the old accounting system and their replacement with the Western German system of taxation, the reduction of costs for intermediate inputs, and the reduction by half of the interest and amortization burdens,[41] this figure drops to 1.84 DM at given factor productivities following monetary union (Akerlof et al. 1991, 13). After monetary union, wage costs have become the most important cost component; they contribute a factor of 0.66 to variable costs (Akerlof et al. 1991, 18).

Due to this gap between production costs and producer prices, the Akerlof study expects only a small percentage of enterprises to be able to survive on their own the period following monetary union. The study rates as potentially viable companies those which are able, at full capacity utilization, to cover their current production costs from their sales of goods at world market prices (Akerlof et al. 1991, 12). Under the assumption of a rise of gross wage and salary sums to 1,545 DM for every person employed on a full-time basis, the Akerlof study sees a chance of survival (Akerlof et al. 1991, 19), at given factor productivities, for only 8.2 percent of the enterprises concerned.

Table 5.4 uses the empirical development of costs and productivities to extrapolate the cost-earnings development of Eastern German enterprises on the basis of Akerlof's "benchmark case". According to Akerlof, an increase or decrease of the gross wage and salary sum or labor productivity by one percentage point changes the variable factor costs by 0.66 percentage points with reference to the "benchmark case" (Akerlof et al. 1991, 18).

Table 5.4: Projection of Cost-revenue Development in Eastern Germany, 1989 Production Potential (Manufacturing)

	"Bench-mark"-projection	1990 (2nd sem.)	1991 (2nd quarter)	1992 (2nd quarter)
Productivity[1] (2nd sem. 1990 = 100)	100.0	100.0	106.0	113.2
Sum of gross wages and salaries[2]	1.545	1.362	1.917	2.335
ø Costs to earn 1 DM	1.84	1.70[3]	2.06[3]	2.30[3]
Costs to earn 1 DM[3] (cumulative share of enterprises)				
< 0.25	0.4	1.6	0.1	0.0
< 0.50	2.5	3.9	0.6	0.1
< 0.75	4.9	6.8	2.8	0.7
≤ 1.00	8.2	14.9	5.3	2.8
< 1.25	19.9	30.0	9.6	5.4
< 1.50	37.5	47.7	22.0	10.1
< 1.75	55.2	66.0	39.6	22.7
< 2.00	73.9	78.5	57.4	40.3
< 2.25	81.8	84.9	74.8	58.1
< 2.50	87.2	89.3	82.4	75.2
< 2.75	90.8	91.0	87.6	82.7
< 3.00	91.2	94.1	90.8	87.8
< 3.25	96.3	96.3	91.8	90.9
< 3.50	99.3	96.3	96.7	92.0
< 3.75	99.6	99.6	99.6	96.3
< 4.00	99.6	99.6	99.7	96.8
< ∞	100.0	100.0	100.0	100.0

1) Real gross domestic product per man-hour.
2) Gross incomes from wage labor in manufacturing. Estimate by Akerlof and real development as per DIW data.
3) Author's calculations, based on DIW data on productivity and sum of gross wages and salaries.
4) Percentage of enterprises, based on persons employed.

Sources: "Benchmark-Case": Akerlof et al. 1991, 97, Table 8; Development of employment and sum of gross wages and salaries in manufacturing: DIW 1992b, 513; author's calculations.

The basis is the real gross wage and salary costs per person employed in manufacturing[42] as per the data of the *Statistisches Bundesamt* or the estimates of the economic research institutes for the second six months of 1990, 1991 (second quarter), and 1992 (second quarter) as well as the change in man-hour labor productivity. On the basis of this development of costs and productivity, an extrapolation from Akerlof's model indicates average costs of 1.70[43] DM for the second half of 1990, 2.06 DM[44] for 1991, and 2.30 DM[45] for 1992 to earn one DM. According to the Akerlof projection's cumulative distribution of enterprises in terms of their losses, only 14.9 percent of the companies concerned would have been able to cover their current costs from their earnings; the figures for 1991 and 1992 would have been 5.3 percent and 2.8 percent respectively[46] (see Table 5.4).

The performance figures of the Treuhandanstalt's enterprises can be used as an indicator for an empirical validation of the Akerlof projection. The performance figures are not entirely comparable, since, with reference to 1989 capital stock, productivity rises are to be expected due to organizational change and improved supply conditions, the closure of especially unprofitable production capacities, and rehabilitation investment. Table 5.5 presents, by industry, the performance figures of a sample of 2,645 Treuhandanstalt's enterprises that employ a total of 709,273 persons, roughly one third of those employed in Treuhandanstalt's enterprises (Treuhandanstalt 1992a). The monthly payroll costs of these enterprises averaged 2,260 DM, compared with the 1,545 DM in the benchmark case of the Akerlof projection. The Treuhandanstalt's enterprises included in the sample showed an average deficit per employee of 17,800 DM. That amounts to 65.8 percent of payroll costs or 26 percent of their sales revenues (Treuhandanstalt 1992a).

The Akerlof projection would lead to the expectation that the payroll costs of the enterprises in the sample, assuming an average productivity rise of 6 percent in Eastern Germany's production potential from 1989 to the second half of 1990, would have given rise to costs of 2.33 DM to earn one DM[47] - whereas the actual figure for the sample enterprises was 1.26 DM (see Table 5.5).

The difference between the Akerlof projection and the empirical findings can be explained in part with reference to the closure of unprofitable capacities: if the number of persons employed is used as a rough indicator for the development of Eastern Germany's production potential (DIW 1991b), Eastern Germany's manufacturing capacities had, in

Table 5.5: Losses of Treuhandanstalt's Enterprises, 1991

Branch of industry	(1)	(2)	(3)	(4)	(5)	(6)	(7)
Agriculture and forestry	2,442	1.25	n.a.	-23.4	-80.0	16,298	2.3
Energy and water supply	2,758	0.99	1.10	1.8	5.4	6,417	0.9
Mining	2,633	1.17	n.a.	-20.9	-66.1	6,206	0.9
Chemicals	2,375	1.64	1.81	-33.1	-116.1	24,017	3.4
Plastics, rubber, asbestos	1,983	1.45	(1.65)	-23.8	-100.0	8,009	1.1
Building materials, fine ceramics, glass	2,192	1.43	(1.87)	-20.2	-76.8	18,633	2.6
Iron, nonferrous metals, foundries, steelworking	2,183	1.29	1.60	-20.4	-77.9	40,277	5.7
Machine-building and vehicle construction	2,156	1.25	2.23			181,358	25.6
Machine-building	2,208	1.22	2.29	-15.0	-56.6	150,810	21.3
Vehicles	1,883	1.48	1.96	-23.1	-102.2	30,548	4.3
Shipbuilding	2,500	1.57	n.a.	-37.1	-123.7	23,866	3.4
Electrotechnics/electronics	2,000	1.47	2.90	-18.7	-77.9	66,600	9.4
Precision mechanics and optics	1,792	1.93	n.a.	-19.1	-88.8	11,967	1.7
Steel and light-metal construction	2,562	1.08	n.a.	-1.0	-3.3	24,997	3.5
Iron, metal, sheet-metal goods, music instruments, toys	1,858	1.58	(3.00)	19.1	-85.6	14,474	2.0
Wood industry	2,408	1.56	n.a.	-29.8	-103.1	17,644	2.5
Printing and paper	1,908	1.35	1.85	-21.8	-95.2	10,466	1.5
Leather and shoe industry	1,575	1.98	n.a.	-25.0	-98.0	12,660	1.8
Textiles and clothing	1,592	1.71	1.80	-19.4	-101.6	62,357	8.8
Food and luxury foods	2,150	1.15	3.23	-18.3	-70.9	23,618	3.3
Construction	3,208	1.04	n.a.	-4.2	-10.9	48,465	6.8
Trade and commerce	2,533	1.08	n.a.	-17.4	-57.2	23,343	3.3
Transport and communications	2,892	1.23	n.a.	-17.2	-49.6	44,500	6.3
Services	2,450	1.16	n.a.	-9.6	-32.7	23,104	3.2
Total	2,260	1.26	(2.33)	-17.8	-65.6	709,276	100.0

(1) Monthly payroll costs
(2) Costs to earn one DM (costs/sales revenues)
(3) Costs to earn one DM, as per Akerlof projection; the figures in brackets indicate that the classification is only approximate.
(4) Annual surplus (or deficit)/employee per thousand DM
(5) Annual surplus (or deficit)/payroll costs in %
(6) Employees
(7) Structure (percentage of employees)
Source: Treuhandanstalt

terms of 1989 figures, declined by 21.8 percent in the second half of 1990, by 34.2 percent in the first half of 1991, and by 54.1 percent in the first half of 1992 (DIW 1992b). According to the cumulative distribution of enterprises in the Akerlof projection, the lower 34.2 percent of the companies gave rise to some 50 percent of the overall costs,[48] so that, under the assumption that the capacities closed down were those with the highest losses, the average costs required by the remaining 65.8 percent of the production potential to earn one DM can be estimated at 1.77 DM. It must also be considered that the Akerlof projection views the 1989 factor productivities and production functions as constant. In fact, improved supply conditions, reorganization of production sequences, concentration of manpower on essential tasks, etc. significantly boosted the productivity of Eastern German enterprises by 1991, even though no major rehabilitation investments were made.

Table 5.6:   *Development of Costs Revenues of Treuhandanstalt's Enterprises, 1991 and 1992*

	1991	1992		
		I	II	III
Payroll costs/month	2,260	2,532	2,989	2,923
Annual deficit/employee	17,791	13,690	19,621	22,000
% of payroll costs	65.6	45.1	54.5	62.7
Annual deficit/sales	26.0	14.7	19.1	23.2
Sample:				
Employees	709,276	389.774	299,582	219,819
% of Treuhandanstalt's holdings	32.2	29.9	26.9	33.9
Enterprises	2,645	1,517	1,190	891
Source: Treuhandanstalt: Monatsinformationen, various editions.				

Even if the average losses are not as high as those projected, based on given labor costs, for 1989 production potentials, an annual deficit of some two thirds of payroll costs is still very high. As Table 5.6 shows, the profitability of the Treuhandanstalt's enterprises did not improved essentially as time progressed: the absolute annual deficit per employee rose by roughly 24 percent from 1991 (17,790) DM to the third quarter of 1992 (22,000), while relative losses declined from 65.6 percent to 62.7 percent in reference to payroll costs and from 26 percent to 23.2 percent in reference to sales.[49]

On the whole, the empirical data confirm the hypothesis stated above: the asset-specific capital of Eastern Germany enterprises, i.e. the capital tied to specific uses, had largely been depreciated. It was no longer possible to produce profitably with the existing capital stock under altered cost and demand conditions. Although some 55 percent of Eastern Germany's production potential had been shut down, the Treuhandanstalt's enterprises were still operating at losses amounting to roughly 60 percent of their payroll costs. The Treuhandanstalt was consequently forced to privatize a capital stock that has become obsolete under the given conditions of cost and productivity.

5.4 The Conditions for Direct Investment in Eastern Germany

Following the depreciation of Eastern Germany's capital stock due to the shocklike change in demand and cost conditions, there were two basic economic options open for further development of Eastern Germany's production potential: the first option was to compensate for the rise in wage levels by subsidizing the factor costs for labor, seeking in this way to save part of the existing production potential (Akerlof et al. 1991; Sinn/Sinn 1991, 158-165). The decision was made not to provide blanket subsidies for wage costs in Eastern Germany; instead, the Treuhandanstalt guaranteed the survival of the great majority of its enterprises by providing them with maintenance subsidies.[50] These maintenance subsidies were used to delay the adjustment process, although this did not compensate for the price-cost squeeze facing Eastern German enterprises. The second option sought to redevelop completely Eastern Germany's production potential by subsidizing the factor costs for capital. This investment-oriented option was the one chosen by the German government (SVR 1991/92, 242; Sinn/Sinn 1991).

Eastern Germany's most important comparative advantage vis-à-vis other transition countries were, apart from the public transfers from Western Germany, the low transaction costs for Western German direct investment. In the view of Rüdiger Dornbusch and Holger Wolf, the Feldstein-Horioka effect (Feldstein/Horioka 1980), according to which national investment rates are determined by national savings rates, due to German unification, holds not for Eastern Germany (Dornbusch/ Wolf 1992, 251).

The extent of direct investment in Eastern Germany depended - the institutional framework assumed as given - on the real returns on and the opportunity costs of investment in Eastern Germany. Opinions differed on the *real return* on investment in Eastern Germany: Horst Siebert of the Kiel Institut für Weltwirtschaft suspected that the union of two economies with different factor endowments gave rise to high integration profits, and that the real returns on investments in Eastern Germany were very much higher than in Western Germany (Siebert 1992, 48; 1991). On the other hand, the expectation of Robert Barro and Xavier Sala-I-Martin, which was based on a long-term empirical study on the convergence of regions, was that integration profits would turn out considerably lower: they anticipated a markedly lower difference between the returns on capital in east and west than did Siebert, and they suspected that Eastern Germany's productive capacity would converge toward the Western German level at a rate of two percent per annum (Barro/Sala-I-Martin 1991). The idea behind the argument of integration profits due to the unification of two economies with different factor endowments is that the factor costs themselves differ. This, however, was precisely the German problem: the rise of factor costs for labor has preceded the rise in productivity, so that higher real returns on capital were not necessarily to be expected in Eastern Germany. *The opportunity costs* for investment in the German currency area raise significantly due to borrowing to finance transfers to Eastern Germany (SVR 1990; Sinn/Sinn 1991). The capital markets anticipated growing burdens on public budgets immediately following the decision in favor of monetary union. The nominal interest rate level of the short-term interest rates in Germany rose from 4.33 to 7.12 percent when the Berlin Wall came down in 1989, reaching levels of 9.2 to 9.8 percent following the decision in favor of monetary union. It was only when, in the period between 1992/1993, the recession began and investment declined perceptibly that the interest rate levels in Germany again fell below seven percent. Not only the absolute interest rate level, the relative level also rose, in particular against the US and Japan: while in Germany the interest rate level rose between 1988 and 1992 from 4.3 percent to over nine percent, it fell in the US from nine percent to 3.3 percent, declining in Japan in the same period from 6.9 to 3.7 percent (SVR 1990; 1991; 1992).

The high real interest rates were accompanied by rising opportunity costs for the purchase and rehabilitation of Eastern German enterprises: the capitalized value of Eastern German enterprises was contingent on whether and to what extent their capital could be put to alternative uses. Rising interest rates were therefore accompanied both by falling capitalized values of investments and a decline in the number of enterprises that could be privatized at a positive price (Sinn/Sinn 1991, 93-96). The German government thus sought, by providing massive capital subsidies, to lower the opportunity costs for the establishment of new enterprises and the purchase of existing enterprises in Eastern Germany. Investment allowances and investment subsidies, which in 1991 at times reached levels of 35 percent of the amount invested and can be set at an overall rate of up to 31 percent for the period extending from 1992 to 1996, special write-offs for investments of up to 50 percent of the amounts invested within one year (SVR 1991, 73; 1992, 192; Treuhandanstalt 1991d, 16), and low-interest loans significantly lowered the capital costs for direct investment in Eastern Germany (Frank 1993). Four allocative effects of these capital subsidies can be distinguished: in the first place, they brought about a reallocation of capital from Western to Eastern Germany. Second, they rewarded the use of capital-intensive technologies, in this way additionally forcing on the in any case drastic reduction of employment by increasing the factor costs for labor (Sinn/Sinn 1991, 165-170). Third, this type of tax-based internal relief provided strong incentives for takeovers as opposed to the establishment of new enterprises and benefited Western German investors as opposed to Eastern German and foreign investors (Frank 1993, 125-127). Fourth, and finally, the costs of rehabilitation investments in pri-

vate and privatized enterprises were reduced in comparison with the
costs of rehabilitation investments made by the companies held by the
Treuhandanstalt, which were unable to avail themselves of most of the
capital subsidies.

The massive subsidization of private direct investment and public investment in Eastern German infrastructure meant a high investment
rate in Eastern Germany in relation to its economic performance. In
1994 the investment rate in Eastern Germany was 61 per cent of GNP,
the joint forecast of the economic research institutes saw a rate of 66
percent of GNP for 1995. In comparison, Western Germany achieves a
rate of investment in fixed assets of 21 percent of GNP (Dornbusch/
Wolf 1992, 249). On the other hand, the Eastern German investment
rate was 25 percent in relation to domestic demand (which includes the
huge transfers from Western Germany). Roughly half of the investments made in Eastern Germany went into the business sector, the
other half being used to finance infrastructure investments of local
authorities, publicly owned corporations like Telekom and the railroad
system, and housing, which was financed largely with public funds (see
SVR 1992; Gemeinschaftsdiagnose 1992).

But as yet the high investment rate in Eastern Germany has not given
rise to the corresponding growth effects hoped for. This is due to the
fact that investments in Eastern Germany had to be matched by a very
much higher depreciation rate for old production capacities owing to
the price-cost squeeze there. According to an estimate of the state and
development of Eastern Germany's production potential presented by
the DIW the gross capital stock of the Eastern German business sector
(without housing) declined in 1992 by 2 percent and increased in 1993
by 2 percent, while gross fixed investment grew by 23 percent and 14
percent, respectively. Only in 1994 and 1995 the gross capital stock
and the production potential grew considerably (see Table 5.7).

Table 5.7: Capital Stock and Changes in Production Potential

	1991	1992	1993	1994	1995
Gross fixed investment in Bn. DM	61	75	85	94	102
change against previous year in p.c.	n.a.	23	14	10	9
Scrapped assets in Bn. DM	59	92	46	44	43
change against previous year in p.c.	n.a.	56	-50	-4	-2
Gross capital stock in Bn. DM	478	470	481	526	580
change against previous year in p.c.	n.a.	-2	2	9	10
Old assets (invested before 1991) in Bn. DM	412	336	267	223	179
change against previous year in p.c.	n.a.	-18	-21	-16	-20
New assets (invested from 1991) in Bn. DM	66	134	214	303	401
change against previous year in p.c.	n.a.	103	60	42	32
Production potential in Bn. DM	270	257	252	262	277
change against previous year in p.c.	n.a.	-5	-2	4	5
Gross value added in Bn. DM	159	176	189	205	223
change against previous year in p.c.	n.a.	10	8	9	9
Use of production potential in percent	59	68	75	78	81
change against previous year in p.c.	n.a.	16	10	4	3
Source: DIW 1994, 761.					

5.5   Conclusions for the Privatization of Eastern German Enterprises

The transformation of the economic system in Eastern Germany exposed Eastern German enterprises to a shock. The abolition of mandatory planning and the institutionalization of a market-oriented monetary constitution with a convertible currency has been linked with a decline in demand in all transition countries. In Eastern Germany, enterprises were exposed to an additional price-cost squeeze due to their integration into the Western German currency area, and this squeeze has lowered producer price levels and dramatically raised the factor costs for labor. Technologies and factor productivities being given, Eastern German enterprises have been unable to produce profitably under these price and cost conditions. The asset-specific share of Eastern Germany's capital stock, which was tied to specific transaction relations and uses, has largely been depreciated by the transformation of the economic framework. The German government lowered the opportunity costs of rehabilitation investments and new investment for Western German enterprises by subsidizing the factor costs for capital. This provided an incentive to buy and rehabilitate even companies that were operating with large current losses. The privileged promotion of direct investment made by Western German enterprises lowered the rehabilitation costs for private investors in relation to the Treuhandanstalt's costs for rehabilitation. This entailed the creation of additional incentives to privatization. The strategy of subsidizing capital rewarded the use of capital-intensive production techniques and further intensified cutbacks in employment in Eastern Germany due to the high factor costs for labor. Under the given framework conditions, the Treuhandanstalt was consequently forced to privatize a capital stock that was largely depreciated; on the other hand, large-scale capital subsidies reduced the opportunity costs for investment in private enterprises.

6   Strategy and Results of Treuhand-Privatization

Eastern Germany's accession to the economic and currency area of the Federal Republic of Germany in two ways affected the initial conditions for privatization. First, this development reduced the transaction costs for direct investments - in particular those made by Western German investors. Second, the price-cost squeeze and the demand shock that emerged following monetary union largely depreciated the existing capital stock of Eastern German enterprises.[1] The Treuhandanstalt decided under these conditions to give priority to a rapid privatization of the enterprises it held, defining this task as the most important objective of its business policy. It expected from rapid privatization the most efficient rehabilitation of the enterprises it held. This chapter examines the most significant elements of the Treuhandanstalt's privatization strategy, and the results it has entailed, against the background of the theoretical framework developed in Chapter 3.

Before analyzing the Treuhandanstalt's privatization strategy, the study examines the scope and value of the Treuhandanstalt's assets as a means of outlining the dimensions of the task of privatization (6.1). The examination of the Treuhandanstalt's privatization strategy will start out with an analysis of the pertinent constraints of privatization under the specific economic and institutional framework given in Eastern Germany (6.2). This is followed by a discussion of the Treuhandanstalt's most important strategic options (6.3) and its choice of privatization procedures (6.4). The specific problems of limited bidding competition (6.5) and the principal-agent relationship between the Treuhandanstalt and its staff members in charge of privatization are then discussed separately (6.6). The chapter concludes with a discussion of the overall outcome of the Treuhandanstalt's privatization activities (6.7).

6.1   The Scope and Value of the Treuhandanstalt's Assets

The property rights to the state economic sector in Eastern Germany were, with very few exceptions, transferred to the Treuhandanstalt by the *Treuhandgesetz* (Treuhand Act) and the Unification Treaty. The Treuhandanstalt's assets consist of three property complexes:

First, the former GDR's *state-owned enterprises* (VEBs) and combines (*Kombinate*) that were entered in the country's official industrial register. The Treuhand Act (*TreuhG*) of July 17, 1990, transformed the former state-owned combines and factories into incorporated enterprises.[2] As of July 1, 1990, the Treuhandanstalt held 8,482 such enterprises. 7,188 of these enterprises were direct Treuhandanstalt holdings and 143 were umbrella companies holding shares in 1,151 subsidiaries (Treuhandanstalt 1992, 35). Due to break-ups and deconcentration efforts, the number has risen to 13,815, 328 of which must in turn be subtracted in that they have been dissolved through mergers and break-ups.[3] As a rule, the former *VEBs* and *Kombinate* included several factories and production sites. The number of plants was estimated to be between 40,000 and 45,000 (Bundesminister der Finanzen 1991, 5; Sinn/Sinn 1991, 82). Aside from the state-owned companies and combines, the state business sector included 23,422 retail businesses, hotels and restaurants, and other service enterprises (Bundesminister der Finanzen 1991, 17; Maurer/Sander/Schmidt 1991, 54). The state-owned business sector likewise included the Deutsche Kreditbank AG (DKB), nearly 100 percent of which was held by the Treuhandanstalt.[4]

Second, the Treuhandanstalt held agricultural and forestry assets consisting of 17.2 billion square meters of farmland and 19.6 billion square meters of forests, which is roughly 28 percent of the farmland and 66 percent of the forested area in Eastern Germany (Treuhandanstalt 1991, 13). The Germany Finance Ministry estimates that 5.1 billion square meters of forests and 10 billion square meters of farmland will remain to be privatized once the claims to restitution filed by local Eastern German authorities and private owners have been settled (Bundes-minister der Finanzen 1991, 28).

Third, and finally, the Treuhandanstalt was placed in charge of the property rights to the GDR's *mining properties* (863 objects (Treu-handanstalt 1992, 24)), 863 state-owned *pharmacies*, the assets of the *Ministry for State Security* (MfS),[5] and the special properties and mili-tary assets of the National People's Army (NVA).[6] Beside these three property complexes, the Treuhandanstalt was also assigned the task of *holding in trust* and administering the assets of the so-called bloc par-ties and mass organizations of the GDR, although these assets were not scheduled to be privatized (Treuhandanstalt 1992, 21).

The total number of persons employed in the enterprises held by the Treuhandanstalt was indicated on July 1, 1990, to be 4.08 million (Kühl/Schaefer/Wahse 1992), which amounted to 46 percent of the persons employed in Eastern Germany at that time. Of the remaining 4.9 million persons in employment, some 1.9 million were at that time employed by the Länder and by local authorities and 2.4 million by the *Reichsbahn* and the telecommunications corporation, both state-owned enterprises. I.e., in terms of employment, the Treuhandanstalt was en-trusted on July 1, 1990, with the property rights to roughly three quar-ters of Eastern Germany's business and industrial sector (not including rails and telecommunications). The share of Eastern Germany's com-mercial capital stock held by the Treuhandanstalt must even be esti-mated somewhat higher, because nearly all of its capital-intensive in-

dustrial and manufacturing enterprises had been transferred to the
Treuhandanstalt. (See Table 6.1).

Table 6.1: Assets of the Treuhandanstalt

I. Nationalized economic sector	
Incorporated enterprises (former *Kombinate* and VEBs)	
as of July 1, 1990[1]	8.482
as of Dec. 31, 1994[2]	13.815
incl.: places of business[3]	ca. 45.000
Small businesses and retail establishments[3]	21.569
of these: Shops	16.230
Restaurants, small hotels	4.260
Bookshops	546
Movie theaters	533
Deutsche Kreditbank (DKB)	1
II. Agricultural and forestry assets[1]	
Agricultural land	17.2 bio. sqm
set to be privatized	10.0 bio. sqm
Forestry land	19.6 bio. sqm
set to be privatized	5.1 bio. sqm
III. Other property transferred[1]	
Mining property	863 objects
MfS assets	n.a.
NVA assets	n.a.
Pharmacy assets	1,853 objects

Sources: 1) Treuhandanstalt, DM-Eröffnungsbilanz as of July 1, 1990, Berlin, Oct. 1992
2) Treuhandanstalt 1994d.
3) Bundesminister der Finanzen (1991).

In connection with monetary union, this concentration of assets gave
rise to countless speculations on the value of the assets held by the
Treuhandanstalt: based on a book value of the Eastern German enterprises of 1,200 billion GDR marks,[7] the estimates made in connection
with economic and monetary union ranged from 900 billion DM (Suhr
1992), and 600 DM (Sinn/Sinn 1991, 70), down to 120 billion DM (IW
1990, 13). It was on this figure that the capital required for privatiza-

tion, and hence the privatization strategy chosen, depended (Sinn/Sinn 1991). It was also a criterion to judge the Treuhandanstalt's efficiency in privatization.

The most comprehensive valuation of Eastern German enterprises undertaken by the Treuhandanstalt was contained in its opening DM balance and its consolidated opening balance (Treuhandanstalt 1992c). The Treuhandanstalt's opening DM balance specified the assets and the liabilities held by the Treuhandanstalt; the consolidated balance was a statement of the Treuhandanstalt's holdings and its other assets based on a simplified consolidation (Treuhandanstalt 1992c, 20). The opening DM balance and the consolidated opening balance, including all of the Treuhandanstalt's assets, liabilities, and risks, concluded with a deficit of 209.3 billion DM (Treuhandanstalt 1992c, 14-17).

This balance included Treuhandanstalt reserves totaling 241.8 billion DM for capital restructuring, rehabilitation and privatization, liquidation, communalization, compensation and value adjustment liabilities as per the so-called *Vermögensgesetz*, and interest payments for the Credit Liquidation Fund, which consolidated the GDR's debt (Treuhandanstalt 1992c, 15, 17). In its opening balance, the Treuhandanstalt specified the value of its holdings as 81.4 billion DM, 2.5 billion DM of which consisted of external shareholdings. This was supplemented by the agricultural and forestry properties of the former GDR (16.1 billion DM), its mining property (1.4 billion DM), the assets and property of the National People's Army (NVA) and the Ministry for State Security (MfS) as well as some other real estate (5.8 billion DM), which amounted to an overall book value of 23.3 billion DM. This amounted all told to a book value of some 102 billion DM for the Treuhandanstalt's holdings and the other assets and properties (Treuhandanstalt 1992, 14). This statement is, however, distorted in that it contained numerous balance aids and the balance of the Deutsche Kreditbank AG, the successor to the GDR's banking system. When the balance of the Deutsche Kreditbank and all balance aids are calculated out, the outcome is a balance total of some 247 billion DM and capital resources - the Treuhandanstalt holdings - of roughly 121

Table 6.2:   Balance-sheet Value of Treuhandanstalt's Holdings and other Assets as of July 1, 1990

Assets (mio. DM)			Liabilities (mio. DM)		
A. Capital assets[1] (Treuhandanstalt holdings)			A. Equity capital[2]		123.276
			of this:		
I. Intangible assets		32	Specials assets for other shareholders[1]	2.482	
II. Tangible assets					
1. Real estate and buildings	86.925		B. Reserves[1]		
2. Other tangible assets	61.344	148.269	1. Reserves for pensions, etc.	2.091	
III. Investments		679	2. Other reserves[3]	89.347	91.438
B. Other THA assets[3] (carried over as per Unification Treaty)			C. Liabilities		
I. Mining property		1.387	1. vis-à-vis banking institutions[4]	8.609	
II. Agricultural and forestry property			2. Liabilities from deliveries and services[1]	14.614	
1. Agricultural property	11.899				
2. Forestry property	4.164	16.063			
III. Other tangible assets			3. Other liabilities[1]	9.533	32.756
1. NVA assets	614				
2. MfS assets	4.478				
3. Pharmacies	626				
4. Other real estate and buildings	54	5.772			
C. Current assets[4]					
I. Inventories		43.512			
II. Claims and other assets					
1. Claims from deliveries and services provided	12.699				
2. Other assets	6.947	19.646			
III. Liquid resources		12.110			
Total:		247.470	Total:		247.470

1) Only Treuhandanstalt's enterprises, without Deutsche Kreditbank AG, as per consolidated Treuhandanstalt opening balance and annex as of July 1, 1990.
2) Author's calculation (remainder)
3) The other reserves of Treuhandanstalt's enterprises include 30 bio. DM for clean-ups of old ecological burdens, 20 bio. DM for the costs of social plans, 10 bio. DM for threatened losses from current transactions, 3 bio. DM for neglected maintenance.
4) In the framework of its opening DM balances, the Treuhandanstalt assumed 38.493 million DM as debt relief; another 20.035 mio. DM was adjusted by the Deutsche Kreditbank in connection with debt consolidation.

billion DM (Brücker 1995, 274). This 121 billion DM represents the
book value of the assets set to be privatized.

The book value of the Treuhandanstalt's assets can at best provide
clues to their actual value. The figures in the Treuhandanstalt's consolidated opening balance were determined on the basis of replacement
values. Seen from the angle of the New Institutional Economics, valuation of enterprises on replacement value methods is problematical. In
Eastern Germany the asset-specific capital of the enterprises concerned
was largely depreciated, and thus any valuation of fixed assets at their
replacement value gave rise to a systematic tendency toward overvaluation. This is true in particular for machines and equipment, which
are as a rule dedicated to specific applications.

On the other hand, German accounting regulations favor a tendency
toward undervaluation of assets. Unlike Anglo-Saxon accounting law,
which is based on the principle of a "true and fair view" in the valuation of enterprises (Moxter 1995, 1103), opening DM balances are based
on the *cautionary principle* (Schnicke 1991; IDW 1991, 182). Balances
based on the cautionary principle state minimum values for assets and
maximum values for liabilities. This principle leads as a rule to book
values for enterprises clearly lower than their actual market value. In

opening DM balances, undervaluation is even fostered by specific incentives in the *D-Markbilanzgesetz*: while as per *D-Markbilanzgesetz*
heavily indebted enterprises are assigned an equalization claim against
the shareholder on the asset side of the balance sheet (Wysocki 1990),
enterprises with a positive balance of their assets and liabilities are de-
prived of part of their capital resources via an equalization liability.[8]
This regulation offers a strong incentive to utilize the approaches and
valuation latitudes provided by the *D-Markbilanzgesetz* to undervalue
enterprises (Sinn/Sinn 1991, 91).

On the whole, the market value of the Treuhandanstalt's holdings was
clearly underestimated in the opening DM balances. For example, real
estate in Eastern Germany was estimated at very low prices in the
opening DM balances. Taking 80 percent of the Western German price

per square meter as a basis, the value of the real estate held by the Treuhandanstalt would have been 241 billion DM instead of the 108 billion DM on which the opening balances were based. There was even more a tendency to undervalue than to overvalue tangible assets and current assets. Under the assumption that a possible overvaluation of the other tangible assets in the opening DM balance is at least compensated for by a cautious valuation of current assets, it may be assumed due to the undervaluation of the Treuhandanstalt's real estate holdings that the value stated in the opening DM balance was underestimated by 80 to 120 billion DM. If this rough assessment is correct, the market value of the assets held by the Treuhandanstalt would have been 200 to 240 billion DM, and, even when the restitution claims filed by private persons and municipalities are taken into account, nearly 70 percent of this could have been privatized.

6.2   Initial Conditions and Constraints

Compared with the other transforming economies, the specific economic and institutional conditions for the transformation of Eastern Germany's economic system have also shifted the effective constraints of privatization: due to the decline in their capitalized value, many Treuhandanstalt's enterprises offer private persons no incentive to participate in privatization by submitting a positive bid (6.2.1). On the other hand, privatization in Eastern Germany is not faced with the macroeconomic constraint of a limited capital supply (6.2.2), and the microeconomic constraint of limited financial resources and economic competence on the part of bidders was relaxed due to the low transaction costs for Western German investors (6.2.3).

6.2.1   The Participation Constraint

The concept *participation constraint* is borrowed from game theory (Arrow 1985, 1189); it denotes the trivial fact that a private bidder will participate in privatization bargaining only if he expects to benefit more from participation than from nonparticipation. The privatization of enterprises is restricted by competition for scarce capital: a private investor will submit a positive bid only when the expected returns of his investment are higher than they would be if he used his capital in any other way. In formal terms the condition

$$\sum_{t=1}^{T} n^{t} (1+i)^{-t} = \geq 0 ,$$

must be met, whereby the left-hand side of the inequation represents the net capitalized value of the enterprise concerned, including the net capitalized value of all investments. The net capitalized value consists of the sum of all expected net payments-in (including proceeds from liquidation) n^t of the existing capital stock and the investments made during the enterprise's lifespan (t = 1,2 ..., T), which are discounted at capital market interest rate i. Capital market interest rate i indicates the opportunity costs of the investment.

The participation constraint was the most important restraint on privatization in Eastern Germany: under the cost and demand conditions that existed following economic and monetary union, the Eastern German enterprises had been producing at high loss levels. The enterprises' asset-specific capital had been largely depreciated by the transformation of Eastern Germany's institutional and economic framework. In their study, George Akerlof et al. come to the same conclusion: under the assumption of putty-clay technologies, the disproportionate rise in the factor costs for labor following monetary union was bound to lead to a negative capitalized vale of Eastern Germany's capital stock, because the choice of technologies was based on different factor combinations (Akerlof et al. 1991, 55-56).

However, capitalized value refers not to an enterprise's current earnings but to its future earnings. It thus depends not (solely) on the existing capital stock but also on the expected capitalized value of rehabilitation investments (Sinn/Sinn 1991, 89). The opportunity costs of rehabilitation investments are affected by two contrary factors: on the one hand, the use of credit to finance transfers to Eastern Germany led to very high interest rates; on the other hand, the opportunity costs for direct investment in Eastern Germany were deliberately lowered through investment subsidies and tax write-offs.

Because of the high current losses incurred by Eastern Germany's enterprises, it had to be expected, in spite of the investment subsidies, that the capitalized values of a large share of the enterprises held by the Treuhandanstalt were below the participation constraint, which defines the point at which there is an incentive for private investors to participate in privatization by submitting a positive bid.

6.2.2   The Macroeconomic Capital Supply

Privatization runs up against the macroeconomic constraint posed by the aggregate financial resources of private households when the capital requirements of privatization are not met by an elastic capital supply.[9] This is the case in most of the transforming economies, where national savings are low and the inflow of foreign capital is restricted due to currency risks and high transaction costs. In Eastern Germany, on the other hand, the economic and monetary union with the Federal Republic lowered the transaction costs for direct investment from Western Germany and opened up access to the international capital markets. The aggregate capital supply should therefore not have posed an effective constraint to privatization in Eastern Germany (Wissenschaftlicher Beirat beim Bundesministerium für Wirtschaft 1991).

It is precisely this assumption that is disputed by Gerlinde and Hans-Werner Sinn in their thesis of an "endogenous price decline" of the assets held by the Treuhandanstalt (Sinn/Sinn 1991, 104-110; Sinn 1991). The privatization of Eastern German enterprises, they forecasted, would lead to an additional demand for capital amounting to 600 billion DM (Sinn/Sinn 1991, 109), and this demand was not matched by an adequate national supply of capital. Nor, the argument continued, were capital imports able to meet the additional demand for capital in the short run, since the international commodity markets were not sufficiently elastic. Consequently, interest rates were to rise, without this entailing any possibilities to mobilize additional capital.

The higher opportunity costs for capital, they argued, would trigger a decline in earning power, thus leading to a drop in the number of Treuhandanstalt's enterprises that were able to be privatized at a positive price (Sinn/Sinn 1991, 105). A number of empirical and theoretical objections can be raised to this thesis of a macroeconomic constraint posed by a limited supply of capital in Germany.

First, the figure of 600 billion DM for the capital required for privatization was exaggerated. In its opening DM balance, the Treuhandanstalt specified the book value of its enterprises and other assets as roughly 121 billion DM. The real estate of the enterprises held by the Treuhandanstalt was obviously undervalued by 80 to 120 billion DM in the opening DM balances, i.e. the market value was closer to 200 to 240 billion DM. At best, 70 percent of these assets could be privatized, i.e. capital requirements could be estimated at 140 to 170 DM. Under ideal conditions in a world without transaction costs, this sum could have been realized by the Treuhandanstalt. It must also be noted that this sum did not fall due in one year but was distributed over several years.

Second, privatization is an exchange of assets. Capital markets would be overburdened only if the buyers used their privatization revenues to finance *additional* spending. If the funds are returned to the capital market, the effect of privatization on the capital markets is neutral (Dluhosch 1991, 416-418). Sinn and Sinn assume that additional government consumption was to be financed with privatization revenues from Eastern Germany (Sinn/Sinn 1991, 105-106). But this argument is not cogent: neither the Treuhandanstalt nor the government was subject to a hard budget constraint. The volume of their spending was determined not by privatization revenues but by the cost-benefit rationale of the political actors involved. It was thus more plausible for the volume of government and Treuhandanstalt spending to be fixed *independently* of privatization revenues, i.e. this needed not lead to *additional* consumption-related spending. From 1990 to 1992 the net borrowing of local authorities, the supplementary and shadow budgets, including the Treuhandanstalt, was some 460 billion DM (SVR 1990; 1992), most of which went for transfer payments to Eastern Germany; this stood against effective Treuhandanstalt privatization revenues of 19.2 billion DM.[10] The burden on the capital market consequently stemmed from the credit-financed state transfers to Eastern Germany, not from privatization revenues.

Third, there are theoretical and empirical arguments (Dluhosch 1991, 419-422; Siebert 1991, 53-59) that cast doubt on the thesis that owing to the inelasticity of international commodity flows, the strain on the German capital market could not be eased by capital imports (Sinn/ Sinn 1991, 108). The additional demand for capital triggered by the process of German unification gave rise to a jump in interest rates and an increased external value of the DM. Adjustment of exchange rates altered relative prices in the domestic and foreign commodity markets. Contrary to the assumption of Sinn and Sinn (Sinn/Sinn 1991, 108), response of the international commodity markets to the change in relative prices was an immediate downward adjustment of the current account balance. Germany's capital account deficit fell from 135.5 billion DM in 1989 to 90.1 billion DM in 1990 in the wake of unification; a surplus of 14.4 billion DM was reached in 1991, followed by a surplus of 124.4 billion DM in the first three quarters of 1992 (SVR 1992). Analogously, the current account surplus fell from 108 billion DM in 1989 to 76 billion DM in 1990; the current account deficit for 1991 was 32.9 billion DM and 32.5 billion DM in the first three quarters of 1992 (SVR 1992). Compared with 1989, in other words, capital imports increased even in 1991 on balance by 150 billion DM and commodity imports grew by 141 billion DM p.a. The hypothesis that the inelasticity of commodity markets ruled out an adjustment of the current account balance to Germany's capital requirements can thus be seen as falsified.

6.2.3   Limited Buyer Competence and Financial Endowment

In Eastern Germany, privatization has also run up against the microeconomic constraint posed by the limited financial resources and competence of individual buyers.[11] While private individuals in Eastern

Germany were practically unable to form capital assets, a circumstance similar to that in the other transition countries, there were in Germany many more investors with both adequate financial resources and the competence required to purchase Eastern German enterprises. Still, it was the scarcity of economic competence and financial resources on the part of buyers that formed the bottleneck to privatization of enterprises with positive capitalized values (Härtel et al. 1991, 12). The number of bidders who had both adequate financial resources to purchase and rehabilitate an enterprise and the economic competences required for the purpose was inversely proportional to the size and complexity of the enterprises concerned. There was thus a competition problem involved in privatization: when key industrial enterprises in Eastern Germany were privatized, the Treuhandanstalt was as a rule forced to bargain with a limited number of bidders.

6.3   The Treuhandanstalt's Privatization Strategy

The open formulation of the *Treuhandgesetz* accorded to the agency extensive scopes of action in selecting its privatization strategy.[12] The choice of a privatization strategy was therefore determined less by legal regulations and restrictions than by objectives bound up with welfare economics and by constraints of the Treuhandanstalt itself. The decision diagram in Figure 6.1 presents the most important strategic options open to the Treuhandanstalt: privatization by *sale* or *cost-free distribution* (6.3.1), privatization *before* or *after* rehabilitation (6.3.2), and its choice of *allocative criteria* (6.3.3).

6.3.1   Sale versus Cost-free Distribution

With the exception of the special case of restitution, which was required by law, the Treuhandanstalt decided against a cost-free distribution of property rights. The rationale of privatization through cost-free distribution of property rights was to abrogate the asset constraint of private households as a means of accelerating the process of privatization. As Chapter 3 discussed at length, privatization through vouchers

Fig. 6.1: Strategic Alternatives of the Treuhandanstalt

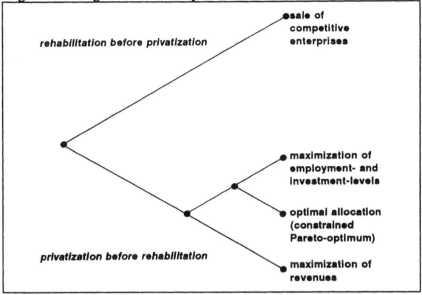

rehabilitation before privatization

●sale of competitive enterprises

● maximization of employment- and investment-levels

● optimal allocation (constrained Pareto-optimum)

privatization before rehabilitation

● maximization of revenues

distributed free of cost involves a trade-off between the acceleration and the allocative efficiency of privatization. Since, due to the low transaction costs for Western German investors in Eastern Germany, the constraint imposed by the financial endowment of bidders played no more than a subordinate role, the pace of privatization would not have profited from a voucher scheme. And for the Treuhandanstalt this would have entailed accepting a much lower degree of efficiency in the allocation and subsequent use of the property rights privatized in this way. A further consideration was that allocation of property rights by means of a voucher procedure would have severely restricted the strategic latitudes open to the Treuhandanstalt: the agency would have been confronted with a great number of anonymous bidders and forced to conclude standardized contracts with them. Complex contracts covering employment and investment guarantees and the clean-up of unregulated environmental burdens could not have been concluded if shares or vouchers had been allocated free of cost.

6.3.2   Privatization Before or After Rehabilitation

The second strategic option open to the Treuhandanstalt was its choice of a rehabilitation strategy. The Treuhandanstalt could either privatize its holdings swiftly, delegating the task of rehabilitation to the private buyers, or itself deconcentrate, restructure, and rehabilitate the enterprises, then selling them as viable and competitive enterprises. Of course it takes considerably more time to privatize rehabilitated enterprises. The strategy of privatizing viable enterprises was chosen for the large-scale privatization programs conducted in Great Britain, France, and Chile in the 1980s (Yarrow 1986; Vickers/Yarrow 1988; Smith 1991). As a rule, shares of the rehabilitated enterprises were put on public offer on the stock exchange (Smith 1991, 9). In these countries, the strategy required at least two to three years for the rehabilitation and preparation of an enterprise for privatization (Smith 1991). These privatization programs are comparable with the task of privatization in Eastern Germany neither in terms of the effort and expense required for rehabilitation nor in terms of the scope of the task: the overall number of enterprises successfully privatized worldwide between 1980 and 1987 is estimated to be below 1,000 (IBRD 1991, Annex 2, 1; Schmid-Schönbein/Hansel 1991, 465).

Having contemplated several other strategic considerations during the presidency of Rainer Maria Gohlke (Schmid-Schönbein/Hansel 1991, 465), the Treuhandanstalt selected the option of rapid privatization (Treuhandanstalt 1991b, 5; 1990, 6; 1991c, 4; Schmid-Schönbein/Hansel 1991, 465; Schmidt 1993, 215). The strategy of rapid privatization was grounded on the assumption that the costs of rehabilitation faced by private investors would be considerably lower than those of the Treuhandanstalt (Treuhandanstalt 1991, 5; Schmid-Schönbein/Hansel 1991, 466). Aside from the transfer of economic and technical knowledge and the mobilization of private capital, what the Treuhandanstalt expected from a rapid privatization was above all the chance for east German enterprises to overcome barriers to market entry (Schmid-Schönbein/Hansel 1991, 465).

The consequence of the Treuhandanstalt's decision not to finance and implement rehabilitation investments DIW 1992a; DIW 1991a) was that the survival of these enterprises was closely bound up with the pace of privatization (Schmid-Schönbein/Hansel 1991, 466): since the price and cost conditions for Eastern Germany's existing production potential, with its given technologies and factor productivities, was to deteriorate over time, any passive adjustment of enterprises to market conditions via layoffs and closures of production capacities would reduced still further the production potential to be privatized. As was demonstrated in Chapter 5, this case entails a growing share of maintenance subsidies per job, which, ceteris paribus, further lowers the capitalized value of the enterprises held by the Treuhandanstalt. The most important postulate of a strategy geared to privatizing Eastern German enterprises before they had been rehabilitated is hence maximization of the pace of privatization.

6.3.3   The Choice of Allocative Criteria

The third strategic decision concerned the choice of *allocative criteria*. The Treuhandanstalt based its allocative decisions on multiple criteria, the price being accorded no more than a subordinate role (Treuhandanstalt 1991d; 1990; Schmid-Schönbein/Hansel 1991, 466). According to Treuhandanstalt publications, sales decisions were based on three groups of allocative criteria: first, the volume of investment and employment commitments; second, price; third, the bidder's economic competence and rehabilitation concept (Treuhandanstalt 1991d, 8-9). The paramount objective was to maximize the volume of employment and investment; the criterion of "fair and just price" (Treuhandanstalt 1990) was clearly subordinated to this aim (Schmid-Schönbein/Hansel 1991, 466). The economic competence of the bidder and the quality and plausibility of his rehabilitation concept had the character of a collateral condition that must be met if the goal of maximizing the volume of employment and investment was to be achieved (Treuhandanstalt 1991d, 8). Consequently, the bidder won whom the Treuhandanstalt, on the basis of the information available to it, could expect to realize the greatest volume of employment and investment.

Agreement on employment and investment commitments and the Treuhandanstalt's use of multiple allocative criteria has come in for severe
criticism (Maskin 1992, 117; Maurer/Sander/Schmidt 1991, 64). The
Treuhandanstalt defended the practice of requiring employment and
investment commitments and its use of multiple allocative criteria in
the following arguments:

> *"What is sold is on the one hand tangible technical
> and economic workforce qualifications and on the
> other hand floor space. This is the reason why the
> buyer's risk is more far-reaching than otherwise
> and why the risk depends much more than otherwise
> on the buyer himself. This implies that the seller
> cannot be certain that the rehabilitation task he
> passes on via privatization will in fact be accom-
> plished. The seller seeks for this reason to reach
> agreement in writing that as many employees as
> possible will be taken over and that the highest
> possible investment sums will be committed. The
> buyer must be compensated for this commitment"*
> (Schmid-Schönbein/Hansel 1991, 466).

The Treuhandanstalt's reasoning was based on two arguments that differed in analytical terms. First, the Treuhandanstalt anticipated a higher
level of allocative efficiency; and second, it intended in this way to
subsidize private investment that would otherwise not have been made.
As was shown in Chapter 3, the allocation-related argument depends
on the behavioral assumptions made: in an abstract model world with
unbounded rationality, the bidder with the highest price would at the
same time be the best entrepreneur for an enterprise. If, on the other
hand, bounded and unequally distributed rationality are assumed, the
person who submits the highest bid need not necessarily find the most
productive use for an enterprise. A conflict can occur between the
goals of maximization of earnings and allocative efficiency. The volume of employment and investment commitments, the economic competence of a bidder, and the quality of business concepts can be indicators for an efficient use of an enterprise. By taking into account multi-

ple information with and without price character, it is therefore possible to heighten allocative efficiency in comparison with the case in which the allocative criteria are restricted to price alone, even if the Treuhandanstalt, under the assumption of bounded rationality, may not have achieved an optimal allocation in the sense of traditional microeconomics. So in other words, if the strict rationality assumptions of traditional microeconomics are dropped, the result is not necessarily a contradiction between the goal of allocative efficiency and the use of multiple allocative criteria.

The Treuhandanstalt's second strategic objective went beyond increasing allocative efficiency under the condition of bounded rationality: by subsidizing rehabilitation investments with negative capitalized values, it aimed to achieve volumes of employment and investment much higher than would have been possible in the profit-maximizing bidder behavior. In the case of positive capitalized values, the bidders were given a price concession for increasing the volume of investment and employment (Treuhandanstalt 1991d, 8); in cases where negative capitalized values were involved, the Treuhandanstalt was prepared to agree to a negative price. The strategic decision to accept even negative bids has led to a sizable extension of the spectrum of enterprises capable of privatization: the most significant barrier to privatization in Eastern Germany, the participation constraint, was shifted with the help of negative selling prices, and this in turn raised the number of privatizable objects.

Subsidizing rehabilitation investments was part and parcel of the Treuhandanstalt's political rationale. From the perspective of welfare economics, it is possible to justify subsidies for rehabilitation investments with negative capitalized values only when these investments entail positive external effects. Following the dramatic slump in production and employment and the closure of large chunks of Eastern Germany's industrial base, positive effects have been achieved through rehabilitation and new investment and the reduction of unemployment associated with them, through cuts in the state and social-insurance transfers necessitated by these problems, and through the realization of agglomerative advantages; these positive effects were internal for working people and their families, for state and region, while they were external for the private investor. But the definition of external effects not only requires an economic actor's choice of action to affect the production and utility function of another economic actor, and to do so without this being taken into account in the action performed by the agent; it also presupposes that this effect cannot be internalized through marketlike or contractual relationships between the economic agents (Weimann 1991, 19; Feess-Dörr 1991, 320). Under the specific conditions prevailing in Eastern Germany, the latter condition was met only to the extent that, due to monetary union, the political framework, and long-term collective wage agreements, the problem of underemployment could not be eliminated via private agreements in markets. Subsidies, be they wage subsidies of the type described in Akerlof's model or be they capital subsidies, were therefore intended as the second best means of realizing effects which, owing to the constraints to which markets are subject, could not be achieved through private agreements (Akerlof et al. 1991).

Providing private investors with rehabilitation subsidies is not the only institutional possibility of realizing positive external effects from rehabilitation investments with negative capitalized values. The fundamental institutional alternative would have been for the Treuhandanstalt itself to take on the task of rehabilitation. But the Treuhandanstalt's overriding strategic decision to privatize as rapidly as possible the enterprises it holds largely eliminated this alternative. In a world without transaction costs, rehabilitation by the Treuhandanstalt would have been equivalent to rehabilitation carried out by a private investor. But when the picture includes opportunism and bounded rationality there is a trade-off between the transaction costs involved in concluding, monitoring, and enforcing rehabilitation contracts with private buyers and the high expected costs of rehabilitation by the Treuhandanstalt as compared with rehabilitation carried out by private investors. It is a complex task to ascertain the comparative costs of subsidizing private rehabilitation investments and rehabilitation by the Treuhandanstalt. Chapter 7 examines the transaction costs and the contract-related costs involved in agreeing on subsidies for private rehabilitation investments with negative capitalized values; Chapter 8 uses a model from game theory to look into the comparative costs of public and private rehabilitation regimes.

6.4   Choice of Privatization Procedures

The spectrum of possible privatization procedures can be broken down into two groups, standard procedures and complex procedures. In *standard procedures* the price of the highest bid is the relevant action parameter. Standard procedures entail the conclusion of complete contracts fully specified in terms of time and subject matter. The package on offer must therefore be specified ex ante and is thus not open to bargaining. The standard procedures include the auctioning off of enterprises, public tender offers of company shares on stock exchanges, and auctions of company shares by means of investment vouchers. In *complex privatization procedures*, the package on offer is specified flexibly through solutions reached in bargaining; in these procedures, action parameters other than price are permissible. Complex negotiated solutions make it possible to agree on complex contracts that are not complete either in terms of time or subject matter. The complex privatization procedures include bilateral and multilateral bargaining as well as management and employee-buyouts and -buyins (Fig. 6.2).

The choice between privatization procedures resulted from the Treuhandanstalt's strategic objectives: the objective of the Treuhandanstalt was not to maximize revenues and returns, it was to increase the volume of employment and investment by subsizing rehabilitation investments with negative capitalized values. Part of the intention was to boost allocative efficiency by including information without price character. The privatization pattern of the Treuhandanstalt was consequently to sell enterprises via *complex negotiations* with one or more interested parties, which could, in the broader sense, include management and employee buyouts and buyins (6.4.1). The Treuhandanstalt restricted as far as possible the use of *standard procedures*. Auction procedures were used only in the so-called small privatization (retail trade, small service enterprises) and in selling small businesses that were of no paramount importance. Despite the existence of a developed capital market, the Treuhandanstalt decided against privatizing company shares on the stock exchange (6.4.2).

Figure 6.2: Privatization Procedures of the Treuhandanstalt

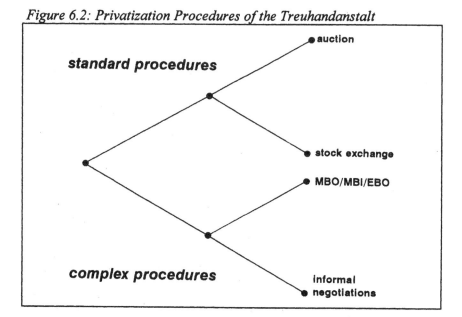

6.4.1   Privatization by Means of Informal Bargaining

Seen in terms of employment and capital assets, the better part of the enterprises held by the Treuhandanstalt was privatized by means of informal bargaining with one or more bidders. As a rule the initiative lay with the bidder. The bidder's business concept (or rehabilitation concept) constituted the basis for sales talks. This business concept had to be based on the continued existence of the enterprise in question, and it was to include a business plan, an investment plan, and a financial plan, as well as an employment plan and a statement of intent on anticipated business relations with suppliers and customers (Treuhandanstalt 1991d, 7). The bidder was expected to provide proof of his financial standing (Treuhandanstalt 1991d, 7). The overall package, i.e. the configuration of the company to be privatized, the bidder's and the

Treuhandanstalt's obligations and liabilities were specified in the talks. The Treuhandanstalt privatized enterprises and business units as well as fixed and circulating assets ("asset deals"), if and to the extent that this did not obstruct the privatization of the remaining units of the enterprise concerned (Treuhandanstalt 1991d, 6).

The Treuhandanstalt sought to sell complete enterprises (Treuhandanstalt 1990; 1991d, 6), although by December 31, 1994, it had, in 14,576 privatization transactions, sold 7,629 minority holdings (Treuhandanstalt 1994b). The Treuhandanstalt concluded complex contracts covering, aside from the price and the terms of payment, buyer employment and investment guarantees, Treuhandanstalt liability commitments for cleanups of unregulated ecological burdens, the implementation of social plans, and provisions on subsequent real estate valuations (Treuhandanstalt 1991d).

Chapter 3 developed three theoretical arguments for the choice of informal privatization procedures: first, it is possible with these techniques to process complex information with and without price character. The Treuhandanstalt at least attempted to increase allocative efficiency by taking account of such complex information as bidder reputation, economic competence, and the quality of bidder rehabilitation concepts, etc. (Schmid-Schönbein/Hansel 1991, 466).

Second, bids could in this way be specified flexibly during the bargaining process. The configuration of the enterprises held by the Treuhandanstalt was, as in the other transforming economies, as a rule not competitive (Hax 1992, 145). The Treuhandanstalt was therefore faced with the alternative of either deconcentrating its enterprises and defining viable corporate configurations before privatizing them or addressing the issue of deconcentration in the bargaining process itself. The second option had the advantage of providing the Treuhandanstalt with additional information on a bidder's utilization concept, thus making it possible to lower substantially the costs of deconcentration (Hax 1992, 146).

Third, and finally, in informal bargaining it was possible to conclude *complex contracts* for which complex information and the mutual identity of the contracting parties were pertinent (Williamson 1985, 78-95). It was for this reason not possible to conclude contracts of this sort using standardized privatization techniques. Conclusion of complex contracts was of central strategic significance to the Treuhandanstalt: aside from agreements on employment and investment commitments (Treuhandanstalt 1991d, 8), the Treuhandanstalt assumed liabilities for eliminating unregulated ecological burdens (Treuhandanstalt 1991d, 11) and was prepared to allow time for payment in cases of buyouts and buyins by management and workforces (Treuhandanstalt 1991d, 12). Provisions on subsequent valuation were frequently agreed on for real estate transactions (Treuhandanstalt 1991d, 10). The rationale behind agreements of this kind was on the one hand to achieve a socially and politically desirable level of employment in Eastern Germany by financing rehabilitation investments with negative capitalized values and on the other hand to use "trading in risk" as a means of achieving an efficient allocation in bargaining between risk-averse investors and a risk-neutral Treuhandanstalt.

One objection often raised to the use of informal privatization techniques and complex privatization contracts is that these techniques restrict bidding competition (Siebert 1992, 97; Maskin 1985, 118). The Treuhandanstalt did in fact for the most part conduct talks with one bidder or a limited number of bidders. On the other hand, the Treuhandanstalt indicated that it was possible for other bidders to join the talks at any time, even during the course of ongoing negotiations (Treuhandanstalt 1991d, 5), and this, as was demonstrated in Chapter 3, distinguishes these bargaining conditions from the case of a bilateral monopoly. Section 6.5 examines in detail the effects and costs of the competitive restraint posed by the Treuhandanstalt's informal bargaining strategy.

Buyouts and buyins by management and employees constitute a special case of privatization by means of complex bargaining. Compared with other bidders, management or employees have the advantage of inside knowledge of the company they wish to take over, though they are as a rule faced with the disadvantage of lacking adequate financial re-sources. In such cases the Treuhandanstalt was prepared to accept a lower equity ratio and thus face the higher commercial risk implied by agreeing on deferred payment schedules with private banks (Treu-handanstalt, Zentrales Controlling, 1994, 3). There were, for two rea-sons, limits to the size of enterprises that qualified for management and workforce buyouts: first, the larger the enterprise, the greater the Treu-handanstalt's risk of being expropriated by management or workforce. Second, corporate rehabilitation requires investment funds which man-agers and workforces were, in view of their limited equity capital, un-able to finance via the capital market. If the Treuhandanstalt financed the rehabilitation investments, this in turn increased its risk of devault due to bancruptcy of buyout firms. Consequently, the Treuhandanstalt largely restricted management buyouts and buyins to small and me-dium-size enterprises: Only 12 percent of MBO and MBI privatizations have been companies employing over 1000 persons (see Table 6.3). By September 30, 1994, 2,697 enterprises had been privatized in manage-ment buyouts; this is 18,5 percent of the companies fully or nearly fully privatized in this period (Treuhandanstalt, Zentrales Controlling, 1994, 3).

Table 6.3: Management Buyouts and Enterprise Size Class

Enterprise size (in employees)	Management buyouts	
	in %	in % (cumulative)
1—49	30.4	30.4
50—99	12.5	42.9
100—499	37.8	80.7
500—999	7.4	88.1
> 1000	11.9	100.0
Source: IAW, 1991.		

6.4.2   Privatization by Means of Standard Procedures

Though the Treuhandanstalt also used auction procedures to privatize a good share of its holdings, this procedure was for the most part restricted to the sale of small businesses. There, too, the Treuhandanstalt made use not of standard auctions but of multiple allocative criteria. The most important action parameter was the level of employment commitments, not price (Maurer/Sander/Schmidt 1991, 58). Unlike the case of standard auctions, the allocative decision was thus made at the discretion of the Treuhandanstalt. Its discretionary scope was, however, restricted by a minimum price set prior to any auction; the price was established on the basis of expert opinions provided by external appraisers and consulting enterprises. The prices actually realized have as a rule been above this reserve price (Maurer et al. 1990, 58). 2000 small businesses employing fewer than 50 persons have been sold at fixed prices; the Treuhandanstalt set employment and investment parameters for the auctions (Siebert 1992, 101). The bidders submitted sealed bids and thus remained anonymous. The contracts finalized were standardized, and the Treuhandanstalt assumed no liability for unregulated ecological burdens, social plans, assumptions of losses, and the like (Siebert 1992, 58). As a rule only the business itself was privatized, the property rights to the real estate remaining with local authorities or private owners (IAW 1991, 46). This was seen as a means of limiting the incentive to liquidate the business with an eye to reselling the real estate.

The Treuhandanstalt restricted its auctions of enterprises to two clearly defined groups of enterprises that were of lesser strategic significance: first, the so-called *small privatization*, i.e. the privatization of retail businesses, movie theaters, restaurants and hotels, and small craftsman's and service businesses. Second, by the middle of 1992 the Treuhandanstalt had used formal competitive bidding techniques to auction off some 2000 small business employing fewer than 50 persons (Siebert 1992, 101).

In general terms, these enterprises met three criteria: first, they were small and clearly defined economic units. The costs of deconcentration

CHAPTER 6 · 165

and the risk of coming up with a noncompetitive package were low in this case. Second, the companies were not overly idiosyncratic, i.e. they placed no excessive demands on the specific competence and financial endowment of bidders. This was the right setting for bidder competition - a necessary condition for the efficiency of auction procedures. Fourth, and finally, these companies had low volumes of employment and capital, a factor that limits the social costs of misallocation. For the Treuhandanstalt, these enterprises were consequently of subordinate strategic importance, and there was thus, in such cases, no particular interest in entering into complex contractual relations with the buyers. The use of auction procedures for these enterprises could, in other words, be justified with the argument of economizing transaction costs.

The disadvantage of auction procedures is that, first, the Treuhandanstalt's package had to be clearly specified prior to the auction and, second, the agency's information-processing capacity was low. The first problem was obviated by restricting auctions to small and clearly defined business units. The Treuhandanstalt attempted to solve the second problem by using multiple allocative criteria and requiring bidders to submit business concepts. But the use of multiple allocative criteria in auctions was problematical. Ex ante, the Treuhandanstalt lacked the information required to assess a bidder's credibility and the rehabilitation concept he submitted. It makes little sense to conclude complex agreements if the parties to them are to remain anonymous. Ex post, the Treuhandanstalt was hardly in a position to safeguard itself against opportunistic behavior on the part of a bidder, because, in relation to the returns involved, the expense involved in monitoring the performance of a contract grows in direct proportion to the number of enterprises and the size of the enterprises privatized. Frequently no penalties for nonperformance were agreed on when enterprises were privatized by auction (Handelsblatt 1993c, 7). If, however, the Treuhandanstalt was unable to secure credible compliance with commitments made on employment and investment, bidders had a strong incentive to negotiate a lower price by exaggerating the volume of employment and investment which they planned to realize. In the terminology of transaction cost theory, the Treuhandanstalt, in agreeing on employment and investment commitments in standard privatization techniques, entered into a complex contractual relationship without being able to protect itself against opportunistic behavior by putting in place adequate monitoring and governance structures.

Interestingly, the Treuhandanstalt has, even though there is a developed capital market in Germany, decided against privatizing company shares on the stock exchange. The decision not to privatize in this way was linked to the German regulations on admission to the stock exchange; these regulations were not met by the enterprises held by the Treuhandanstalt (Sinn/Sinn 1991, 100; Siebert 1992, 98). But there are indications that the Treuhandanstalt would not have chosen this approach even if there were in Germany an institutionalized market for venture capital (junk shares) that met the terms of the statute on admission to the stock exchange (Sinn/Sinn 1991, 100).

The advantage of privatizing company shares on the stock exchange is the possibility of diversifying portfolios, which allows an efficient allocation of risk. There are also disadvantages: in the first place, it is only possible to privatize competitive enterprises, i.e. the companies must be deconcentrated and rehabilitated *prior to* privatization (Smith 1991, 9; Siebert 1992; Schmid-Schönbein/Hansel 1991, 465). The strategy of swiftly privatizing enterprises before they have been rehabilitated would consequently have constituted a barrier to privatization on the stock exchange. In the second place, privatization on the stock exchange would have forced the Treuhandanstalt to deal with anonymous bidders whose economic competence and business concepts were irrelevant to the allocative decision involved. Third, the Treuhandanstalt would in this case have been unable to insist on complex contracts and would consequently have had to privatize without either employment and investment guarantees or any obligation to clean up unregulated wastes. Fourth, and finally, the separation of ownership and control entails a number of problems concerning the rehabilitation of the enterprises concerned: the more widely ownership is dispersed, the greater the principal-agent problems involved in managing an enterprise. If the success of rehabilitation investment is highly uncertain, the problem of control and information is even greater than it is for enterprises operating more or less profitably. All in all, it must be assumed that the transaction costs involved in the separation of ownership and control were much higher for the enterprises held by the Treuhandanstalt than they are for other enterprises, and thus privatization of company shares on the stock exchange would have involved costs very much higher than the revenues that could be realized by means of diversified portfolios.

Only one Eastern German enterprise was traded on the stock exchange once it had been privatized: the Sachsenmilch AG, whose shares were traded in cooperation with the Südmilch AG in Stuttgart (Hoffmann 1992, B5). Even this was possible only because a parent company from the west held the majority of the shares. And this corporation was forced to initiate foreclosure proceedings around one year after it had been admitted to the stock exchange. Some of the parent company's managers were under investigation for fraudulent investment and subsidy practices (FAZ 1993c, 14; Handelsblatt 1993d, 13; 1993e, 14). This may be coincidence, but it does illustrate graphically the principal-agent problems that arise when the property rights to an enterprise about which little is known are broadly dispersed via the stock exchange.

6.5   Limited Bidding Competition

Privatization in Eastern Germany involved little competitive intensity. Where small and medium-sized enterprises were concerned, the Treuhandanstalt as a rule bargained with one bidder only (Härtel et al. 1992, 20-21). The Treuhandanstalt's bargaining position was further weakened by its time preference: rises in factor costs, high current losses, and the decision to forego rehabilitation investments were detrimental to the competitiveness of the Treuhandanstalt's enterprises over the course of time. The survival of a good number of enterprises therefore depended on their being privatized swiftly. This is the reason why, in a bilateral monopoly, a bidder can secure for himself the lion's share of the net returns of privatization, as was demonstrated in the analysis of the Ståhl-Rubinstein game in Chapter 3.

Chapter 3 distinguished between two causes for the restraint of bidding competition: first, the idiosyncratic character of an enterprise as a commodity and, second, the procedures used for privatization. The first aspect, competitive restraint, is contingent on the size of the enterprise in question and the asset specificity of its capital. The Treuhandanstalt could influence the size of its enterprises by deconcentrating them. Measured in terms of competitive corporate configurations, the depth and pace of the deconcentration carried out by the Treuhandanstalt was relatively low. 1990, the Treuhandanstalt's corporate portfolio consisted of some 8,500 enterprises, which in turn included roughly 40,000 places of business. Owing to deconcentration and split-ups, the overall number of enterprises rose to 13,815 by December 31, 1994, and 328 of these were in turn dissolved through merger and split-up (Treuhandanstalt 1994).

Deconcentration was limited by the Treuhandanstalt's costs in defining viable corporate configurations and breaking up the enterprises it held. The advantage of informal privatization procedures was of course that they make it possible to carry out deconcentration with an eye to bidder requirements. Nevertheless, enterprise size and a lack of depth of deconcentration constituted a significant obstacle to privatization, in particular where the units concerned were medium-size enterprises (e.g. in the machine-building industry) (Härtel et al. 1992, 15-16).

The second cause of restrained bidding competition is concerned with the choice of a privatization procedure. The Treuhandanstalt sold off the better part of its enterprises in informal bargaining with one or a limited number of bidders. In economic terms, this approach is controversial in that privatization by means of informal bargaining is seen as entailing pronounced restraints on competition (Siebert 1992, 97-102). The *Sachverständigenrat* called on the Treuhandanstalt to activate bidding competition and to employ auction techniques wherever possible (SVR 1991).

Following Schumpeter, Chapter 3 developed the hypothesis that competition can also be effective as a latent threat. To the extent that the bargaining process is open and further bidders can enter the talks at any time by submitting a bid of their own, the outcomes of bilateral bargaining converge toward competitive conditions. As long as the bargaining process was open, the outcome was no longer dependent on the number of bidders with which the Treuhandanstalt bargained, the key factor was the likelihood that another bidder joined the bargaining process. What was at issue was thus not whether the Treuhandanstalt privatized its holdings through informal bargaining but whether it provided the bargaining process with an open structure.

In describing its privatization strategy, the Treuhandanstalt claimed that new bidders were able at any time to enter the bargaining process by submitting a bid of their own (Treuhandanstalt 1991d, 5). On the other hand, a study published by the *Hamburger Weltwirtschaftsarchiv* (HWWA) and based on observation of the Treuhandanstalt's bargaining practices arrived at an entirely different conclusion: in its opinion, the Treuhandanstalt was too quick to enter into a strategic alliance with one bidder or consortium of bidders, thereby gravely weakening its bargaining position (Härtel et al. 1992, 21). The Treuhandanstalt did not, it was claimed, bargain simultaneously with several bidders, thus ruling out from the outset any other privatization options (Härtel et al. 1992, 20). This phenomenon, it was further claimed, could be observed especially often in talks with Western German companies active in oligopolistic markets (Härtel et al. 1992, 21). The HWWA pointed to four exemplary cases to prove its contention: the award of the Petrolchemie und Kraftstoffe AG to a consortium consisting of VEBA, DEA, and AGIP/ELF/TOTAL, the bargaining between Carl Zeiss Jena and Carl Zeiss Oberkochen, the sale of the Zwickauer Batterie GmbH to the Varta Batterie AG, and the privatization of the shipbuilding industry (Härtel et al. 1992, 16-41). One indicator of the low level of competitive intensity was also the small percentage of foreign investors involved in privatization in Eastern Germany: by February 28, 1993, foreign bidders accounted for 10.2 percent of the enterprises privatized, 9.9 percent of the investment commitments, and 8.7 percent of the employment guarantees agreed upon (Treuhandanstalt, Zentrales Controlling, 1993a, 109).

If the findings of the HWWA study are representative for the Treuhandanstalt's privatization strategy, the conditions for latent bidding competition outlined in Chapter 3 were not given. The risk that a competitor would receive the award would then have tended toward zero for the bidder engaged in bargaining. When the Treuhandanstalt was pressed for time, the bidder could, as in the case of a bilateral monopoly, expropriate the lion's share of the net returns of privatization. If the bidder took up an oligopolistic position in the privatized enterprise's market segment, this also entailed the risk that a market adjustment strategy emerged (Härtel et al. 1992, 38-40). But the consequence of the high costs entailed by competitive restraints in privatization would not be the concern of a privatization strategy based on informal bargaining, the issue would have been to lower the barriers to the entry of additional bidders.

6.6   Principal-agent Problems Facing the Treuhandanstalt

Another important argument against privatization through informal bargaining is the lack of transparency of such transactions. The Treuhandanstalt was exposed to the risk that its employees might expropriate a share of its assets. The principal-agent problem faced by the Treuhandanstalt differed from the classical "hidden action" model (Arrow 1986, 1184) in one important respect: in the classical principal-agent problem, an outcome π, for example an enterprise's profit, is contingent on an action of agent a and the relevant environmental states of action θ [$\pi = \pi (a, \theta)$]). The principal can observe the outcome of the action, but not the action itself and the relevant environmental states (Arrow 1986, 1188). The problem facing the Treuhandanstalt was that it, unlike in the case of a classical principal-agent relationship, was unable to assess the outcome of privatization. The Treuhandanstalt had insufficient information on the value of its enterprises. Without an exact valuation, however, it was impossible to assess the outcome of bargaining, for instance the proceeds of the sale or commitments on employment and investment (Arrow 1986, 1193). Incentive models developed for the classical principal-agent problem were therefore bound to fail here: in a classical principal-agent model, an agent receives, depending on her risk preference, a share of (observable) return π based on a remuneration model previously specified (Arrow 1986, 1188-9). Since the Treuhandanstalt, without an exact valuation of its enterprises, could not judge the net returns of privatization, i.e. the difference between the actual proceeds and its reserve price, it could base its considerations only on the gross revenues. But if an incentive model was based on gross revenues, an employee could increase her earnings not only by raising the proceeds per object but also by lowering the prices and increasing the number of objects privatized. As the principal, the Treuhandanstalt was unable to distinguish between these cases because of the informational edge enjoyed by its agent. According to principal-agent theory, the use of incentive models makes little sense in cases in which the outcome of the action of an agent cannot be assessed exactly (Arrow 1986, 1194).

The Treuhandanstalt used incentive models affected by precisely this problem: it gave its employees premiums based on the amount of the privatization revenues realized, the employment and investment commitments given, and the number of enterprises privatized (Handelsblatt 1992b, 4). The *Bundesrechnungshof* (federal accounting office) has sharply criticized this bonus system, because

> *"(...) there is a lack of adequate criteria for formulating and weighting performance objectives and evaluating the achievement of these objectives"* (Handelsblatt 1992f, 6).

The central principal-agent problem faced by the Treuhandanstalt in its privatization activities was of course collusion among its employees and the bidders. This problem was intensified by the use of Western German managers as privatization agents; these managers often conducted sales talks with their former or future enterprises (Härtel et al. 1992, 12-15). Even receipt of information on the bids submitted by competitors or the Treuhandanstalt's reserve price could provide Western German enterprises with strategic bargaining advantages (Härtel et al. 1992, 13).

Numerous cases of criminal collusion between Treuhandanstalt employees and bidders have come to the attention of the public (Suhr 1991; Christ/Neubauer 1991; Kampe 1993; Der Spiegel, 1991a, 122-127; 1991b, 135-136; FAZ 1992c, 16). But what is even more important than criminal offenses committed by employees of the Treuhandanstalt is the use of noncriminal acts to expropriate Treuhandanstalt assets: the more complex the privatization negotiations and contracts involved, the greater were the discretionary latitudes open to employees. When the contracts and allocative criteria concerned were complex, unjustified concessions made to bidders, i.e. expropriations of Treuhandanstalt assets, were for the most part the responsibility of Treuhandanstalt agents and were therefore relatively difficult to sanction by due process of law. As was pointed out above, the principal-agent problem could not be solved through formal incentive models as a result of the inadequate information available on the value of the enterprises concerned. The Treuhandanstalt could limit any expropriation of its assets only by installing an internal control system that monitored the individual acts of its agents. A control system of this sort could be based on social norms, with agents being dismissed for serious offenses. The degree to which the Treuhandanstalt's objectives were supported by the agency's personnel was essentially contingent on these persons' acknowledgment of its business policy. The Treuhandanstalts' brief term of activity and the short periods of employment did, however, reduce the chances of providing any social integration for employees. The incentives for loyalty toward the Treuhandanstalt's objectives were therefore low for many of the agents entrusted with the task of privatization. In the sense of game theory, what is involved here are 'endgames' played against the Treuhandanstalt, because for an agent the end of a transaction was effectively one step toward the end of his transaction-based relationship with the Treuhandanstalt.

Expropriation of state-owned property by agents assigned to privatize this property is an unavoidable risk in a program involving the privatization of just about the whole of an economy's productive property. Compared with standard procedures, the strategy of informal bargaining and sale no doubt opened up additional opportunities for expropriation in that this strategy's transparency was lower than that involved in formal privatization procedures. There was a trade-off here between the efficiency and speed of informal procedures and their low level of transparency. The high costs of opportunistic behavior on the part of Treuhandanstalt employees were transaction costs stemming from the decision to privatize swiftly and the choice of informal privatization procedures. They could be limited, but not done away with.

6.7   A Balance of the Treuhandanstalt's Privatization Activity

When it was dissolved in December 31, 1994, the Treuhandanstalt had largely concluded its task of privatization: some 70 percent of its stock of enterprises had been privatized, reprivatized, or transferred to municipalities. The remaining enterprises are for the most part in the process of liquidation or foreclosure; merely 1.6 percent of the Treuhandanstalt's enterprises remain to be privatized. These figures provide little information on the capital stock that has been privatized. According to its annual financial statements, the Treuhandanstalt had, on December 31, 1994, privatized, reprivatized, or transferred to municipal ownership some 57 percent of the capital it held (6.7.1). On average, the revenues from privatization, amounted only to the book-value of the Treuhandanstalt's holdings (6.7.2). It is not possible to draw any cut-and-dried inferences from these data, although they do indicate on the one hand that employment and investment commitments were subsidized to a considerable extent by means of price rebates and on the other hand that the Treuhandanstalt's bargaining stance and tactics were not very efficient (6.7.3).

6.7.1   Scope of Privatization

Basically, the Treuhandanstalt's privatization activity breaks down into three complexes: first, small-scale privatization, with its 23,422 businesses - retail establishments, hotels and restaurants, cinemas, pharmacies, and small crafts and service enterprises. Second, privatization of the former state-owned enterprises and industrial combines, the number of which grew, owing to divestiture, from an approximate original figure of 8,500 to 13,815 by December 31, 1994, and 328 of which were merged and thus dissolved (Treuhandanstalt 1994b). Third, and finally, privatization of real estate and buildings not required for business operations (*Treuhand-Liegenschafts-Gesellschaft* mbH - TLG) and agricultural and forestry property (*Bodenverwertungs- und -verwaltungs GmbH* - BVVG - and *Treuhand-Forstbetriebs-GmbH* - TGF).

The so-called *small privatization* was completed by the middle of 1991. 15,250 (65.1 %) of these 23,422 items were privatized for the most part by auction. The remaining 8,172 items were either closed outright or could not be privatized because their leases were canceled (Bundesminister der Finanzen 1991).

By December 31, 1994, 6,321 of the 12,354 enterprises making up the former *state-owned economic sector* had been fully privatized, as had the majority holdings of 225 enterprises; in *numerical terms* this is 53 percent of the Treuhandanstalt's portfolio. The Treuhandanstalt's holdings were also reduced through 1,588 reprivatizations (12.9 %), 265 transfers of enterprises into municipal property (2.1 %), 70 deliveries as per existing property law (0.4 %), and 157 liquidations (1.3 %). In other words, the Treuhandanstalt reduced its holdings by 8,601 enterprises, 69.6 percent of its overall portfolio. Almost 95 % of the remaining 3,735 enterprises (3,562, 30.4 % of the overall portfolio) is set to be liquidated. What remains with the Treuhandanstalt' successor organizations is a net stock of 192 enterprises, or 1.6 percent of the overall portfolio (Treuhandanstalt 1994b). (See Table 6.4).

The number of enterprises privatized gives little indication of the actual scope of privatization. The share of the capital stock privatized by the Treuhandanstalt is calculated in Table 6.5. The table shows that on December 31, 1994, some 39 percent of the Treuhandanstalt's holdings as per corrected opening DM balance had been privatized; 18 percent had been reprivatized and communalized and one third had been adjusted for to the initiation of liquidation and foreclosure proceedings. 9.4 per-

Table 6.4: State of Privatization as of December 31, 1994

		in %
I. Small privatization[1]		
Total number of objects	23.422	100.0
Privatized objects	15.250	65.1
of these:		
shops	10.740	45.9
Restaurants/small hotels	2.300	9.8
Pharmacies	1.417	6.0
Bookshops	475	2.0
Movie theaters	318	1.4
Closed/not privatized for other reasons[2]	8.172	34.9
II. Former nationalized enterprises and combines		
Total portfolio	13.815	
Dissolved by merger/split-up	328	
Mining properties (rights)	502	
THA property shares	484	
Treuhandanstalt holding in audit	1	
Other companies outside gross stock	146	
Total (gross stock)	**12.354**	**100.0**
Privatized, completely/majority stakes	6.546	53.0
of these: completely privatized	6.321	51.2
majority stake privatized	225	1.8
Reprivatizations	1.588	12.9
Communalizations	265	2.1
Provisional writs of possession	45	0.4
Completely liquidated	157	1.3
Stock reduced[3]	8.601	69.6
Stock	3.753	30.4
of these: liquidation/foreclosure in process	3.561	28.8
Net stock	192	1.6
of these: management KGs	63	0.5
III. Results		
Gross revenues (in mio. DM)	65,000	
Investment commitments (in mio. DM)	211,100	
Employment commitments	1,508,000	

1) State following conclusion of the small privatization, June 30, 1991
2) For the most part cancellation of lease, no transfer to municipalities and private landlords
3) Unlike the case here, the Treuhandanstalt counts all enterprises set to be liquidated as not part of its stock of enterprises.

Sources: Bundesminister der Finanzen 1991; Treuhandanstalt 1994b; FAZ 1994, 10.

cent of its holdings remained with the Treuhandanstalt. In numerical terms, on the other hand, 46 percent of the enterprises had been privatized either fully or for the most part at this point of time, while 14 percent had been reprivatized and recommunalized and 24 percent were set to be liquidated. In other words, there are sizable deviations here between the privatization figures and the value of the capital stock that was privatized (see Table 6.5).

Real estate turned out to be the slowest aspect of privatization. By December 31, 1993, 21 percent of the agricultural and forestry assets and 21 percent of the properties not required for operation had been sold. 42.9 percent of the assets of the *Nationale Volksarmee* and 43.9 percent of the assets of the Ministry for State Security, a sizable share of which consisted of real estate, was privatized or reprivatized. On the other hand, 86.3 percent of the mining properties - for the most part mining rights - and 96.8 percent of the pharmacy properties were successfully privatized. The reasons for th e slow progress in privatizing properties and real estate may also have been the slow pace at which restitution claims made by former owners were processed (see Table 6.6).

The major part of the privatization process in Eastern Germany was thus completed. When the Treuhandanstalt was dissolved on December 31, 1994, 65,895 of the 4.08 million persons originally employed still held jobs in Treuhandanstalt's enterprises, umbrella companies, and the subsidiaries of the Treuhandanstalt (Kühl/Schäfer/Wahse 1992). The percentage of employment provided in Eastern Germany by the Treuhandanstalt and its holdings thus declined to 1 percent compared to 48 percent in 1990. Of the 65,895 persons employed by the Treuhandanstalt and its holdings on December 31, 1994, 44,280 held jobs in enterprises yet to be privatized, and 17,791 of these were in turn employed in management Kgs.

Table 6.5: Changes in the Treunhandanstalt's Holdings

	State					
	31/7/90	31/12/91	31/12/92	31/12/93	31/12/94	Σ 1994 -1990
	- in mio. DM -					
Holdings according to opening DM balance	78,909	77,838	77,611	76,102	76,301	76,301
adjustments	-	-1,073	-225	-1,509	199	-2,608
Increase due to capital inflows and direct takeovers of holding companies	-	596	1,437	1,139	-662	2,510
Adjusted holdings[1]	78,909	78,432	79,048	77,241	75,639	75,639
Adjustment for the holdings of management KGs	-	-	-	-1,783	n.a.	-1,783
Reduction due to privatization	-	11,814	19,415	25,134	29,567	29,567
in % of holdings[2]		15.1	24.6	32.5	39.1	39.1
Reduction due to communalization/ reprivatization	-	-6,428	10,832	13,243	13,591	13,591
% of holding[2]		8.2	13.7	17.1	18.0	18.0
Reduction due to adjustment for liquidation	-	14,622	15,797	18,806	25,296	25,296
in % of holdings[2]		18.6	20.0	24.3	33.4	33.4
Remaining THA holdings	78,909	45,568	33,004	20,058	7,185	7,185
in % of holding[2]	100.0	58.1	41.9	26.0	9.5	9.5

1) Holding as per opening DM balance and increases due to capital inflows and direct takeovers of holding companies.

2) Corrected holdings per year.

Sources: Treuhandanstalt: Annual financial statements, 1990/91 and 1992, 1993, 1994, (Treuhandanstalt 1993b; 1994a; 1995); author's calculations.

Table 6.6: Changes in Agricultural and Forestry Assets

	31/7/90	31/12/91	31/12/92	31/12/93	Σ 1993/90
		- in mio. DM -			
Adjusted holdings as per opening DM balance[1] Agricultural and forestry assets	16,063	15,959	16,202	16,166	16,166
Mining assets	1,387	1,388	1,388	1,388	1,388
NVA assets	614	614	614	614	614
MfS assets	4,478	4,478	4,793	4,793	4,793
Pharmacy assets	626	626	626	626	626
Other properties and buildings	54	335	636	2,062	2,062
Total[2]	23,213	23,400	24,259	25,649	25,649
Reductions due to privaization, reprivatization, and communalization of agricultural and forestry assets	-	649	892	1,952	3,401
in % of holdings		4.0	5.5	12.1	21.0
Mining property	-	406	516	244	1,198
in % of holdings		29.3	37.2	17.6	86.3
NVA assets	-	100	56	108	264
in % of holdings		16.3	9.1	17.6	42.9
MfS assets	-	47	286	1,771	2,104
in % of holdings		7.5	6.4	36.9	43.9
Pharmacy assets	-	396	141	69	606
in % of holdings		63.3	22.5	11.0	96.8
Other properties and buildings	-	179	236	154	569
in % of holdings		53.4	37.1	7.5	27.6
Total[2]	-	1,777	2,127	4,298	8,202
in % of holdings		7.6	8.8	16.8	32.0

1) Holdings as per opening DM balance and increases due to capital inflows and
   direct takeovers of holding companies.
2) Slight deviations can arise due to the process of rounding off.

Source: Treuhandanstalt 1993b; 1994a; author's calculations.

6.7.2   Privatization Revenues

The Treuhandanstalt indicated that its gross revenues from privatization amounted to 36.953 billion DM as of December 31, 1994; it received employment commitments for 1.5 million jobs and investment commitments covering 211.1 billion DM. Against these revenues stand the obligations contracted by the Treuhandanstalt which are shown in the balance as reserves. The annual accounts show that the Treuhandanstalt achieved privatization returns as high as the net present value of its enterprises according to the opening DM balance. In 1992 and 1993 revenues amounted only to 55.3 and 36.4 of the net present values, respectively. In 1994 revenues were with 250 percent of the net present values much higher than in the previous years due to the privatization of objects in infrastructure. For the remaining assets, there are no net present values as per opening DM balance. Here the reduction of assets was shown in the balance in average prices equal to the level of the privatization returns, which makes it impossible to draw any conclusions on the ratio between privatization revenues and balance-sheet value (see Table 6.7).

The ratio of the privatization revenues to the balance-sheet values of the assets privatized is the only empirical category available to evaluate the Treuhandanstalt's privatization activity. But the cogency of this category is also limited in that on the one hand balance-sheet value and market value of the enterprises and assets in question may deviate considerably and on the other hand the obligations contracted by the buyers and the Treuhandanstalt are unknown. The privatization revenues are nevertheless low if we consider the tendency to undervaluation in the opening DM balances. Three hypotheses can be used to explain this phenomenon: first, the market value of the Treuhandanstalt's enterprises may have been equivalent to their net asset value as per balance sheet when the opening DM balances were presented on July 1, 1990. What speaks against this hypothesis is, however, that the enterprises were very cautiously valued in the opening DM balances. All indicators suggest that in the balances capital assets with low asset specificity such as properties and buildings were shown distinctly below their market value (see Chapter 6.1).

Table 6.7: Privatization Revenues

	12/31/1991	12/31/1992	12/31/1993	12/31/1994	Σ 1990-93
Revenues from the privatization of enterprises	11,801	4,200	2,082	11,187	29,270
Reduction of assets	11,814	7,601	5,719	4,433	29,567
Returns in % of values as per opening DM balance[1]	99.9	55.3	36.4	252.4	99.0
Privatization revenues from other assets[2]	1,972	1,657	1,551	2,367	7,547
Total revenues[3]	13,773	5,857	3,789	13,534	36,953

1) Net present value of enterprises as per corrected opening DM balance.
2) Agricultural and forestry assets, mining property, NVA/MfS assets, pharmacy assets, other properties and buildings.
3) Deviations due to incomplete records.

Sources: Treuhandanstalt 1993c; 1994a.; 1995.

Second, the low privatization revenues might perhaps be regarded as a result of the Treuhandanstalt's privatization strategy. As was demonstrated above, the Treuhandanstalt's time preference led to very high costs associated with competitive restraints, and thus the lack of openness marking the bargaining process made it possible for many buyers to pocket sizable rents. Also, the lack of Treuhandanstalt control over the agents entrusted with privatization evidently led to sizable losses of revenues.

Third, and finally, the goal pursued by the Treuhandanstalt was not maximization of revenues but maximization of employment and investment in Eastern Germany. Private rehabilitation investments were subsidized through negative sales prices and prices rebates. The level of the subsidies in individual cases that have become public and the Treuhandanstalt's low privatization revenues indicate that the figures involved go into tens of billions.

6.7.3   Conclusions

The Treuhandanstalt has largely achieved the primary goal of its business policy, viz. "to use privatization as a means of reducing as far as possible the entrepreneurial activity of the state" (Treuhandanstalt 1990, 1) The Treuhandanstalt's enterprises accounted for less than 1 percent of overall employment in Eastern Germany at the end of 1994. When the Treuhandanstalt was dissolved, the enterprises it held were of no more than marginal importance to Eastern Germany's economy. The Treuhandanstalt's strategy of restricting standardized competitive bidding procedures to smaller and - at the utmost - medium-sized companies and privatizing the main part of its holdings through informal bargaining evidently contributed to a quickening of the pace of privatization in Eastern Germany.

The Treuhandanstalt evidently turned to account the comparative advantages involved in informal privatization procedures: flexibly structured packages, consideration of complex information in arriving at allocative decisions, agreement on complex contracts. But these advantages stand against the disadvantage that bilateral bargaining can have an inhibitive impact on competition. Such inhibitive effects can, as was discussed at length in Chapter 3, be minimized by opening up the framework of the bargaining process. The findings of empirical case studies and the low levels of privatization revenues realized by the Treuhandanstalt do, however, indicate that the barriers to the entry of further competitors into ongoing privatization talks were very high. The Treuhandanstalt might therefore have, in practice, reached bargaining results that converge more toward the case of bilateral monopoly than toward the case of bidding competition.

The strategy of swift privatization without doubt led to high costs. The decision against far-reaching rehabilitation investments successively undermined the competitiveness of the Treuhandanstalt's enterprises. Privatization became a race against time. As was demonstrated in Chapter 3 using the Ståhl-Rubinstein game, the time pressure faced by the Treuhandanstalt led to a weakening of its strategic bargaining position and a reduction of its privatization revenues. But even more important than diminished revenues is the fact that the decision against making rehabilitation investments led to a drop in the production and employment capacities of the Treuhandanstalt's enterprises (see also Chapter 8).

The low level of privatization revenues realized indicates that the Treuhandanstalt on the one hand provided sizable subsidies in exchange for employment and investment commitments by private investors, while on the other hand the agency's bargaining strategy and tactics gave rise to considerable losses of revenues. An economic evaluation would be considerably easier if the Treuhandanstalt had created more transparency regarding the scope of the rehabilitation subsidies granted to private investors in the form of price rebates and other subsidies.

7   Transaction Costs of Rehabilitation Contracts

The transformation of Eastern Germany's economic framework has largely depreciated the capital stock of the firms there. Since the currency union with Western Germany, the firms held by the Treuhandanstalt have been making large losses, and these have continued to grow. The survival of Eastern German firms could be ensured only by making them competitive, which could be accomplished only by investing substantial sums in their rehabilitation. The Treuhandanstalt for the most part decided against financing rehabilitation itself, opting instead for a "privatization of rehabilitation" (Treuhandanstalt 1991d, 4) This strategy entailed substantial subsidies for private investors in the form of price rebates and negative prices. In terms of welfare economics, these subsidies can be justified only if the rehabilitation investments are expected to give rise to positive external effects.[1] This chapter will examine neither the welfare-economic effects of rehabilitation investments nor their influence on the factor combinations chosen. Instead, the chapter will seek to analyze the transaction costs involved in concluding privatization contracts containing provisions on rehabilitation subsidies. It is assumed for the sake of simplicity that the Treuhandanstalt was familiar with the social benefits of rehabilitation investment, though it can just as well be assumed that the matter has been settled by a political decision.

First, the contractual problem the Treuhandanstalt was facing will be described from the angle of transaction cost theory (7.1); then the costs of agreeing on rehabilitation subsidies will be examined in a game-theory model with perfect information (7.2). The final section will report briefly on the initial empirical findings of the Treuhandanstalt's contract-controlling unit (*Vertragscontrolling*) on the fulfillment of rehabilitation contracts (7.3).

7.1   The Contractual Problem

In a world without transaction costs and with complete contracts, the Treuhandanstalt could have fixed the volume of rehabilitation investments in such a way as to balance marginal social utility against marginal social costs and then compensated the private investor by providing him with a subsidy for the costs of realizing this volume of investment. The buyer would have responded by choosing the welfare-maximizing investment level. In a world with bounded rationality and opportunism, on the other hand, the problem is that a firm's relevant business conditions were uncertain and the costs of rehabilitation investments were the buyer's private knowledge. The buyer therefore had a strong incentive to overstate to the Treuhandanstalt the costs of the rehabilitation investments required and obtain a part of the rehabilitation subsidies as an information rent.

Both before and after it entered into a contract, the Treuhandanstalt was faced with the risk of being expropriated of its rehabilitation subsidies. *Ex ante*, the Treuhandanstalt was faced with the risk that a buyer would provide distorted information on his rehabilitation costs. The information on the capitalized value of rehabilitation investments, and thus the costs of realizing positive external effects, were unequally distributed between Treuhandanstalt and the buyer. The Treuhandanstalt had to provide an investor with a subsidy at least as high as the private costs he will incur in realizing a given volume of investment that lay above his private optimum. Since the costs of rehabilitation investments were an investor's private knowledge, he has the chance to obtain an information rent. But the buyer's information rent prior to signing the contract was contingent upon bidding competition. The greater the competition, the higher the bidder's risk, when he provided distorted information, of losing out to a competitor who submitted a more favorable bid combination. Under the assumption of perfect competition, it was thus rational - or, in the jargon of game theory, incentive-compatible - to provide truthful information on the expected capitalized value of his rehabilitation investments (Gresik/Satterthwaite 1989). In general terms, the ex ante risk faced by the Treuhandanstalt in agreeing to price rebates and negative prices was no different from that involved in other sales negotiations. Under the assumption of imperfect competition a bidder would here too seek to gain a rent by providing distorted information on his reserve price.

The actual risk faced by the Treuhandanstalt in agreeing to pay rehabilitation subsidies emerged after a contract had been finalized. The *ex post risk* was the result of imperfect information over the firm's business conditions following the conclusion of a contract. The information on the relevant economic environment that emerged after the contract had been concluded were distributed asymmetrically between investor and Treuhandanstalt — the investor was familiar with his firm's business and cost conditions, the Treuhandanstalt was not. Once the contract was signed, the investor could demand that it be revised by maintaining that the firm's business state had deteriorated substantially vis-à-vis the assumption that prevailed when the contract had been agreed upon. The demand for a reduction of the volume of investment and employment agreed upon could be underlined with threats of bankruptcy. In this case, the Treuhandanstalt was faced with a strategic dilemma aptly described by Ralf Neubauer in *Die Zeit* as follows:

> *"If it comes to the crunch, the Treuhandanstalt is in a position not to be envied. If it wastes no time in collecting the penalties owed to it, it may risk driv-*

ing the firms affected into bankruptcy and losing not just a few, but all the jobs concerned. If it is altogether too soft, it is faced with the threat of being buried by an avalanche of after-the-fact bargaining" (Neubauer 1993, 18).

The difference between the Treuhandanstalt's ex post risk and ex ante risk was to be found in altered competitive conditions: while ex ante a bidder's opportunistic behavior was held in check by competition with other bidders, ex post the situation was that of a bilateral monopoly between Treuhandanstalt and buyer. Oliver Williamson referred to this as a *"fundamental transformation"* (Williamson 1985, 61-63). Any longer-term contract not fully specified in terms of time and subject matter, and thus open to adjustment to contingent business events, constitutes a bilateral relationship between two parties which is vulnerable to opportunistic behavior. In this case, both parties will seek to protect themselves against the risk of opportunistic behavior after the contract has been concluded by selecting suitable "governance structures" (Williamson 1985, 72-78). Various institutional options were open to the Treuhandanstalt: one possibility was vertical integration, i.e. the Treuhandanstalt rehabilitated its firms itself. If vertical integration was ruled out and a bilateral contractual relationship between buyer and Treuhandanstalt was assumed as given, what was called for was an adequate form of contract that would generate on both sides a *mutual* interest in cooperative behavior (Williamson 1985, 167).

According to Williamson, contracts can best be adapted cooperatively by providing a transaction with reciprocal support via asset-specific investments (Williamson 1985, 169-175). A transaction-specific investment constitutes a credible commitment in that if the transaction relationship is terminated due to uncooperative behavior, the asset-specific capital of both parties will be depreciated. This was not true of the transaction between Treuhandanstalt and buyer: the buyer did employ asset-specific capital, but this was not bound to his transaction relationship to the Treuhandanstalt. As a substitute for a transaction-specific investment, the Treuhandanstalt came to an agreement with the buyer on a penalty for the case that the buyer failed to comply with his obligations. In the sense of transaction cost theory, pecuniary safeguards such as contractual penalties cannot be interpreted in any centralist-legal sense as a clear-cut obligation, but must be viewed more in the sense of the terms "hostage" (Williamson 1985, 169). The Treuhand-anstalt could, but was not obliged to, claim the penalty if the buyer breached the agreement on employment and investment guarantees. Adjustments made to a contract were, as it were, effected in the shadow of the law (Williamson 1985, 164), they did not follow the exact wording of the contract. This assumption was confirmed by the Treuhandanstalt's contractual practice: in numerous publications, the Treuhandanstalt made it clear that it was willing to accept adjustments to the contracts it concluded and that it would enforce penalties only in exceptional cases involving uncooperative investor behavior.[2] If business conditions deteriorated, the investor was allowed to fall short of the volume of investment and employment agreed upon, or at least prolong the time frame.[3] In the sense of transaction cost theory, agreements on rehabilitation subsidies are thus the classic example of a complex contract whose time and subject matter are not perfectly specified.

Compared with reciprocal asset-specific investments, pecuniary safeguards such as contractual penalties are unstable. While asset-specific investments generate on both sides a long-term interest in cooperation, pecuniary safeguards give rise to the risk of expropriation when they, in the short term, can improve one actor's position (Williamson 1985, 179).

The contractual problem involved in subsidizing private rehabilitation investments was essentially a problem bound up with the asymmetrical distribution of information between buyer and Treuhandanstalt. Since there was no mutual interest in cooperative behavior, it is possible to use the means of game theory to analyze the strategic equilibrium of both actors under the assumption of imperfect and asymmetrically distributed information.

7.2 An Analysis of Rehabilitation Contracts by Game-theory

Strategic games with asymmetrical information are dealt with by a specific branch of game theory, "mechanism design" (Fudenberg/Tirole 1992, 243-318; Holler/Illing 1993, 331-353; Myerson 1983; Myerson/Satterthwaite 1983). Mechanism can be understood as a contract or incentive scheme offered by an uninformed principal to an informed agent with the aim of inducing the agent to disclose truthfully his private information (Fudenberg/Tirole 1992, 243). Mechanism design is often applied to problems involving the efficient design of auctions, monopolistic price discrimination, taxation and the supply of public goods, and the internalization of external effects. In our case the Treuhandanstalt is the principal who offers the private buyer a rehabilitation contract with the aim of achieving positive political or social effects by subsidizing rehabilitation investments with negative capitalized values.

The formal structure of the model developed here is in part derived from a model developed by Klaus Schmidt to analyze the comparative effects of private and state regimes of ownership in the provision of public goods (Schmidt 1991). But the assumptions made in the model developed here differ fundamentally from Schmidt's as regards the information structure and the binding obligations taken on by the Treuhandanstalt when it granted subsidies for rehabilitation.

7.2.1 Description of the Model

The Treuhandanstalt's strategic dilemma can be depicted as follows using the means offered by game theory: every rehabilitation investment has a social benefit $b(i)$ for the Treuhandanstalt, and this benefit is contingent on the level of the rehabilitation investment. Rehabilitation investment costs c are equivalent to their negative capitalized value for the private investor. The costs are dependent on the level of the investment and the firm's business states [$c(i, \theta)$]. For the sake of simplicity, the number of possible business states θ is restricted to two:

in business state l rehabilitation investment costs are low due to the firm's favorable demand and cost conditions, whereas they are high in unfavorable business state h. The ex ante probability that favorable business state l will occur is p; the probability that the unfavorable business state will occur is $1-p$. For each business state there is one *ex post-efficient* investment volume $i^*(\theta)$, at which the difference between social costs and benefits is maximized[4]:

$$(7.1) \qquad max \quad b\left(i(\theta)\right) - c\left(i(\theta), \theta\right) \qquad\qquad i(\theta) \geq 0.$$

The Rehabilitation of Treuhandanstalt's firms has thus largely been restricted to passive adjustment measures such as the streamlining of product lines, the closure of factories and production capacities, lay-offs, etc. (DIW/IfW 1991b; 1991a; Schmid-Schönbein/Hansel 1991). Within one year after economic and monetary union, the employment level of the Treuhandanstalt's firms had dropped from 4.08 million to 1.372 million, while the firms privatized by the Treuhandanstalt employed 285,000 persons. In December 31, 1994, the Treuhandanstalt employed no more than 66,000 persons while in the privatized firms 930,000 persons were employed. This means a drop in employment of some three million workplaces or 75 percent in the firms either privatized or remaining with the Treuhandanstalt (see Table 8.3).

The optimal investment volume i^* is reached in balancing out marginal benefits $b(i)$ and marginal costs $c(i(\theta), \theta)$ of the rehabilitation investments concerned:

$$(7.2) \qquad b'\left(i^*(\theta)\right) = c'\left(i^*(\theta), \theta\right) \qquad \theta \in \{l, h\}.$$

The business state that has in fact emerged is, however, the buyer's private knowledge; the Treuhandanstalt's a priori knowledge is probability p that the favorable state h will emerge. If the contract was concluded with the favorable business state in mind and the rehabilitation agreement includes optimal investment volume i^*, the buyer has an incentive to claim after the fact that the unfavorable business state has emerged and to demand that the Treuhandanstalt adjust the contract. The Treuhandanstalt is in this case faced with a strategic dilemma: if unfavorable state h has in fact emerged, then realization of a lower investment volume $i*(h) < i*(l)$ would be ex post-efficient in that under the altered business states the marginal costs would be higher than the marginal utility of the investment volume agreed upon:

$$(7.3) \qquad b\left(i^*(h)\right) - c\left(i^*(h), h\right) > b\left(i^*(l)\right) - c\left(i^*(l), h\right)$$

Since the costs of an ex post-inefficient investment volume have to be borne by the buyer, the Treuhandanstalt could insist on the investment volume agreed upon and enforce the corresponding penalty. But the buyer can add weight to his demand for an adjustment of the contract by threatening bankruptcy. In the case of bankruptcy the social benefits drop to zero $[b(0) \equiv 0]$, so that the Treuhandanstalt would be better off waiving the penalty than insisting on enforcing it:

$$(7.4) \qquad b\left(i^*(h)\right) - s > b(0) + k - s.$$

But if, contrary to the buyer's claim, the favorable business state has emerged ($\theta = 1$), the Treuhandanstalt would be better off if it enforced the penalty than if it decided against doing so:

$$(7.5) \qquad b\left(i*(h)\right) + k - s > b\left(i^*(h)\right) - s.$$

7.2.2   Optimal Contract Design (Mechanism Design)

For the Treuhandanstalt the problem of mechanism design is that the agency is forced to enter into a contract with the buyer that contains incentives for him to provide truthful information on the business states that have emerged, and this, ex ante, maximizes the agency's expected benefits. The rehabilitation contract offered by the Treuhandanstalt to its buyers contains three action parameters: simplified investment volume $\hat{i}^p$, rehabilitation subsidy s, and contractual penalty k, whereby $\hat{i}^p(\theta)$ is contingent on an a priori assumption on the prevailing business state and $k(i)$ depends on the volume of investment realized ex post by the buyer $[M = \{\hat{i}^p(\theta), s, k(i), \theta \in \{l,h\}\}]$. As owner, the buyer, once he has entered into the agreement and observed the business state that develops, chooses the volume of his investment. Penalty k can be enforced only if the buyer's actual volume of investment is lower than that agreed upon $[i < \hat{i}^p]$ (see Fig. 7.1).

As far as the rest of the model is concerned, it is of interest that this mechanism entails, implicitly or explicitly, an agreement on the volume of investment in both business states: in the privatization contract, the Treuhandanstalt can stipulate an explicit agreement on the volume of investment either for both business states $\hat{i}^p(\theta)$ or only for favorable business state $\hat{i}^p(l)$. In the latter case, however, the rehabilitation contract will also contain an implicit agreement on investment volume $\hat{i}^p(h)$ in the unfavorable business state: in stipulating penalty $k(i)$, the

Figure 7.1: Rehabilitation Game with Asymmetrical Information

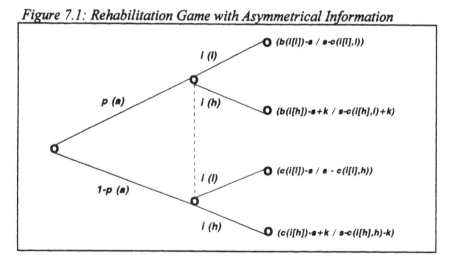

Treuhandanstalt agrees on transfer volume t $[t\ (\hat{i}^p(h)) = s - k(\hat{i}^p(h))]$ for the unfavorable state h. The investor would be worse off if he realized a higher volume of investment under the unfavorable business state

higher than that subsidized through the Treuhandanstalt's transfer payments. In this sense, the privatization contract, in stipulating a contractual penalty, contains an implicit agreement on the level of rehabilitation investments, even if no explicit volume of investment has been agreed upon for the unfavorable business state. In the extreme case, the Treuhandanstalt can reclaim its entire subsidy if the contract is not fulfilled, thus making it rational for the investor to realize an investment volume of zero under unfavorable business states $[i^P(h) = 0]$.

Both parties have von Neumann-Morgenstern utility functions and are risk-neutral. The Treuhandanstalt's utility function consists of the social benefits of rehabilitation investments and its transfer payments to the buyer:

$$(7.6) \qquad U^{tha} = b(i) - t(i) = b(i) - s + k(i),$$

and the buyer's utility function is made up of the Treuhandanstalt's transfers and the costs of rehabilitation investments:

$$(7.7) \qquad V^P = t(i) - c\left(i(\theta), \theta\right) = s - k(i) - c\left(i(\theta), \theta\right).$$

The problem of contract design facing the Treuhandanstalt is to stipulate the action parameters of the rehabilitation contract in such a way as to induce the buyer to provide truthful information on the business state that has actually developed. To achieve this end, the mechanism must contain two constraints: first, truthful information on the actual business states must be *incentive-compatible*, i.e. in revealing his private information on the actual business state, the buyer must be at least as well off as he would be if he did not reveal this information:

$$(7.8) \quad s - c\left(i(\theta), \theta\right) - k(i) \geq s - c\left(i(\theta'), \theta\right) - k(i) \quad \forall \theta', \theta \in \{l, h\},$$

whereby θ' is a buyer statement on the actual business state that does not correspond to the truth.

Second, for the buyer the rehabilitation contract must meet the criterion of *individual rationality*, i.e. the agreement with the Treuhandanstalt must not place him in a position better than that he would achieve without it (*participation constraint*):

$$(7.9) \qquad s - c\left(i^P(\theta), \theta\right) - k(i) \geq 0 \quad \forall\, \theta \in \{l, h\}.$$

The Treuhandanstalt must then, under the given constraint, solve the following maximization problem:

$$(7.10) \qquad \max_{i^P(\theta), s, k(i)} \left\{ p\left[b\left(i^P(l)\right) - s\right] + (1 - p)\left[b\left(i^P(h)\right) - s + k(i)\right] \right\}$$

under the constraints of (7.8) and (7.9).

This is a classical problem of mechanism design (Fudenberg/Tirole 1992, 253-257). Dealing with an agent's private information, the principal has to find a mechanism in which truthful revelation of his private information constitutes an equilibrium strategy. According to the so-called *revelation principle* (see Dasgupta/Hammond/Maskin 1979; Myerson 1979; Fudenberg/Tirole 1992, 255), there is for each game a direct mechanism accepted by all agents before they obtain their private information. For this mechanism, truthful revelation of private information as soon as it is received constitutes a Bayes-Nash equilibrium (Fudenberg/Tirole 1992, 255).

The incentive compatibility constraint can be met only when the Treuhandanstalt cedes to the buyer, as a subsidy, the information rent he would be able to realize by providing false information on the actual business state and choosing a lower volume of investment. If the unfavorable business state occurs, the buyer is unable to obtain an information rent by providing false information [*(r(h)* = *0*]. Under the favorable business state, on the other hand, the buyer, by realizing the volume of investment implicitly or explicitly agreed upon for the unfavorable business state $i^P(h) < i^P(l)$, can obtain information rent r(l)

$$(7.11) \qquad r\left(l\right) = c\left(i^{P}(h),h\right) - c\left(i^{P}(h),l\right).$$

The Treuhandanstalt must therefore stipulate both rehabilitation subsidy and contractual penalty in such a way as to rule out the possibility that the buyer may improve his position by providing false information when the favorable business state emerges. In the unfavorable state, on the other hand, the Treuhandanstalt is forced to offer him only the benefit of his reserve utility $[r(h) = 0]$. The subsidy is then equal to the buyer's costs for realizing the rehabilitation subsidies plus the information rent:

$$(7.12) \quad s = c\left(i^{P}(l),l\right) + r\left(l\right) = c\left(i^{P}(l),l\right) + c\left(i^{P}(h),h\right) - c\left(i^{P}(h),l\right).$$

Contractual penalty $k(i)$ for volume of investment $i^{P}(h)$ is stipulated in such a way that the Treuhandanstalt's remaining transfers are equal to the buyer's costs for his rehabilitation investment under the unfavorable business states, i.e.

$$(7.13) \quad k\left(i^{P}(h)\right) = s - c\left(i^{P}(h),h\right) = c\left(i^{P}(l),l\right) - c\left(i^{P}(h),l\right).$$

If the Treuhandanstalt stipulates rehabilitation subsidies and contractual penalty in this way, the buyer, if he reduces his investment volume $i^{P}(h)$ under the unfavorable state h, will achieve the same payoff he would receive if he realized the investment volume $i^{P}(l)$ agreed upon:

$$(7.14) \quad s - c\left(i^{P}(l),l\right) = s - k\left(i^{P}(h)\right) - c\left(i^{P}(h),l\right) = c\left(i^{P}(h),h\right) - c\left(i^{P}(h),l\right).$$

The Treuhandanstalt can influence the level of the buyer's information rent via the *volume of investment* it stipulates. If it is to realize ex post-efficient investment volume $i(\theta) = i^{*}(\theta)$, the Treuhandanstalt is forced, under the favorable business states, to cede to the buyer information rent $c(i^{*}(h), h) - c(i^{*}(h), l)$. Any agreement of this kind would be rational only if the Treuhandanstalt is indifferent toward its transfers to the buyer. The Treuhandanstalt's transfers are, however, not cost-free and make up part of its utility function. The Treuhandanstalt can minimize its transfers to the buyer by subsidizing only a suboptimal volume of investment: The buyer's information rent $c(i(h),h) - c(i(h),l)$ is contingent on the level of the volume of investment subsidized under the *unfavorable* business state h. The Treuhandanstalt can influence the volume of investment under the unfavorable business state either directly, via a stipulation in the privatization contract, or indirectly, via the level of the penalty agreed upon (see above). The buyer's information rent under the favorable business state depends on the direct or indirect agreement reached on the volume of investment to be made under the unfavorable business state: the lower the subsidy provided by the Treuhandanstalt under the unfavorable state h, the lower the buyer's information rent under the favorable state l. When the unfavorable state develops, on the other hand, the buyer has, in view of the Treuhandanstalt's remaining transfers, only an incentive to realize suboptimal investment level $i^P(h) < i^*(h)$. In other words, the Treuhandanstalt is faced with a trade-off between minimizing its transfers to the buyer and realizing an ex post-efficient volume of investment.

The optimization problem for the direct or indirect agreement on investment volume $i^P(h)$ for the unfavorable business state is then

$$(7.15) \quad \max_{i^P(h) \geq 0} \left\{ (1-p) \cdot \left[b\left(i^P(h)\right) - c\left(i^P(h),h\right) \right] - p \cdot \left[c\left(i^P(h),h\right) - c\left(i^P(h),l\right) \right] \right\}$$

Optimal investment volume $i^P(h)$ is achieved in the balance of marginal costs and marginal benefits,[5] i.e. at

$$(7.16) \quad b'\left(i^P(h)\right) = c'\left(i^P(h),h\right) + \frac{p}{1-p} \cdot \left[c'\left(i^P(h),h\right) - c'\left(i^P(h),l\right) \right]$$

under the constraint of

$$(7.17) \quad b\left(i^P(h)\right) - c\left(i^P(h),h\right) - \frac{p}{1-p} \cdot \left[c\left(i^P(h),h\right) - c\left(i^P(h),l\right) \right] \geq 0.$$

If the constraint in formula (7.17) is fulfilled, the Treuhandanstalt will stipulate the penalty in such a way that the remaining transfers are equal to the costs of the rehabilitation investments under the unfavorable business state $[t(i^P(h)) = s - k(i^P(h)) = c(i^P(h),h)]$. If the secondary condition is not fulfilled, the Treuhandanstalt will stipulate a penalty equivalent to the rehabilitation subsidy $[t(i^P(h)) = s - k(i^P(h)) = 0]$. In the latter case, it is rational for the investor, under the unfavorable business states, to forego all rehabilitation investments with negative capitalized values $[i^P(h) = 0]$.

Investment volume $i^P(l)$ agreed upon for the favorable business state has no influence on the buyer's information rent, so that the Treuhandanstalt can set the investment volume at the first-best optimum

(7.18) $$b'\left(i^P(l)\right) = c'\left(i^P(l)\right)$$

i.e. $i^P(l) = i^*(l)$.

The optimal rehabilitation contract (mechanism) then has the form

$$s = c\left(i^P(l), l\right) + r = c\left(i^P(l), l\right) + c\left(i^P(h), h\right) - c\left(i^P(h), l\right)$$

(7.19) $k = \begin{cases} s & \text{if} \\ b\left(i^P(h)\right) - c\left(i^P(h),h\right) - \dfrac{p}{1-p}\cdot\left[c\left(i^P(h),h\right) - c\left(i^P(h),l\right)\right] > 0. \\ s - c\left(i^P(h),h\right) = c\left(i^P(l),l\right) - c\left(i^P(h),l\right) & \text{else} \end{cases}$

$$i^P(l) = i^*(l)$$

and $i^P(h)$ is defined by (7.16) under the constraint of (7.17).[6]

This contract (mechanism) is only plausible if the government can credibly commit itself to the enforcement of the contract. A contract is safe against subsequent *renegotiations* when the rewards and sanctions to which the principal is committed are credible even when, following implementation of the mechanism, the agent has truthfully revealed his private information. The criterion of credibility is that no party can improve its position at any stage of the game by breaking the agreement to which it is committed. If the principal's rewards and sanctions are not credible, the agent will be better off not to reveal truthfully his private information. In our case, the Treuhandanstalt must therefore credibly commit itself to pay the rehabilitation subsidies and to enforce the contractual penalty. As far as the rehabilitation subsidy is concerned, this poses no problem, in that the Treuhandanstalt cedes the subsidy to the buyer upon conclusion of the contract and can reclaim it in the form of a penalty only if the buyer is in breech of his contractual obligations. The assumption is more problematical in the case of a contractual penalty. The proposed contract proceeds on the assumption that the Treuhandanstalt is committed to an agreement covering an ex post-inefficient investment volume under unfavorable business state [i^P (h) < i^* (h)]. Under unfavorable state h, the buyer could invest optimal volume $i^*(h)$ and demand that the Treuhandanstalt reduce the penalty. But because this investment has already been made, the Treuhandanstalt has no incentive to waive the penalty. The buyer would then be obliged to bear the costs of optimal investment volume [$c(i^*(h))$ > $c(i^P(h))$]. In other words, enforcement of the penalty is credible only if, under the unfavorable state, the buyer invests more than $i^P(h)$. But there is one exception: the investor would have to threaten credibly to initiate bankruptcy proceedings in the event that the Treuhandanstalt should enforce the penalty. In this case, the Treuhandanstalt would be worse off in enforcing the penalty than it would be in waiving it. However, no such threat on the part of the investor is credible to the extent that the investor, in selecting the volume of investment he is prepared to make under the unfavorable business state, would not have been worse off if he had chosen investment volume $i^P(h)$ < $i^*(h)$, which is covered by transfers. The Treuhandanstalt would therefore have to interpret any realization of a higher volume of investment as a signal indicating that it has been provided with incorrect information. The assumption made in the model is that the Treuhandanstalt will be unable to observe, even ex post, the business state that has actually emerged, and if this assumption is correct, the mechanism is safe against demands for renegotiation.

With the given mechanism, the Treuhandanstalt will then realize the payoff

$$
\begin{aligned}
U^{tha} &= p \cdot \left[b\left(i*(l)\right) - c\left(i*(l),l\right) - r(l) \right] + (1-p) \cdot \left[b\left(i^P(h)\right) - c\left(i^P(h),h\right) \right] \\
(7.20) \qquad &= p \cdot \left[b\left(i*(l)\right) - c\left(i*(l),l\right) - c\left(i^P(h),h\right) + c\left(i^P(h),l\right) \right] + (1-p) \cdot \\
& \qquad\qquad\qquad \left[b\left(i^P(h)\right) - c\left(i^P(h),h\right) \right]
\end{aligned}
$$

while the buyer's payoff will be

$$
(7.21) \qquad V^P = p \cdot r(l) = p \cdot \left[c\left(i^P(h),h\right) - c\left(i^P(h),l\right) \right] + (1-p) \cdot 0.
$$

The model developed here suggests three conclusions: first, the volume of investment realized by both parties under the assumption that each will maximize its benefits is not ex post-efficient. True, ex post-efficient investment level $i^P(l) = i*(l)$ will be achieved under favorable business state, but suboptimal investment level $i^P(h) < i*(h)$ will be realized under unfavorable state h.

Second, with the given mechanism it is possible for a firm to end up with no rehabilitation subsidies under the unfavorable business state, even though this would be ex post-efficient. This would be the case if the Treuhandanstalt, having taken the buyer's information rent into account, fails to achieve positive benefits, even though a positive net benefit would be realized without the information rent. This is formally the case if

$$
\begin{aligned}
(7.22) \qquad & b\left(i^P(h)\right) - c\left(i^P(h),h\right) - \frac{p}{(1-p)} \cdot \left[c\left(i^P(h),h\right) - c\left(i^P(h),l\right) \right] < 0 \\
& \text{and} \quad b\left(i^P(h)\right) > c\left(i^P(h),h\right).
\end{aligned}
$$

In the extreme case, refusal to provide rehabilitation subsidies can lead to the liquidation of firms even though it would be ex post-efficient for them to continue to operate. This feature is unavoidable under the assumption that the Treuhandanstalt's information is imperfect.

Third, the buyer will achieve only his reserve benefit under the unfavorable cost conditions, whereas under the favorable conditions he will receive information rent $[r(l) = c(i(h),h) - c(i(h),k)]$, a sum which must be paid by the Treuhandanstalt.

In other words, the Treuhandanstalt is faced with the trade-off of ceding to the buyer high transfer payments as an information rent or accepting an ex post-inefficient volume of investment. This finding confirms a theorem established by Roger Myerson and Mark Satterthwaite according to which, given bilateral transactions with asymmetrical distribution of information, there is no mechanism that can satisfy the restrictions imposed by the participation constraint, incentive compatibility, *and* the "budget equilibrium" (Myerson/Satterthwaite 1983). The budget equilibrium constraint requires that the principal's transfer payment not be higher than the agent's costs (Fudenberg/Tirole 1992). Thus in our example the Treuhandanstalt's rehabilitation subsidies may not be higher than the buyer's rehabilitation costs—which is not possible under the assumption of asymmetrically distributed information on the rehabilitation costs that have actually been incurred.

In other words, compared with an ideal world without transaction costs, the Treuhandanstalt can, if it takes account of the asymmetrical distribution of information between investor and itself, realize no more than a suboptimal volume of investment by *privatizing the task of rehabilitation*, which means that it will be able to internalize only part of the positive external effects of the rehabilitation investments. Furthermore, the investor will obtain part of the rehabilitation investment as an information rent. The efficiency of this outcome can, however, only be assessed in the light of given institutional alternatives if Harold Demsetz' „Nirvana error" (Demsetz 1969) is to be avoided. With this in mind, chapter 8 compares the contractual and transaction costs of this private rehabilitation regime with rehabilitation carried out by the Treuhandanstalt.

7.3   Empirical Findings

The Treuhandanstalt's practice of subsidizing rehabilitation investments was of considerable weight: up to December 31, 1994, the Treuhandanstalt had reached agreement on investment commitments amounting to 211,1 billion DM and employment guarantees covering some 1.5 million jobs (Treuhandanstalt 1994d). 706,000 of these 1.5 million guaranteed jobs were covered by contractual penalties, and another 231 were secured by written agreement (Kachel 1994, 40; Ziller 1994, 9). The situation was similar for investment commitments: the vice-president of the Treuhandanstalt, Hero Brahms, indicated that only some 60 percent was covered by contracts, while 70 percent of these commitments were secured with contractual penalties (SPD-Bundestagsfraktion 1994; Ziller 1994, 9). There is no empirical data available on the overall volume of the rehabilitation subsidies paid for investment and employment commitments. Nor was the amount of the subsidies explicitly set out in the privatization agreements, a factor that impairs transparency. The available empirical indicators suggest that that these subsidies were at least two-digit billion figures: the level of the price rebates granted by the Treuhandanstalt is unknown, the only leads available being the volume of negative prices at which firms have been sold. In three rehabilitation complexes - two shipyards in Mecklenburg-Western Pomerania, the EKO steel works in Eisenhüttenstadt, and the Carl Zeiss optical works in Jena - did the Treuhandanstalt agree to sell at negative prices amounting to a total of eight billion DM (Siebert 1992, 90). In privatizing the chemical industry (Leuna, Bitterfeld), the Treuhandanstalt agreed in writing to guarantees amounting to four billion DM (Siebert 1992, 90).

The findings of the Treuhandanstalt's contract-controlling department that have become known indicate that the agency was faced with substantial problems in enforcing rehabilitation commitments: a study conducted by the Treuhandanstalt's contract-controlling department for

1991 and covering 3,550 privatization agreements that had come into effect in 1991 indicated that 17 percent of the firms had not complied with employment guarantees and 10 percent had not met their investment commitments (Frankfurter Rundschau 1992, 9; Handelsblatt 1992e, 18). All told, however, the overall level of employment in the firms investigated was 10 percent higher than stipulated in the privatization contracts (Handelsblatt 1992e, 18). For 1992, the Treuhandanstalt, basing its findings on an investigation of 5,146 contracts, came to the conclusion that 20 percent of the firms covered were not complying with their employment and investment commitments (FAZ 1993a, 15; Handelsblatt 1993c, 7). All in all, it was claimed, the investment and employment commitments were overfulfilled in 1992 as well. The survey refered only to investment commitments agreed to in writing, and thus the overall picture was somewhat less favorable (FAZ, 1993a, 15; Handelsblatt, 1993c, 7). For 1993 and 1994, years for which a major share of the rehabilitation investments agreed upon were scheduled to be implemented, the Treuhandanstalt anticipated a perceptible rise in cases of noncompliance (FAZ, 1993a, 15; Handelsblatt, 1993c, 7).

In its contractual practice, the Treuhandanstalt failed as a rule to enforce the penalties stipulated. In 3,000 of the roughly 12,300 privatization agreements concluded thus far, the Treuhandanstalt had entered into new bargaining talks, and 400 of these cases were termed "difficult." (Handelsblatt 1993c, 7). The number of penalties for which suits have had to be filed was, however, low; in 126 cases penalties were claimed and in nine cases employment and investment guarantees were set to be enforced (Handelsblatt 1993c, 7). It was part of the Treuhandanstalt's declared policy to claim penalties only in exceptional cases.[7] As a rule, guarantees could be postponed, and the Treuhandanstalt was sometimes willing to waive completely part of the commitments agreed upon (Handelsblatt 1993b, 13; FAZ 1992e, 15; Handelsblatt 1992e, 18). By June of 1993, the Treuhandanstalt had taken back objects it had privatized in thirty cases in which the buyers failed to comply with their contractual commitments (FAZ 1993b, 15; Handelsblatt 1993b, 13). These were as a rule cases in which the firms were threatened by bankruptcy due to illegal withdrawals of liquid funds by their owners (FAZ 1993b, 15).

It is impossible to form a clear-cut judgment on the basis of this incomplete information. But it is clear that in practice the Treuhandanstalt, as described in the model presented above, was faced with the
strategic dilemma of having to decide on the enforcement of contractual penalties without being in possession of perfect information on the
economic situation of the firms concerned (Neubauer 1993, 18). It consequently had to be expected that part of the rehabilitation subsidies
were appropriated by private investors and that the volumes of investment actually realized were suboptimal. One serious flaw in the Treuhandanstalt's contractual practice was the lack of transparency on the
scope of rehabilitation subsidies: it was neither possible for the public
to judge what it returns in exchange for the subsidies granted by the
Treuhandanstalt nor was the agency in a position to evaluate the privatization contracts negotiated by its agents. This has led to an unnecessary exacerbation of the principal-agent problems involved.

8   Rehabilitation versus Privatization: A Comparative Analysis

8.1   The Economic Controversy

The primacy of privatization in the Treuhandanstalt's business policy
was the subject of a heated economic controversy. The issue was not
the objective of privatization but the question whether the Treuhandanstalt should rehabilitate the firms it held before it sold them off. In
the *Treuhandgesetz*, the law governing the Treuhandanstalt, the legislative chose to leave this question open.[1] One camp, represented by the
Sachverständigenrat (SVR 1990, §§517-519; 1991a, §§20-28; 1991b,
§§485-496; 1992, §§303-304), the economic research institutes (Gemeinschaftsdiagnose 1990, 626; 1991a, 250; 1991b, 615; 1992a, 224-
225; 1992b, 63-65; 1993a, 264), and numerous other economists (Lipp
1990, 11; Hax 1992, 149-151; Siebert 1992, 103-111), called for a
clear-cut priority for rapid privatization, demanding that the Treuhandanstalt refrained as far as possible from rehabilitating the firms it held.

Their antipodes, represented chiefly by economists of the *Memoran-dum-Gruppe,* called for the Treuhandanstalt to rehabilitate resolutely the firms it held in order to preserve Eastern Germany's industrial structure (Arbeitsgruppe Alternative Wirtschaftspolitik 1992, 129-130; Priewe/Hickel 1992, 183-184; Priewe 1991, 208-215).

In essence, the first camp based its call for the Treuhandanstalt to re-frain from rehabilitating Eastern German enterprises on three argu-ments. First, the *informational efficiency* of a centralized organization like the Treuhandanstalt was said to be far too low to be able to process the detailed information required for any successful rehabilitation (Siebert 1990, 16; Lipp 1990, 11; SVR 1990; Hax 192, 147). On the other hand, privatization should lead to much higher informational ef-ficiency in that - following Hayek - it "stimulates competition for the discovery of promising rehabilitation conceptions" (SVR 1990, § 516). In the second place, it was argued, abrogation of the market's selection function via the Treuhandanstalt's *soft budget constraint* would lead to a politicization of investment decisions and subsidization of obsolete structures (SVR 1991a, 21; 1990, § 517; 1992, § 296; Hax 1992, 147; Siebert 1990, 105). The allocative efficiency of private firms, whose survival is determined by the market, was consequently claimed to be far greater (Siebert 1990, 117). Third, and finally, the intensity of the incentive provided by private ownership was regarded as much higher than that of state-owned property, and thus rapid privatization would lead to a more efficient deployment of capital (SVR 1990, § 29; Siebert 1990, 117). Rehabilitation by the Treuhandanstalt, the argument con-tinued, was therefore substantially more costly than rehabilitation con-ducted by private owners (Lipp 1990, 11).

The Treuhandanstalt should, on this view, consequently have accorded clear priority to privatization and restricted its support to the preserva-tion of privatizable firms. Firms for which no private buyer could be found should have been liquidated (SVR 1991a, 17).

The opposing camp based its argument on the structural and employ-ment effects of rehabilitation investments. Following economic and monetary union, the necessary conditions for the operation of a market economy, they claimed, were no longer given in Eastern Germany as a result of high factor costs, the poor infrastructure situation, and the collapse of export markets in the former COMECON countries (Priewe/Hickel 1991, 184; Arbeitsgruppe Alternative Wirtschaftspolitik 1992, 129-130). That no buyer had been found at the outset of this adjustment process was, the argument goes, no indication that a firm was beyond rehabilitation (Priewe/Hickel 1991, 184). The idea of rehabilitation by the Treuhandanstalt would have been to "buy time" (Arbeitsgruppe Alternative Wirtschaftspolitik 1992, 129) to bridge over the adjustment period (Priewe/Hickel 1991, 184). It was here argued that the economic costs of rehabilitation by the Treuhandanstalt were lower than the costs of deindustrialization in Eastern Germany (Priewe/Hickel 1991, 184-185). The Treuhandanstalt should therefore have rehabilitated the firms for which, in the short run, no buyers could be found and taken over their operating losses for an initial period. The assumption of losses should successively have been reduced as a means of exerting pressure in the direction of restructuring (Arbeitsgruppe Alternative Wirtschaftspolitik 1992, 129-130). As soon as such firms were rehabilitated, the property rights to them should have been broadly dispersed via the stock exchange or some other proprietary conceptions (Arbeitsgruppe Wirtschaftspolitik 1992, 129-130; Priewe 1991, 214).

So the rehabilitation debate addressed two different problems: while the first camp stressed the comparative efficiency advantages involved in private ownership regimes as opposed to public ones, the second camp pointed to the negative social and economic effects of the slump in employment and production in Eastern Germany. Chapter 5 demonstrated that the cost and demand conditions that emerged following economic and monetary union had largely depreciated the asset-specific capital of Eastern German firms. Integration into the larger German labor market and the politically determined factor costs of labor had not given rise to the expectation that a full-employment equilibrium would emerge in the foreseeable future (Akerlof et al. 1990). The hypothesis developed in the last chapter was that under these conditions rehabilitation investments had positive external effects. The rational core of the rehabilitation debate was then to be sought in the question whether these positive external effects of rehabilitation investments could better have been realized by a private rehabilitation regime or a public one.

What is not disputed is that the Treuhandanstalt, with its centralized organizational structure, was not in possession of the capacities required to rehabilitate the enterprises it holds (Gemeinschaftsdiagnose 1992a, 224; Priewe 1991, 214). The problem of rehabilitation did not, however, result from the centralization of decision-making. In theory, the Treuhandanstalt could have decentralized operative decisions on rehabilitation and restricted its own role to central strategic decisions.[2]

Under the assumption that the necessary organizational conditions were given, the question as to the relative advantages of private and public rehabilitation regimes leads back to the starting point of the study: Can the state achieve the same as *and* more than a private owner? Can the state, by mimicking the capital market, achieve the same level of productive efficiency as private firms *and* also, via selective intervention, internalize the positive external effects of rehabilitation investments?

János Kornai and Oliver Williamson have developed two closely linked arguments that speak against the hypothesis that the state, through selective intervention, can achieve the same level of productive efficiency as a private owner. First, the capital market's selective function is abrogated by the soft budget constraint of state-owned enterprises. This is unavoidable in that closure of state-owned companies is not an accidental event that the persons affected are bound to accept; it is, rather, the outcome of a bargaining process. It is not only ex post but ex ante, in relevant decisions on production and investment, that the soft budget constraint alters the behavior of economic subjects (Kornai 1980; Williamson 1985, 171-173). In addition, the attempt to internalize the positive external effects of rehabilitation investments is necessarily bound up with an assumption of losses, which opens up additional scopes of action to the management of the firms concerned. Second, the intensity of the incentives provided by state-owned property is substantially lower (Williamson 1985, 154-175). This applies both for private incentives, in that management is unable to appropriate residual income, and for negative sanctions, which are largely obviated by the soft budget constraint.

It must therefore be expected that public-sector rehabilitation of enterprises by the Treuhandanstalt gives rise to nontrivial transaction costs in the form of efficiency losses and misallocations. On the other hand, as was demonstrated in the last chapter, even subsidizing private rehabilitation investment itself, which is necessarily linked with an asymmetrical distribution of information between Treuhandanstalt and buyer, gives rise to high transaction costs in the form of suboptimal investment levels and an information rent obtained by the buyer. In other words, in a world with transaction costs there is no first-best solution to the problem of reaping the positive political and social effects of rehabilitation investments in Eastern Germany. The following section uses the tools of game theory to examine from a comparative-static angle the relative transaction costs of public- and private-sector rehabilitation regimes (8.2); the last section of this chapter assesses the Treuhandanstalt's rehabilitation strategy both against the background of this analysis and in terms of dynamic aspects (8.3).

8.2 A Comparative Analysis of the Transaction Costs of Private- and Public-rehabilitation Regimes

8.2.1 Description of the Model

The last chapter used a model based on game theory to examine the costs of the asymmetrical distribution of information between Treuhandanstalt and a private buyer where the subsidization of private-sector rehabilitation investment is concerned. This model is here extended to include two additional aspects as a means of analyzing the comparative advantages and disadvantages of public- and private-sector rehabilitation regimes: first, the problem of the soft budget constraint and, second, the problem of the different incentive structures of alternative ownership regimes. As a means of rendering the latter accessible to differentiated treatment, the section deals with two regimes of private ownership in addition to the issue of rehabilitation conducted by the Treuhandanstalt: sale to an entrepreneur who himself assumes the property rights and the rights of decision, and sale to a rentier or group of rentiers who delegate their decision-making rights to a professional manager.

Just as in the model in the last chapter, every rehabilitation investment here has for the Treuhandanstalt a positive political or social benefit $b(i)$ that can be realized fully only through implementation of investment projects with negative capitalized values. The negative capitalized values are the social costs $c(i, \theta)$ of realizing the positive social effect of rehabilitation investments. For the sake of simplicity, only two business states are assumed here as well [$\theta \in \{l, h\}$]. In favorable state l, the costs of rehabilitation investments are low, whereas under unfavorable state h they are high [$c(i,l) < c(i,h)$]. The welfare-maximizing investment level $i^*(\theta)$ then reemerges in the equilibrium of marginal social utility and marginal costs, i.e. at[3]

$$(8.1) \qquad b'(i^*(\theta)) = c'(i^*(\theta), \theta) \quad \theta \in \{l, h\}.$$

The model is here played in four periods: in the first period the Treuhandanstalt as principal chooses the rehabilitation regime and proposes a rehabilitation contract (*mechanism*) to its agents. If the agents agree to the contract, the first period is concluded. The choices involved are: rehabilitation by the Treuhandanstalt (regime 1), sale to an entrepreneur (regime 2), and sale to a rentier or group of rentiers (regime 3). The private rehabilitation regimes provide for a subsidy for rehabilitation investments with negative capitalized values, and these subsidies are safeguarded by a contractual penalty. Each rehabilitation regime is a subgame for itself.

In the second period, the manager or entrepreneur first chooses between different actions a aimed at rehabilitating the firm concerned. Each action a is linked to a nonpecuniary effort $\phi(a)$ of the manager or entrepreneur that can be understood as an investment in the firm's productive efficiency. Activity level a is contingent on the pecuniary and nonpecuniary incentives offered by each regime of ownership. The distribution of the probability of the two business states $\theta(a)$ is in turn contingent on this activity level. The higher the activity level and the quality of the actions of the manager or entrepreneur, the higher the probability $p(a)$ that the favorable state will emerge; or conversely, the lower the effort and the quality associated with actions a, the higher the counterprobability $1-p(a)$ that unfavorable state h will emerge. The choice of actions a is the private knowledge of the manager and the entrepreneur, and this cannot be observed by the Treuhandanstalt. Nature accordingly chooses the firm's business state $\theta(\theta \in \{l,h\})$.

In the third period, the owners, i.e., depending on rehabilitation regime, the Treuhandanstalt, the entrepreneur, or the rentier, decide on the choice of investment volume $i(\theta)$. The various rehabilitation regimes differ with regard to the information available to the owners on the business state that has emerged.

Figure 8.1: Alternative Rehabilitation Regimes

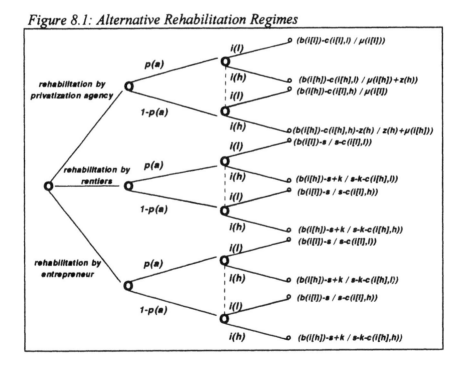

Finally, in the fourth period the parties are paid off in accordance with the agreements previously made. All parties have a von Neumann-Morgenstern utility function and are risk-neutral. (See Fig. 8.1)

8.2.2   Rehabilitation by the Treuhandanstalt

If the Treuhandanstalt decides to rehabilitate its enterprises itself, it is faced with two problems: an allocation problem and an incentive problem. If the Treuhandanstalt has perfect information on rehabilitation costs $c(i(\theta), \theta)$, the solution of the allocation problem is trivial. The agency chooses the optimal investment level $i^*(\theta)$ from formula (8.1). The assumption of perfect information would, however, strongly over-simplify the Treuhandanstalt's decision problem. What must be expected is that the Treuhandanstalt's manager has an informational edge over the agency as far as the rehabilitation of his firm is concerned, and he can deploy this advantage strategically. Under these information conditions, the allocation problem constitutes a mirror image of the private rehabilitation regime discussed in the last chapter: while a private owner will seek to obtain an information rent by *over*estimating his rehabilitation costs, a Treuhandanstalt's manager will attempt to achieve additional investment by *under*estimating the rehabilitation costs. Management has an existential interest in underestimating rehabilitation costs, especially when a firm is threatened with closure.

For transition countries, János Kornai described this phenomenon as „investment hunger" (Kornai 1980). Yet similar phenomena have also been observed in major Western corporations (Williamson 1985, 283; Jensen 1986, 323-329). The phenomenon of investment hunger is a result of the manager's utility function. The manager derives his utility not only from his pecuniary income but also from social and profes-sional recognition, power, identification with his work and his firm, etc. (Jensen 1986, 329). All these factors are positively correlated with the size of the firm concerned, and this results in an "expansion drive" which in turn leads to the firm's investment hunger (Kornai 1980, 193). The phenomenon of expansion drive is associated with the soft budget constraint under which a firm operates: while in firms with a hard

Figure 8.2: Rehabilitation by the Treuhandanstalt

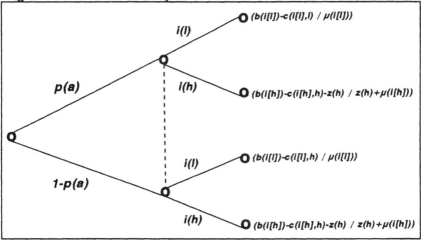

budget constraint investment hunger is restrained by the threat of bank-ruptcy, the demand for investment is infinite in an enterprise with a perfectly soft budget constraint (Kornai 1980, 194, 309).

In order to integrate the phenomenon of investment hunger into the model, the manager's utility function is here expanded to include a nonpecuniary factor $\mu(i)$ on top of the manager's pecuniary income; this factor summarizes all of the manager's nonpecuniary utility factors that correlate positively with firm size:

$$(8.2) \qquad V^m = m + \mu\left(i^{tha}(\theta)\right) - \phi\,(a)$$

The incentive problem is initially bracketed out and the activity level of the Treuhandanstalt's manager is assumed as given $[a = \bar{a}]$, whereby, for the sake of simplicity, all $p(\bar{a})$ or $1-p(\bar{a})$ are rendered as p and $1-p$, respectively. As the owner, the Treuhandanstalt decides on investment volume $i^{tha}(\theta)$ on the basis of the agency's manager's information on the business state that has emerged. Business state θ is the Treuhandanstalt manager's private knowledge. In view of the given utility function, the Treuhandanstalt's manager has a strong incentive to use distorted information on the costs of rehabilitation $[c(i^{tha}(\theta'),\theta) < c(i^{tha}(\theta),\theta)]$ to induce the Treuhandanstalt to invest more than would be optimal as a means of increasing his nonpecuniary utility $\mu(i^{tha}(\theta), \theta)$.

As in the case of the private rehabilitation regime, the contractual problem facing the Treuhandanstalt is that it must induce its manager to provide truthful information on the business state that has emerged if it is to achieve an ex post-efficient allocation. The mechanism that the Treuhandanstalt can propose to its manager consists of the two action parameters: investment volume i^{tha} and a premium $z(\theta)$, which the Treuhandanstalt can pay its manager $[M = \{i^{tha}(\theta), z(\theta), \theta \in \{l, h\}\}]$.[4] The Treuhandanstalt' maximization problem then reads

(8.3)
$$\max_{i^P(\theta)z(\theta)} \left\{ p \cdot \left[b\left(i^{tha}(l)\right) - c\left(i^{tha}(l), l\right) - z(l) \right] + (1-p) \cdot \left[b\left(i^{tha}(h)\right) - c\left(i^{tha}(h), h\right) - z(h) \right] \right\}$$

under the constraints of *incentive compatibility*

(8.4) $\quad z(\theta) + \mu\left(i^{tha}(\theta), \theta\right) \geq z(\theta') + \mu\left(i^{tha}(\theta'), \theta\right) \quad \forall \theta, \theta' \in \{l, h\}$

and individual rationality (*participation constraint*)

(8.5) $\qquad z(\theta) + \mu\left(i^{tha}(\theta)\right) \geq 0 \qquad \forall \theta \in \{l, h\}$.

θ' denotes a statement made by the Treuhandanstalt's manager on the business state that has emerged which does not correspond to the truth. The constraint of incentive compatibility can be met only if the Treuhandanstalt cedes to its manager, as a pecuniary income, the information rent which he could obtain by underestimating the costs. The information rent he obtains under the unfavorable business states must therefore be at least as high as the benefit he would realize if he made a false statement on the business state that has emerged, i.e.

(8.6) $\qquad z(h) \geq \mu\left(i^{tha}(l)\right) - \mu\left(i^{tha}(h)\right)$.

The Treuhandanstalt manager's utility function is, however, his private knowledge. It is therefore assumed that the Treuhandanstalt will cede to its manager the utility differential that he would obtain as an information rent by providing truthful information:

$$(8.7) \quad z(h) = \left[b\left(i^{tha}(h)\right) - c\left(i^{tha}(h),h\right) \right] - \left[b\left(i^{tha}(l)\right) - c\left(i^{tha}(l),h\right) \right]$$

The Treuhandanstalt can cede this rent to the manager at the end of the game, once the payoffs, and thus also the business states that have actually emerged, have become known. In practice, this would amount to profit-sharing, or, in our case, i.e. the realization of rehabilitation investments with negative capitalized values, the payoff of the manager could be tied to a reduction of the firm's actual losses at the end of a business year. As long as the premium $z(h)$ is at least as great as the differential of the manager's nonpecuniary utility for the Treuhandanstalt's volume of investment in the favorable and the unfavorable states $[z(h) \geq \mu(i^{tha}(l)) - \mu(i^{tha}(h))]$, the mechanism is incentive-compatible.[5] In the favorable business states, the manager has, even without an information rent, an incentive to provide truthful information on the actual business state, and thus, under these conditions, there is no need to cede an information rent to him $[z(l) = 0]$.

The utility that remains to the Treuhandanstalt is then, in the unfavorable business state

$$(8.8) \quad \begin{aligned} U^{tha}\left(i^{tha}(h)\right) &= W\left(i^{tha}(h)\right) - z(h) \\ &= \left[b\left(i^{tha}(h)\right) - c\left(i^{tha}(h),h\right) \right] - \left[\left(b\left(i^{tha}(h)\right) - c\left(i^{tha}(h),h\right)\right) - \right. \\ &\qquad \left. \left(b\left(i^{tha}(l)\right) - c\left(i^{tha}(l),h\right)\right) \right] \\ &= b\left(i^{tha}(l)\right) - c\left(i^{tha}(l),h\right) \\ &\quad \forall z(h) \geq \mu\left(i^{tha}(l)\right) - \mu\left(i^{tha}(h)\right) \end{aligned}$$

and in the favorable state

$$(8.9)\quad U^{tha}\!\left(i^{tha}(l)\right) \;=\; W\!\left(i^{tha}(l)\right) \;=\; b\!\left(i^{tha}(l)\right) - c\!\left(i^{tha}(l),l\right)$$

whereby $W(i^{tha}(l))$ denotes the net social gains $[b(i^{tha}(l))-c(i^{tha}(l),l)]$ in the favorable state l and $W(i^{tha}(h))$ stands for the net social gains $[b(i^{tha}(h))-c(i^{tha}(h), h)]$ in the unfavorable state h.

Once the manager has informed it of the firm's business and cost conditions, the Treuhandanstalt chooses investment volume $i^{tha}(\theta)$. Like the case of the private rehabilitation regime, the Treuhandanstalt, by distorting the volume of investment, i.e. by choosing a volume of investment that is not ex post-efficient, can limit the manager's information rent. Due to the manager's information rent, the utility remaining to the Treuhandanstalt in the unfavorable business state is contingent on the volume of investment made in the favorable state. If the Treuhandanstalt credibly undertakes to realize a suboptimal volume of investment in the favorable business state, it can reduce the manager's information rent in the unfavorable state.

In the favorable business states, the maximization problem facing the Treuhandanstalt when it stipulates investment volume $i^{tha}(l)$ is

$$(8.10)$$
$$\max_{i^{tha}(l)\geq 0}\left\{p\cdot\left[b\!\left(i^{tha}(l)\right)-c\!\left(i^{tha}(l),l\right)\right]+(1-p)\cdot\left[b\!\left(i^{tha}(l)\right)-c\!\left(i^{tha}(l),h\right)\right]\right\}.$$

Optimal investment volume $i^{tha}(l)$ is then reached by balancing out the Treuhandanstalt's marginal utility and marginal costs,[6] i.e. at

$$(8.11)\quad b'\!\left(i^{tha}(l)\right) = p\cdot c'\!\left(i^{tha}(l),l\right) + (1-p)\cdot c'\!\left(i^{tha}(l),h\right),$$

under the constraint of

$$(8.12)\quad b\!\left(i^{tha}(l)\right) - p\cdot c\!\left(i^{tha}(l),\, l\right) - (1-p)\cdot c\!\left(i^{tha}(l),h\right) \;\geq\; 0.$$

If the constraint in formula (8.12) is not fulfilled, the Treuhandanstalt will choose investment volume $i^{tha}(l) = 0$, because in this case the rehabilitation gains, taking into account the manager's information rent, are lower than the agency's costs. Since the manager's information rent is not influenced by the Treuhandanstalt's volume of investment in the unfavorable business state, the agency can choose the ex post-efficient investment volume $i^{tha}(h) = i^*(h)$. At given expense level $\bar{a}$, the optimal mechanism $M\ \{i^{tha}(\theta),\ z(\theta)\}$ is then

$$z(h) = b\left(i^{tha}(h)\right) - c\left(i^{tha}(h),h\right) - b\left(i^{tha}(l)\right) + c\left(i^{tha}(l),h\right)$$

$$z(l) = 0$$

(8.13)
$$i^{tha}(l) = \begin{cases} 0 \ \ if \\ b\left(i^{tha}(l)\right) - p \cdot c\left(i^{tha}(l),l\right) - (1-p) \cdot c\left(i^{tha}(l),h\right) < 0 \\ i^{tha}(l) \ \ in\ the\ reverse\ case \end{cases}$$

$$i^{tha}(h) = i^*(h)$$

and investment volume $i^{tha}(l)$ is defined by formula (8.12).

The Treuhandanstalt's second problem is the manager's *incentive structure*. The probability that the favorable business state will emerge is contingent on the manager's efforts. In a world without transaction costs, the welfare-maximizing activity level a^* would be determined by solving the maximization problem

(8.14) $\max\limits_{a \geq 0} \left\{ W(a) = p(a)\ W^*(l) + (1-p(a))\ W^*(h) - \phi(a) \right\}$

whereby $p(a)$ and $1-p(a)$ denote the probability and the counterprobability as functions of the activity level of the manager at which the firm's favorable and unfavorable cost conditions occur, $W^*(\theta) = b(i^*(\theta)) - c(i^*(\theta), \theta)$ describes the social utility of the rehabilitation investments, $\phi(a)$ represents the effort-level of activity a. The activity optimum is then reached in balancing out marginal effort and marginal utility, i.e. at:[7]

$$(8.15) \qquad p'(a*) \cdot \left(W*(l) - W*(h)\right) = \phi'(a*)$$

In a world with transaction costs, on the other hand, a lower level of activity on the part of the Treuhandanstalt's manager must be expected in that the manager is unable to appropriate the entire social benefit of the rehabilitation investments. It is assumed that the Treuhandanstalt is unable to observe its manager's individual acts. As was noted above, the manager's utility function consists of the pecuniary factors w and z and the nonpecuniary factor $\mu(i^{tha}(\theta))$. In the face of competition in the labor market for managers, the manager's fixed salary w is reduced to his reserve utility, which is here normalized as 0, i.e.

$$(8.16) \quad w = \phi\left(a^{tha}\right) - p\left(a^{tha}\right) \cdot \mu\left(i^{tha}(l)\right) - \left(1 - p\left(a^{tha}\right)\right) \cdot \left[z(h) + \mu\left(i^{tha}(h)\right)\right]$$

The mechanism developed above has the drawback that the information rent which the Treuhandanstalt is forced to cede to its manager if he is to inform the agency truthfully on the business state that has emerged diminishes his incentives to bring about a favorable business state. In the unfavorable state, the manager receives pecuniary premium $z(h)$, while the benefit that accrues to him in the favorable state is purely nonpecuniary:

$$(8.17) \qquad V^{tha}\left(p(a)\right) = \mu\left(i^{tha}(l)\right) - \mu\left(i^{*}(h)\right) - z(h)$$

If the mechanism proposed above is incentive-compatible, i.e. if $z(h) \geq \mu(i^{tha}(l)) - \mu(i^{tha}(h))$, the manager has no incentive to invest personal effort in the firm's productive efficiency, so that, ceteris paribus, his activity level will drop to zero.[8]

Under the given mechanism, the Treuhandanstalt's manager then, on the whole, realizes the benefit

$$V^{tha} = w + p\left(a^{tha}\right) \cdot \mu\left(i^{tha}(l)\right) + \left(1 - p\left(a^{tha}\right)\right) \cdot \left[z(h) + \mu\left(i \cdot (h)\right)\right] - \phi\left(a^{tha}\right)$$

(8.18)   or

$$V^{tha} = w + p(0) \cdot \mu\left(i^{tha}(l)\right) + \left(1 - p(0)\right) \cdot \left[z(h) + \mu\left(i * (h)\right)\right] - \phi(0)$$

respectively.

The Treuhandanstalt's benefit being

$$U^{tha} = p(0) \cdot W\left(i^{tha}(l)\right) + \left(1 - p(0)\right) \cdot \left[W\left(i * (h)\right) - z(h)\right] - w$$

(8.19)

$$= p(0) \cdot \left[b\left(i^{tha}(l)\right) - c\left(i^{tha}(l), l\right)\right] + \left(1 - p(0)\right) \cdot \left[b\left(i^{tha}(l)\right) - c\left(i^{tha}(l), h\right)\right] - w$$

$$\forall \; z(h) \geq \mu\left(i^{tha}(l)\right) - \mu\left(i^{tha}(h)\right)$$

Under the assumption of imperfect information, three conclusions can be drawn from this outcome on rehabilitation conducted by the Treuhandanstalt: first, the Treuhandanstalt's rehabilitation regime fails to achieve an ex post-efficient volume of investment, provided that the Treuhandanstalt is not indifferent to transfers to its manager. In the favorable business state, investment volume $i^{tha}(l) < i*(l)$ is suboptimal, whereas in the unfavorable state the Treuhandanstalt is free to choose ex post-efficient investment level $i^{tha}(h) > i*(h)$.

Second, the Treuhandanstalt is forced to cede to its manager a pecuniary premium $z(h) = [b(i*(h)) - c(i*(h),h] - [b(i^{tha}(l)) - c(i^{tha}(l),h)]$ if it is to implement an incentive-compatible mechanism.

Third, and finally, the pecuniary premium z annuls the manager's incentives to improve the firm's cost conditions. Assuming that the mechanism is incentive-compatible, the manager will be just as well off when the unfavorable business state emerges as he would be if the favorable state occurred. His incentive to invest personal effort in the firm's productive efficiency therefore drops to zero. In other words, the Treuhandanstalt's rehabilitation regime entails both low allocative efficiency and a low level of productive efficiency.

The mechanism proposed here presupposes that the Treuhandanstalt is able to accept credibly two strategic conditions: first, it must give a credible commitment that it is willing, ex post, to cede to its manager the pecuniary premium $z(h)$ as his information rent. Second, the Treuhandanstalt must oblige itself strategically to realize the ex post-efficient investment volume $i^{tha}(l) < i*(l)$ as soon as it has been truthfully informed by its manager on the business state that has emerged.

The Treuhandanstalt can consent credibly to the first undertaking by, for instance, entering into a contractual bond with its manager, by, in Oliver Williamson's terminology, ceding to him a "hostage." The second undertaking is far more problematical in that implementation of the ex post-efficient investment volume $i^{tha}(l) = i*(l)$ would give rise to a situation in which the Treuhandanstalt was better off once the manager had provided the agency with truthful information. If in turn the manager anticipates this, it is no longer optimal for him to provide the Treuhandanstalt with truthful information. Under the conditions of game theory, the Treuhandanstalt's strategic undertaking to implement an ex post-inefficient volume of investment would be credible only if the game were one that it reiterated infinitely. Perhaps it is possible to interpret in this way the strategic bargaining situation of the Treuhandanstalt in its dealings with the numerous firms it holds. If, on the other hand, the Treuhandanstalt fails to oblige itself credibly vis-à-vis the firms it holds to implement the ex post-inefficient volume of investment, it will be forced to cede to its manager the higher information rent

$$
(8.20) \quad \begin{aligned}
&\left[b\big(i*(h)\big) - c\big(i*(h),h\big)\right] - \left[b\big(i*(l)\big) - c\big(i*(l),h\big)\right] > \\
&\left[b\big(i*(h)\big) - c\big(i*(h),h\big)\right] - \left[b\big(i^{tha}(l)\big) - c\big(i^{tha}(l),h\big)\right].
\end{aligned}
$$

8.2.3   Rehabilitation by an Entrepreneur

The most important benefit of privatization is the higher intensity of the incentives provided by private ownership. When privatization is carried out by an entrepreneur who consolidates in one person the rights of ownership and decision, this give rise to expectations of high levels of incentive intensity, because the entrepreneur is entitled to appropriate the returns stemming from his actions. As was demonstrated in the last chapter, what results from a private rehabilitation regime is an ex post-inefficient allocation of rehabilitation investments and an information rent for the private owner. In contrast to rehabilitation by the Treuhandanstalt, the private owner is able to obtain an information rent by *over*estimating the costs of rehabilitation.

Figure 8.3: Private Rehabilitation Regimes

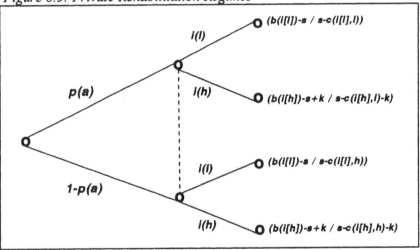

Under these conditions, and at given entrepreneur activity level a, the optimal mechanism $M \{s, k, \hat{t}^P\}$ developed in chapter 7.2 reads

$$s = c\left(i^P(l),l\right) + r(l)$$

$$= c\left(i^P(l),l\right) + c\left(i^P(h),h\right) - c\left(i^P(h),l\right)$$

$$k = \begin{cases} s \ \ \text{if } b\left(i^P(h)\right) - c\left(i^P(h),h\right) - \dfrac{p}{1-p} \cdot r < 0 \\[2mm] s - c\left(i^P(h),h\right) = c\left(i^P(l),l\right) - c\left(i^P(h),l\right) \\[1mm] \text{in the reverse case} \end{cases}$$

(8.21)

$$i^P(l) = i^*(l)$$

and $i^P(h)$ was defined by

(8.22) $b'\left(i^P(h)\right) = c'\left(i^P(h),h\right) + \dfrac{p}{1-p} \cdot \left[c'\left(i^P(h),h\right) - c'\left(i^P(h),l\right)\right].$

Under these conditions, the Treuhandanstalt reaches the payoff

(8.23)
$$U^{tha} = p \cdot \left[b\left(i^*(l)\right) - c\left(i^*(l),l\right) - c\left(i^P(h),h\right) + c\left(i^P(h),l\right)\right] + (1-p) \cdot$$
$$\left[b\left(i^P(h)\right) - c\left(i^P(h),h\right)\right]$$

In other words, under the unfavorable cost conditions the volume of investment is suboptimal under this rehabilitation regime. The central difference between private rehabilitation and rehabilitation by the Treuhandanstalt is, however, to be sought not in allocative efficiency but in the *intensity of the incentives* involved. In order to induce the private owner to reveal truthfully the business state that has emerged, the Treuhandanstalt is forced to cede to him the information rent

(8.24) $r = p \cdot \left[c\left(i^P(h),h\right) - c\left(i^P(h),l\right)\right].$

The entrepreneur faces the following maximation problem in fixing his activity level a^P:

$$(8.25) \quad \max_{a^P \geq 0} \left\{ p\left(a^P\right) \cdot \left[c\left(i^P(h),h\right) - c\left(i^P(h),l\right) + \mu\left(i*(l)\right) - \mu\left(i^P(h)\right) \right] - \phi\left(a^P\right) \right\}$$

The optimal entrepreneur activity level then results at the equilibrium of the marginal return and the marginal utility of his activities,[9] i.e. at

$$(8.26) \quad p'\left(a^P\right) \cdot \left[c\left(i^P(h),h\right) - c\left(i^P(h),l\right) + \mu\left(i*(l)\right) - \mu\left(i^P(h)\right) \right] = \phi'\left(a^P\right).$$

In other words, the given incentive structure gives rise to the expectation of an entrepreneur activity level substantially higher than that encountered in the case of the Treuhandanstalt's manager, because under the unfavorable cost conditions the latter is just as well off as he would be under the favorable cost conditions. The entrepreneur can realize an information rent only in the favorable business state, and his nonpecuniary benefit is greater in the favorable business state than it would be in the unfavorable state. But in contrast to the activity level under the first-best conditions in a world without transaction costs, the activity level is suboptimal in that if the nonpecuniary incentives are bracketed out, the entrepreneur's information rent is lower than the differential of the welfare level in the favorable and the unfavorable business state, i.e.

$$(8.27) \quad c\left(i^P(h),h\right) - c\left(i^P(h),l\right) \; < \; W^*(l) - W^*(h).$$

In view of the given mechanism, the entrepreneur can then realize the benefit

$$
\begin{aligned}
(8.28) \quad V^P &= p\left(a^P\right) \cdot \left[c\left(i^P(h),h\right) - c\left(i^P(h),l\right) + \mu\left(i*(l)\right) \right] + \left(1 - p\left(a^P\right)\right) \cdot \mu\left(i^P(h)\right) - \phi\left(a^P\right) \\
&= p\left(a^P\right) \cdot \left[r + \mu\left(i*(l)\right) \right] + \left(1 - p\left(a^P\right)\right) \cdot \mu\left(i^P(h)\right) - \phi\left(a^P\right)
\end{aligned}
$$

and the Treuhandanstalt

$$U^{tha} = p(a^P) \cdot \left[b(i*(l)) - c(i*(l),l) - c(i^P(h),h) + c(i^P(h),l) \right]$$
$$(8.29) \qquad\qquad + (1 - p(a^P)) \cdot \left[b(i^P(h)) - c(i^P(h),h) \right]$$

respectively.

Comparison of this private rehabilitation regime with rehabilitation carried out by the Treuhandanstalt leads to the following conclusions: first, neither of the rehabilitation regimes reaches an ex post-efficient allocation of rehabilitation investments. While under the private rehabilitation regime the investment level is suboptimal in the *un*favorable business state, the investment level is suboptimal in the favorable state when rehabilitation is carried out by the Treuhandanstalt. For this reason, the probability that a firm will not be rehabilitated in the first place is, ceteris paribus, greater under the private rehabilitation regime than in the case in which the Treuhandanstalt conducts the rehabilitation.

Second, the Treuhandanstalt is forced under both rehabilitation regimes to pay an information rent to its agents if it is to implement an incentive-compatible mechanism. In the case of private rehabilitation, the entrepreneur is, in the favorable business state, not compensated with a rehabilitation subsidy for the costs he incurs in realizing rehabilitation investments with negative capitalized values; instead, he too receives an information rent $r = c(i^P(h), h) - c(i^P(h), l)$. Under the Treuhandanstalt's regime, the agency's manager receives in the unfavorable state an information rent in the form of a pecuniary premium $z(h) =$ $[b(i*(h)) - c(i*(h), h)] - [b(i^{tha}(l)) - c(i^{tha}(l), h)]$. Which of the two rents is higher depends on the specific conditions involved.

Third, the entrepreneur's incentives to invest in his firm's productive efficiency in order to bring about the favorable business state are much higher than those of the Treuhandanstalt's manager. This is the reason why a private rehabilitation regime, ceteris paribus, gives rise to expectations of a productive efficiency greater than would be expected under a public-sector rehabilitation regime, while allocative efficiency is low under both of these rehabilitation regimes.

In other words, there are, under the assumptions made here, advantages for the private rehabilitation regime. This finding is tied to the assumption that the Treuhandanstalt, even though it is the owner of the firms it holds, is just as poorly informed on rehabilitation costs as it would be if rehabilitation were carried out by a private firm. On the other hand, the assumption - often encountered in the literature on the supply of public goods - that the owner is always perfectly informed of his costs entails for the choice of a rehabilitation regime a trade-off between allocative and productive efficiency: the Treuhandanstalt would then, in contrast to a private rehabilitation regime, achieve an ex post-efficient allocation of rehabilitation investments, while productive efficiency would, in consideration of the given incentives, be lower than the productive efficiency to be reached under a private rehabilitation regime (Schmidt 1991, 21-22). Both of these are idealized assumptions that may be chosen for heuristic reasons. In reality, the Treuhandanstalt has in both cases information on rehabilitation costs, although this information is imperfect and strategically distorted to boot. If, in practice, the Treuhandanstalt as owner should actually be in possession of privileged access to information, the benefit of the higher level of allocative efficiency resulting from this fact would have to be weighed against the drawback of a lower level of productive efficiency.

8.2.4   Rehabilitation by a Rentier

One important comparative advantage of the private rehabilitation regime discussed above is thus to be sought in the entrepreneur's stronger incentives to invest in his firm's productive efficiency. Yet not every private ownership regime implies such strong incentives. As was discussed at length in Chapter 3, the separation of the rights of ownership and decision alters the incentive structure in private firms. This section will therefore look into the consequences of a sell-off to a private rentier or group of rentiers who hire a professional manager to run and rehabilitate their firm. What is behind this analysis is the idea that that selling off to rentiers who appropriate the firm's residual income might on the one hand weaken management's incentives vis-à-vis entrepreneur privatization, while on the other hand the hard budget constraint of a private firm could expose a professional manager to incentives and sanctions different from those faced by the manager of a Treuhandanstalt's firm.

In ideal terms, it can be assumed that the budget constraint of a Treuhandanstalt's firm is (largely) soft, while privatized firms will (largely) be faced with a hard budget constraint. This is an abstraction to the extent that on the one hand Treuhandanstalt's firms are also threatened with closure and on the other hand the budget constraint of private firms is not perfectly hard, either. The Treuhandanstalt has entered into renegotiation in 3,000 cases involving not only prolongation and cancellation of the employment and investment commitments agreed upon but also additional financial transfers to ailing firms and, in some cases, even the return of such firms to the Treuhandanstalt. Still, it is not implausible to assume that the budget constraint of private firms is substantially harder than that of the firms held by the Treuhandanstalt.

In analogy to the Treuhandanstalt's rehabilitation regime, the model presented here assumes that the owners (rentiers) are responsible for making the decisions on investment levels, while the managers have an informational edge over the owners. The costs of rehabilitation investments are the private knowledge of the managers. As in the case of the private rehabilitation regime, it is assumed here that the Treuhandanstalt will conclude rehabilitation contracts with the buyers and that these contracts will stipulate a rehabilitation subsidy s, an investment volume i, and a contractual penalty k.

Under this rehabilitation regime, the manager's payoffs differ from those of the manager of a Treuhandanstalt's firm: although the manager's utility function likewise consists of his pecuniary income m and a nonpecuniary benefit μ contingent on the size of the firm concerned, i.e.

$$(8.30) \qquad V^m = m + \mu\left(i^r\right) - \phi\left(a^m\right),$$

the manager's income is affected by the unfavorable business state. While the Treuhandanstalt's soft budget constraint assures a firm's survival even when it has invested too much under unfavorable cost conditions, a private firm with a hard budget constraint will in this case be driven into bankruptcy: the Treuhandanstalt's payments will not be enough to cover the costs of a volume of investment which, in the favorable business state, would be optimal, i.e.

$$(8.31) \qquad t(h) = s - k = c\left(i^r(h), h\right) < c\left(i^r(l), h\right).$$

Under the assumption of a perfectly hard budget constraint, any misinvestment is sanctioned by the market, driving the firms concerned into bankruptcy. Any underestimation of rehabilitation costs will therefore have negative consequences for the manager: he will be dismissed, lose his business reputation and the benefits that would accrue to him from a successful management of his firm. In formal terms, bankruptcy reduces the manager's nonpecuniary utility to zero. His dominant strategy - as opposed to that of his counterpart in the Treuhandanstalt's firm - will be to truthfully reveal to the owners the actual business state and to avoid any misallocation:[10]

$$(8.32) \qquad V^m\left(c\left(i^r(l'), h\right)\right) = \mu(0) < V^m\left(c\left(i^r(h), h\right)\right) = \mu\left(i^r(h)\right)$$

Consequently, the owners are not forced to pay the manager an information rent, and thus his pecuniary income is restricted to his fixed salary w. To select optimal activity level a^m with this incentive structure, the manager has to solve the following maximization problem:

$$(8.33) \quad \max_{a^m \geq 0} \left\{ p\left(a^m\right) \cdot \mu\left(i^r(l)\right) + \left(1 - p\left(a^m\right)\right) \cdot \mu\left(i^r(h)\right) - \phi\left(a^m\right) \right\}$$

The manager's optimal activity level is reached in a private firm in balancing out his private marginal utility and his marginal costs[11], i.e. at

$$(8.34) \qquad p'\!\left(a^m\right)\cdot\left[\mu\!\left(i^r(l)\right)-\mu\!\left(i^r(h)\right)\right]=\phi'\!\left(a^m\right),$$

This activity level of the manager in a private firm is consequently higher than that of the manager of a Treuhandanstalt's firm, but lower than the activity level of the entrepreneur, who, in addition, is also able to appropriate an information rent as a residual income ($a^{tha} = 0 < a^m < a^p < a*$).

In the model developed here, rentier and manager are both equally well informed, because the manager's dominant strategy is to reveal truthfully the cost conditions to the owners. On the other hand, the Treuhandanstalt does not know what business state has emerged in the rentier-owned firm. The rentiers can therefore obtain the same information rent as the entrepreneur in the favorable business state, and thus the Treuhandanstalt will implement the same mechanism as it would under the rehabilitation regime of entrepreneur privatization (see Chapters 8.2.3 and 7.2). In the case of rehabilitation by a rentier, the volume of investment will thus be the same as the volume of investment involved when privatization is conducted by an entrepreneur, i.e. $i^r(\theta) = i^p(\theta)$. The following payoffs then result for the three parties:

$$(8.35) \quad V^m = p\!\left(a^m\right)\cdot\mu\!\left(i*(l)\right)+\left(1-p\!\left(a^m\right)\right)\cdot\mu\!\left(i^r(h)\right)+w-\phi\!\left(a^m\right)$$

$$(8.36) \quad V^r = p\!\left(a^m\right)\cdot\left[c\!\left(i^r(h),h\right)-c\!\left(i^r(h),l\right)\right]-w$$

$$(8.37) \quad\begin{aligned}U^{tha} = {}&p\!\left(a^m\right)\cdot\left[b\!\left(i*(l),l\right)-c\!\left(i*(l),l\right)-c\!\left(i^r(h),h\right)+c\!\left(i^r(h),l\right)\right]\\ &+\left(1-p\!\left(a^m\right)\right)\cdot\left[b\!\left(i^r(h)\right)-c\!\left(i^r(h),h\right)\right]\end{aligned}$$

The Treuhandanstalt's utility differs only in one respect from that involved in the other private regime of rehabilitation: with the given incentive structure, the private manager's activity level is lower than the private entrepreneur's, and thus, ceteris paribus, productive efficiency will be lower than in the case of rehabilitation by an entrepreneur. But on the other hand, the hard budget constraint of the privately owned firm increases both activity level and productive efficiency, raising their levels substantially above those encountered when rehabilitation is carried out by the Treuhandanstalt. But this model leaves out of consideration the returns made possible by the separation of the rights of ownership and decision. Under the assumption that the Treuhandanstalt's firms do not qualify to be traded on the stock exchange, i.e. the transaction costs stemming from the separation of the rights of ownership and decision exceed the possible returns, this model can be interpreted as a formal representation of the hypothesis that privatization through dispersion of company shares does not constitute an adequate privatization procedure.

The central factor behind the lower productive efficiency of Treuhandanstalt's firms is their soft budget constraint: if the Treuhandanstalt could credibly undertake ex ante to close its firms even if this were ex post-inefficient, it could achieve the level of productive efficiency possible in the case of privatization by a rentier. But an undertaking of this kind is, for two reasons, not credible: first, the Treuhandanstalt would be worse off due to an ex post-inefficient allocation resulting from a closure than it would be if it realized an ex pot-efficient allocation and decided against closure. Second, the closure of a firm by the Treuhandanstalt calls for a political justification that would hardly be possible in the case of an ex post-inefficient allocation.

8.3   The Treuhandanstalt's Rehabilitation Policy

The static analysis of private- and public-sector rehabilitation regimes above leads to the conclusion that, under the assumption of positive external effects of rehabilitation investments, no ex post-efficient volume of investment is realized under either of the two ownership regimes. On top of the soft budget constraint and the incentive structure of the Treuhandanstalt's firms, however, rehabilitation under a public-sector regime gives rise to expectations of a lower level of productive efficiency than would be anticipated under a private-sector rehabilitation regime. The decision problem faced by the Treuhandanstalt as regards the rehabilitation of its firms was, however, more complex than it appears under the model conditions of a static analysis of alternative rehabilitation regimes. The starting point of the rehabilitation process was the fact that the Treuhandanstalt was the owner of the firms it held. Under the assumption of nontrivial transaction costs, privatization is a time-intensive process. This gave rise to the question of how the firms were to be dealt with until they were privatized. The proposal of the *Sachverständigenrat* that the Treuhandanstalt should have closed all firms that were unable to be privatized (SVR 1991a, 17) presupposed that the Treuhandanstalt was able to judge ex ante which firms were privatizable and which were not. This, however, imputes to the Treuhandanstalt an economic competence that, in other places, is rightly disputed.

Under dynamic conditions, the Treuhandanstalt was faced with two decision problems: first, it was forced to choose between firms that could be rehabilitated and firms not able to rehabilitation. Since nearly all of the enterprises held by the Treuhandanstalt were operating in the red, this selection decision was complex. The privatization criterion proposed by the *Sachverständigenrat* was not an adequate decision aid in that in a world with transaction costs and bounded rationality privatization is a time-consuming and cost-intensive process. Second, aside from paying maintenance subsidies, the Treuhandanstalt had to decide on the implementation of rehabilitation subsidies. And the implementation of rehabilitation subsidies confronted the Treuhandanstalt with a trade-off: on the one hand, a decision against rehabilitation investments under dynamic conditions weakened the competitiveness of the Treuhandanstalt's firms. This led both to a drop in the prices for these firms and a high shutdown rate of production capacities. On the other hand, no efficient use of the funds invested could have been expected when the Treuhandanstalt itself was in charge of rehabilitation.

In its self-presentations, the Treuhandanstalt described the guiding principles of its business strategy as "rapid privatization - resolute rehabilitation - cautious liquidation" (Treuhandanstalt 1991a, 5) This Treuhandanstalt self-description will not bear up under closer scrutiny. The Treuhandanstalt's business policy is better characterized by the following key points: first, payment of maintenance subsidies tended to safeguard the survival of the agency's firms without regard to their economic performance in the first phase after monetary union (8.3.1). Second, the Treuhandanstalt for the most part declined to finance rehabilitation investments, and the possibility open to its firms to borrow in the financial markets was largely restricted (8.3.2). Third, the Treuhandanstalt had built up an apparatus designed for a rational selection of firms, and this apparatus, following protracted information and bargaining processes, decided on the firms that would be given a chance to survive. In cases in which a decision was made in favor of liquidation, the agency generally prolonged the time required for closure (8.3.3).

8.3.1   Payment of Maintenance Subsidies

As was discussed at length in Chapter 5, the asset-specific capital of Eastern German firms has largely been depreciated by the price-cost-squeeze that occurred following economic and monetary union. Without any public subsidies, the great majority of these firms would have gone into bankruptcy following German monetary union. Following monetary union, the Treuhandanstalt had no information on the extent to which its firms were capable of rehabilitation. Under these conditions, it decided in favor of starting out by securing, more or less indiscriminately, its firms' survival by providing them with global credit guarantees (Schmid-Schönbein/Hansel 1991, 463). In the first three months following economic and monetary reform, it provided so-called "liquidity guarantees" amounting to 25.4 billion DM (Bundesminister der Finanzen 1991, 6), some 15 billion of which was used by the firms for safeguarding loans (Treuhandanstalt, Zentrales Controlling, various reports). In September 1991, the volume of these non-earmarked global guarantees reached its highest level, 28.5 billion DM, 22.9 billion of which was used for safeguarding loans (Treuhandanstalt 1992c; 1993c).

The instrument of global guarantees was successively replaced with other financial instruments such as individual tied guarantees and loans by the Treuhandanstalt. A sharply reduced stock of firms held by the Treuhandanstalt still saw the agency providing, in February 1993, a volume of 14.2 billion DM, 12.6 billion of which was claimed in the form of credit[12]. Until December 31, 1994, when the Treuhandanstalt was dissolved, it provided 45.8 billion DM as loans to its subsidiaries and accepted a relief on "old" liabilities with a volume of 73 billion DM. (See Table 8.1)   ·

Under the economic pressure that emerged following economic and monetary union, the Treuhandanstalt was thus forced to institutionalize a soft budget constraint for its firms and to abrogate the selective function of the capital market. The Treuhandanstalt delegated its selection decisions to a bureaucratic apparatus which decided on the survival of the firms on the basis of fixed rules and bargaining procedures.

Table 8.1: Payments of the Treuhandanstalt to its Enterprises

	12/31/1991	12/31/1992	12/31/1993	12/31/1994
	- DM millions -			
guarantees	27,545	23,913	17,638	n.a.
export liabilities	1,694	2,560	2,606	n.a.
intermediary finance of foreign trade firms	1,343	2,288	-	n.a.
shareholder's loans	19,940	30,685	43,200	45,813
of this: interest bearing loans	13,200	16,478	12,751	n.a.
non-interest loans	6,720	14,207	30,449	n.a.
corrections for non-performing loans	11,574	22,025	36,340	31,317
other corporate loans	8,366	8,669	6,860	14,496
compenzation demands according § 24 DM-BilG	15,534	15,076	12,851	311
debt relief on "old credits"	49,922	56,682	63,100	73,000
Sources: Treuhandanstalt 1993; 1994a; 1995; author's calculations.				

8.3.2   Finance of Investments

A closer analysis of the financial relations between the Treuhandanstalt
and the firms it held shows that although the agency paid generous
maintenance subsidies, it abstained for all practical purposes from financing investments. The transfers made by the Treuhandanstalt to its
firms were made up basically of four financial instruments: first, the
above-mentioned global guarantees, which were intended to safeguard
the liquidity of the firms concerned. The liquidity credits may not be
used for rehabilitation investments. Second, the Treuhandanstalt's
firms were financed via individual tied guarantees and loans. The
greater part of these funds was used to redeem the liquidity guarantees.[13] As of February 28, 1993, only 1.150 billion DM of the shareholder's loans of the Treuhandanstalt was earmarked to finance investments; the agency had also provided a total of 6.479 billion DM for
individual guarantees, and 2.513 billion DM of these funds was made
available for investment credits.[14] Third, the Treuhandanstalt was often
forced to take over the funding of social plans and the liquidation costs
of its firms. By February 28, 1993, the Treuhandanstalt had spent 7.053
billion DM for social plans and 728 million DM for the liquidation of
firms.[15]

Fourth, and finally, the Treuhandanstalt provided to those of its firms
that are seen as capable of rehabilitation equity capital in the amount
customary for the industry concerned; this was done in the form of debt
redemption either within the framework of the firms' opening DM balances or in connection with their privatization. The agency had in this
way taken over old credits of its firms amounting to 73 billion DM (see
Table 8.1).

The chances of Treuhandanstalt's firms to obtain credit without any
guarantees were low (Schmid-Schönbein/Hansel 1991, 466). Also, the
Treuhandanstalt restricted, on the basis of a catalogue of transactions
requiring approval, all investment decisions that went beyond pure replacement investment and most long-term obligations its firms were
allowed to enter into (Treuhandanstalt 1991d). All in all, this business
policy led to a high degree of investment attentism: the Treuhandan-

stalt indicated the volume of investment of its firms as 6,000 DM per person employed for 1991 (Treuhandanstalt/Zentrales Controlling 1993b, 9.3) and 11,000 DM for 1992.[16] In a representative survey of the manufacturing industry, the Deutsches Institut für Wirtschaftsforschung (DIW) and the Kieler Institut für Weltwirtschaft (IfW) found for the Treuhandanstalt's firms an investment volume of 11,070 DM (1991) and 12,860 DM (1992) per person employed, while private firms invested 25,330 DM (1991) and 40,040 DM (1992) per person employed (DIW/IfW 1991b, 718) (see Table 8.2).

Table 8.2:   Investment and Ownership in Eastern Germany's Manufacturing Sector (Investments in DM per Employee)

	1991	1992
- investments in DM per employee -		
Treuhandanstalt's firms	11.070	12.860
Private firms	25.330	40.040
of these:		
Independent firms	20.590	27.530
Subsidiaries of Western German firms	29.570	54.100
Subsidiaries of foreign firms	28.570	39.100
Privatized or reprivatized firms	23.340	29.870
Firms private before 1990	20.354	33.740
Firms established after 1989	47.360	132.40
All firms	18.000	26.060
Source: DIW/IfW 1992, 718.		

Rehabilitation of Treuhandanstalt's firms has thus largely been restricted to passive adjustment measures such as the streamlining of product lines, the closure of factories and production capacities, layoffs, etc. (DIW/IfW 1991b; 1991a; Schmid-Schönbein/Hansel 1991). Within one year after economic and monetary union, the employment level of the Treuhandanstalt's firms had dropped from 4.08 million to 1.372 million, while the firms privatized by the Treuhandanstalt employed 285,000 persons. In December 31, 1994, the Treuhandanstalt employed no more than 66,000 persons while in the privatized firms 930,000 persons were employed. This means a drop in employment of some three million workplaces or 75 percent in the firms either privatized or remaining with the Treuhandanstalt (see Table 8.3).

Table 8.3:   Employment in Treuhandanstalt's Firms and Ex-Treu-
             handanstalt's Firms

	THA's firms	Ex-THA's firms	total
- thousand employees -			
7/31/1990	4,080	-	4,080
12/31/1991	1,372	285	1,657
12/31/1992	408	1,047	1,455
12/31/1993	186	962	1,148
12/31/1994	66	930	996

Source: Söstra/IAB 1994; author's calculations.

8.3.3   Rational Selection

The Treuhandanstalt had successively built up at its head office a strategic apparatus that decided on the survival of the agency's firms on the basis of rehabilitation and business concepts This process can be characterized as one of *rational selection*: Firms categorized by the Treuhandanstalt as capable of rehabilitation have been endowed with equity capital in keeping with their size and the industry in which they are active. The Treuhandanstalt had taken over part of their old loans and current operating losses. The declining percentage of global guarantees and the rising percentage of individual loans and guarantees made available by the Treuhandanstalt were indications of the progressive development of this selection process (see Table 8.1). Firms classified as capable of rehabilitation have been provided with the equity capital customary in their fields of activity, even if they were not rehabilitated by the Treuhandanstalt. Schmid-Schönbein and Hansel describe the Treuhandanstalt's role as that of a "financial holding company" that manages its firms almost entirely with a view to their balance-sheets (Schmid-Schönbein/Hansel 1991, 463). Rehabilitation investments, on the other hand, have not been financed, partly as a means of keeping the firms open for projects of their future owners, partly in order to avoid any inefficient allocation of the resources employed (Schmid-Schönbein/Hansel 1991).

General foreclosure or liquidation proceedings have been initiated for all firms not classified as capable of rehabilitation. By December 31, 1994, such proceedings had been initiated against some 3,700 firms, that is, some 30 percent of the firms originally held by the agency. This firms represented 33.4 percent of the equity capital of the Treuhandanstalt's holdings according to the DM-opening balance sheets. In only 12 percent of these cases did the Treuhandanstalt choose the path of formal bankruptcy proceedings, while 88 percent of its firms were set to be liquidated. According to information of the Treuhandanstalt, in cases of foreclosure proceedings 21.7 percent of the jobs concerned have been saved, and in cases of de facto liquidation proceedings 28.3 percent have survived. The Treuhandanstalt provided time for liquidation; by December 31 of 1994, only 157 of the 3,718 firms categorized as not capable of rehabilitation had been liquidated.

The process in which the Treuhandanstalt used rational criteria to select viable firms confirms the hypothesis of János Kornai and Oliver Williamson on the "soft budget constraint" that tends to prevail in state-owned enterprises, but also in other large-scale bureaucratic organizations (Williamson 1985). It can generally be observed that the selection function of the capital market has been consciously abrogated and subjugated to control and justification mechanisms elaborated in the Treuhandanstalt's headquarters. Although this approach has often been criticized (SVR 1991), it has been unavoidable under the specific conditions in Eastern Germany: under the conditions of a hard budget constraint, the greater part of the firms held by the Treuhandanstalt would have had to be closed. The Treuhandanstalt has instead prolonged, and in part rendered unnecessary, the process of closure by providing massive maintenance subsidies.

Second, the Treuhandanstalt has subjected its firms' demand for investment to strong financial and administrative restrictions. If the Treuhandanstalt had more generously funded rehabilitation investments, it would, under the assumption of a largely soft budget constraint, have been faced with an infinite demand for investment on the part of its firms. The Treuhandanstalt was not in possession of a strategic apparatus that could have been used for an efficient allocation of investment funds among its firms. It therefore decided, almost without exception, against making available funds for rehabilitation investments. There is no doubt that this has entailed high costs (Schmid-Schönbein/Hansel 1991): necessary rehabilitation and modernization investments have been delayed or canceled entirely. Firms unable to be privatized quickly became less competitive. On the other hand, rehabilitation by the Treuhandanstalt would, as was demonstrated by the model developed above, have led to an inefficient allocation and use of the resources made available. The costs involved in delaying rehabilitation investments must be seen in relation to the costs of lower productive and allocative efficiency within the Treuhandanstalt.

One of the reasons why the Treuhandanstalt has decided largely against rehabilitating the firms it held was a lack of organizational capacities. The one exception is the so-called limited management partnerships (*Management-Kommanditgesellschaft*), which were developed at a very late juncture, and then only to a limited extent. In limited management partnerships some 15 firms were subordinated to a holding company, at which the Treuhandanstalt held the majority stake and a private operating company (*private Betreibergesellschaft*) held a minority stake. The private operating company took over the management of the holding company and participated in the privatization revenues. Their share of the privatization revenues decreased during the process of privatization. The model of limited management partnerships was designed by the Treuhandanstalt for the rehabilitation of firms which were in short-term not privatizable but had good prospects for survival. The deconcentration and assignment of firms to such holding companies was itself a time- and cost-intensive process. But no rehabilitation was conceivable without the establishment of clearly structured business units within which the information required for resource allocation could be processed. This is the reason why there was, in the initial phase, no alternative to the Treuhandanstalt's attentism in this respect. But perhaps the firms could have been organized earlier into clearly structured units that would have involved lower costs for the allocation of investment funds. Rehabilitation by the Treuhandanstalt would in this case still have involved high transaction costs, although in a number of cases this approach would have been more beneficial than the Treuhandanstalt's decision not to fund any rehabilitation investments at all.

9   Conclusions

The Treuhandanstalt is leaving behind a mixed legacy. On the one hand, its overall economic-policy objective of rapidly reducing the state sector's share of production and employment in Eastern Germany has been achieved. Measured in terms of the book value of its capital resources, the agency privatized, reprivatized, or communalized sixty percent of the firms it held. At the Treuhandanstalt's disclosure in the end of 1994 only some 66,000 of the 4.08 million persons originally employed there were still working for the Treuhandanstalt or the firms it held. The share of the Treuhandanstalt's enterprises in overall employment in Eastern Germany has dropped from an original figure of 48 percent in 1990 to a figure of around one percent. On the other hand, the privatization process in Eastern Germany has been associated with an unparalleled reduction of production capacities and jobs: roughly one third of the firms concerned were shut down, and current estimates indicate that around three million of the four million jobs in firms held or formerly held by the Treuhandanstalt have been cut.

Any evaluation of the Treuhandanstalt's activity is faced with the problem of having to differentiate between the consequences stemming from the transformation of the institutional and economic framework and the effects of privatization. Only in a qualified sense can the drop in production and employment figures be ascribed directly to the Treuhandanstalt's privatization and rehabilitation strategies. Eastern Germany's accession to the economic and currency area of the Federal Republic of Germany had a crucial impact on the framework that was to determine the course of privatization and economic development. As was demonstrated in Chapters 6 and 7, the introduction of the D-mark as a currency and the adoption of Western Germany's institutional system lowered the transaction costs for direct investment, thus substantially contributing to an acceleration of the privatization process. One of the most important constraints of privatization in other countries in the process of transformation, the limited supply of capital, could be eased in this way. At the same time, however, the cost and price shock experienced after economic and monetary union led to a devaluation of the asset-specific capital of Eastern German enterprises, thus triggering a dramatic drop in production and employment. Beyond by high public-sector transfers and private investment from Western Germany, Eastern Germany's economy has now picked up, and the annual overall production growth figures currently range between three and eight percent.

In view of the given framework, two fundamental issues arise that are crucial to any evaluation of the Treuhandanstalt's privatization strategy: first, the question as to the efficiency of the Treuhandanstalt's allocation of property rights and, second, the question of a rehabilitation strategy adequate to Eastern German conditions.

The question of the allocative efficiency of different privatization procedures was discussed at length in the first section of this study. Privatization of a state economic sector is a time- and cost-intensive process. Firms are not homogeneous goods that can be allocated efficiently with the aid of standardized auction procedures. Depending on the asset specificity of the capital and the size of the firm concerned, the process places great demands on the economic competence and the financial resources of bidders. Under the assumption that rationality is bounded and unequally distributed across individuals, it cannot be expected that the highest bidder will necessarily find the most productive use for a firm. Under these conditions, informal bargaining has comparative advantages vis-à-vis standardized privatization procedures in that the multiplication of information flows and the processing of complex information without price character possible with such procedures make it possible to achieve higher levels of allocative efficiency. The ability to process information without price character does not imply that a hyperrational privatization agency will arrive at a more exact reserve price than a bidder; it simply implies that, based on the information available, it is possible to arrive at an ordinal rank-order judgment between competing bidders. Informal privatization procedures have two further advantages over standardized procedures: first, they reduce the transaction costs of privatization in that, as opposed to standardized procedures, the firms need not in this case be deconcentrated prior to privatization, and this makes it possible to work out a flexible package in the course of bargaining. Second, this procedure makes it possible to conclude complex contracts.

Basically, the Treuhandanstalt privatized its large and medium-sized firms through informal bargaining; it is only the strategically less significant small businesses and service firms that were auctioned off using formal bidding procedures. Privatization was based on multiple allocative criteria, including, apart from price, the bidder's business concept, his personal reputation, and the volume of employment and investment commitments he was willing to make. Under the framework conditions specific to Germany, this was an adequate strategy. Eastern Germany's joining Western Germany's economic and currency area lowered the transaction costs for direct investment from Western Germany, and this meant a supply of capital for privatization in Eastern Germany far greater than that available in other countries of East and Central Europe. The advantage of a broad dispersion of company shares possible when firms are privatized on the stock exchange or via vouchers, i.e. the lower level of the demands placed on the financial resources of potential bidders, was not of any particular weight in Eastern Germany. But in deciding against a broad dispersion of company shares, it was possible to avoid the principal-agent problems associated with this technique and thus to arrive at a more efficient allocation of property rights.

One central problem of privatization in Eastern Germany was limited bidding competition. Restrictions on competition in the process of privatization resulted on the one hand from the asset specificity of the capital and the size of the firms involved and the specific demands placed on bidder competence and financial resources and on the other hand from the choice of a privatization procedure. Privatization through informal bargaining can be conducted efficiently only with one bidder or a limited number of bidders. The theoretical part of this study developed the argument that competition can also be effective as latent competition, as a mere threat. This, however, implies that there is a sufficient degree of probability that another bidder will join the bargaining process. Whether the Treuhandanstalt succeeded in giving the bargaining process an open shape and using its bargaining strategy to avoid competitive restraints is a question that would have to be decided by a large-scale empirical investigation. Some of the cases under public discussion and the case studies of the Hamburg *Weltwirtschaftsarchiv* do, however, indicate that the Treuhandanstalt often weakened its bargaining position by entering prematurely into strategic commitments with a bidder or a cartel of bidders. Competitive restraints in bargaining on privatization not only reduce privatization revenues, they can also lead to strategic market adjustments entailing the closure of production capacities when the bidder in question has a dominant market position.

Measured in terms of the book value of the assets privatized, the Treuhandanstalt's privatization revenues showed a distinct downward trend with the exemption of 1994: whereas in 1990 and 1991 its privatization revenues were in line with the book values of the firms privatized as shown in the opening DM balance sheets, these revenues dropped in 1992 to 55 pfennig and in 1993 to 36 pfennig for one D-mark of book value. In 1994 the Treuhandanstalt realized due to the privatization of valuable assets in infrastructure revenues of 285 percent of the book value. Still, the absolute level of the privatization revenues does remain low. Although the net asset values shown in the opening DM balances need not necessarily constitute an adequate indicator for the market value of Eastern German firms, plausibility-related arguments would seem to indicate that that the opening DM balances tended more to underestimate the market value of the Treuhandanstalt's assets than otherwise.

Basically there are two explanations for the low level of privatization revenues: first, there is reason to assume that in many cases the Treuhandanstalt weakened its own bargaining position and failed to implement efficiently its privatization strategy. Three factors were important here: restricted bidding competition, the pressure of time with which the agency was faced, and principal-agent problems between the Treuhandanstalt and its employees.

The second explanation of the low level of privatization revenues is the subsidies granted by the Treuhandanstalt to buyers in the form of price rebates and negative prices in return for employment and investment guarantees. Although the level of these subsidies is unknown, the figures involved certainly go into the tens of billions.

The second fundamental issue bound up with the Treuhandanstalt's business policy concerns its rehabilitation strategy. Until its extraction this issue formed the center of the economic-policy controversy surrounding the Treuhandanstalt: while the one side demanded that the agency refrain completely from making rehabilitation investments, the other side criticized its lack of effort in rehabilitation. The issue of the comparative advantages of private and public rehabilitation regimes leads back to the point of departure of this study. Chapter 1 used two theoretical arguments to justify privatization: first, the *coherence* of an economic order that coordinates the plans of its economic agents decentrally, via markets, requires a monetary constraint at the macrolevel and a hard company budget constraint at the microlevel. Theoretical considerations and the empirical experience gained from market-socialist reforms in the transition countries indicate that, in the long run, a hard budget constraint cannot be enforced against a state economic sector which dominates the production and employment of the economy concerned. Second, it must be expected that, owing to their incentive and sanction structure, firms under private ownership achieve a higher level of *X-efficiency* than enterprises in the public sector. Whether private firms, as opposed to state-owned enterprises, also reach a higher level of allocative efficiency depends on whether or not external effects are involved and what institutional alternatives are available to internalize these effects.

In being integrated with Western Germany's economic and currency area, Eastern Germany was faced with a coherence problem of a lesser magnitude. As opposed to the other transition countries, there was no risk involved here that the soft budget constraint of the state economic sector might endanger macroeconomic stability. However, the soft budget constraint of the firms held by the Treuhandanstalt and the incentive problems facing state-owned property give rise to lower expectations of efficiency in rehabilitation carried out by the Treuhandanstalt. Furthermore, following monetary union the Treuhandanstalt was without the organizational capacities required to rehabilitate its firms. Only in the form of limited management partnerships (*Management-Kommanditgesellschaften, KGs*) was an organizational model developed that could be used to allocate investment funds among firms in keeping with economic criteria and to monitor the uses to which such funds are put.

The Treuhandanstalt largely decided against rehabilitating the firms it held, instead restricting its role to distributing maintenance subsidies and subsidizing private rehabilitation investments. This gives rise to the question whether these funds might not have been employed more efficiently to rehabilitate firms directly. Under the assumption of information asymmetrically distributed between the private investor and the Treuhandanstalt, the study demonstrated with the aid of a model derived from game theory that the private investor will be able to obtain part of rehabilitation investments in the form of an information rent and that the investment level reached will be a suboptimal one. Still, in comparative-statical terms the private rehabilitation regime turns out to be more beneficial than rehabilitation carried out by the Treuhandanstalt: the information involved is distributed asymmetrically not only between the Treuhandanstalt and the private investor but also between the agency and the managers of its firms. The manager of a Treuhandanstalt firm can use his informational edge to acquire additional investment funds by underestimating the costs of rehabilitation. In transition countries, this phenomenon is familiar under the name of investment hunger. The asymmetrical distribution of information between the Treuhandanstalt and its manager therefore leads to a nonoptimal volume of investment, just as it does when private rehabilitation investments are subsidized. Moreover, the different incentive structures to be found under private and state regimes of ownership give rise to expectations of lower X-efficiency on the part of Treuhandanstalt's firms than would be the case with a privately owned firm. In comparative-static terms, private rehabilitation regimes are more likely to produce efficiency advantages even when rehabilitation subsidies are used to internalize external effects.

In dynamic terms, the outcome is not so cut and dried. Since privatization is a time- and cost-intensive process, the Treuhandanstalt's decision not to invest in rehabilitation has without doubt been a factor of high costs. Empirical studies show that the decision not to provide funds for rehabilitation has successively weakened the competitiveness of Treuhandanstalt's firms as compared with privately owned and privatized firms. The costs stemming from the decision to refrain from investing in rehabilitation are, however, matched by the very high costs involved when the Treuhandanstalt allocates and monitors funds for investment. The question whether the Treuhandanstalt might have saved a good part of Eastern Germany's production potential if it had chosen a different rehabilitation strategy will thus have to remain an open one.

In all, this study has come to the assessment that the state economic sector has fewer possibilities to efficiently control and manage firms. Efficiency may thus be expected from a privatization of the state economic sector. However, an increase of production efficiency—this is proven not least by the experience made in the course of the transformation process in Eastern Germany—does not necessarily go hand in hand with the achievement of other welfare-economic objectives such as full employment or high rates of economic growth.

Notes

Chapter 2

1   For a definition of the concept of "reform" as opposed to system changes that might be described as a "perfection" of mandatory planning, see Bauer (1987), pp. 12-15.

2   See Kornai (1986), pp. 1687-1737; Kornai (1992), pp. 474-512.

3   The two theoretical solutions, the auctioneer in Walras and so-called "recontracting" in Edgeworth, presupposes that the transaction is only completed when an equilibrium has been reached.

4   See Hayek 1948; 1950; Lavoie 1988; Richter 1992; Murrell 1983; Temkin 1989.

5   See for the dynamic concept of equilibrium of the Austrian school Kirzner 1973; Wegehenkel 1981; Mises 1949.

6   Public choice theory is will not be given any further consideration here.

7   This problem will be dealt with at length in Chapter 3.3.4.

8   On this, see the model of the comparative advantages of private and public rehabilitation regimes developed in Chapters 7 and 8.

Chapter 3

1   The problem involved in the separation of ownership rights and control rights is discussed in section 3.3.3 in connection with privatization via the stock exchange.

2   See Chapter 6.1.2.

3   The problem of the separation of ownership and control will also be addressed in the discussion on privatization on the stock exchange and by means of vouchers (see 3.3.4/3.3.5).

4   Chapter 6.3.1 presents a detailed description of the informal sales procedures as practiced in Eastern Germany.

5   A bidder's reserve price is the maximum prices he is prepared to pay. At this maximum value the bidder is just as well off in the case that he buys an object as in the case that he does not.

6   The contractual problem is discussed at length in Chapter 7.

7   See Chapters 6.2 and 7 on this point.

8   For details, see Chapter 6.5.

9   Auctions sometimes also allow other action parameters. This problem will be addressed below.

10   The second-bid auction is also named after its inventor, William Vickrey.

11   The attribute of symmetry is given when the bidders are not distinguished by discernible features that would permit conclusions on the probability distribution of their bids.

12   In this context "shading" refers to a bid lower than the bidder's reserve price.

13   On this point, see Chapter 3.4.

14   "The directors of such companies (joint stock companies - H.B.), however, being the managers rather of other peoples money than their own, it cannot well be expected, that they should watch over it with the same vigilance with which the partners in private copartnery frequently watch over their own." Smith 1776/1937, 700.

15   On the profitability of Eastern German enterprises, see (Chapter 5).

16   The issue of the distributive justice of different privatization procedures will be discussed in the following chapter.

17   Formally: $U_i (s_i^*, s_{-i}^*) \geq U_i (s_i', s_{-i}^*)$, where U_i is the utility of player i, s_i^* and s_{-i}^* the equilibrium strategy of player i and his fellow-player, and s_i' a deviation from the equilibrium strategy.

18   The following relation holds between discount factor δ and discount rate i (the internal interest rate): $\delta = 1(1+i)$. At an interest rate of i = 0, δ = 1, and for i = 1 (100%), δ = 0.5.

19   Fig. 3.2 presents the effects of different privatization agency discount factors in a bargaining equilibrium on the payoffs of both parties given a constant bidder discount factor of δ_b = 0.9.

Chapter 4

1   "In justice of fairness the original position of equality corresponds to the state of nature in the traditional theory of social contract. This original position is not, of course, thought of as an actual historical state of affairs, much less as a primitive condition of culture. It is understood as a purely hypothetical situation characterized so as to lead to a certain conception of justice." Rawls 1971, 12.

2   See also Chapter 5.3.1.

3   See Chapter 3.4.

4   See Chapter 3.3.3.

5   See Chapter 3.3.1.

6   This is true, for instance, of Eastern Germany, see Chapter 6.

7   See Chapter 3.3.6.

Chapter 5

1   See Chapter 3.2.

2   § 18, para. 1, para. 2 GDR Civil Code, June 19, 1975.

3   The law was adopted on March 7, 1990 (Gbl. DDRI, p. 141), and allowed the foundation of private companies and private investment in enterprises. It transformed "people's property" into a variable holding element that has a status equal to that of private property. The state at the same time relinquished its monopoly in decisions relating to the foundation, organization, and assignment of companies and economic activities

4   Treaty on the Creation of a Monetary, Economic, and Social Union between the Federal Republic of Germany and the German Democratic Republic (the so-called "Staatsvertrag") of May 18, 1990, BGBl. II, p. 537.

5   Art. 1, para. 2, Treaty: "The cornerstone of the economic union is the social market economy as the economic order shared by both parties to the Treaty. It is characterized in particular by private property, competition, free price formation, and, fundamentally, full freedom of movement for labor, capital, goods, and services; this does not rule out legal approval for special forms of property that permit participation of the public sector or other economic institutions, as long as this does not entail discrimination of private legal entities. It makes allowance for the needs of environmental protection." It is here that the Treaty diverges from the economic neutrality of the constitution (Grundgesetz) of the Federal Republic. See. Münch, I.v. (1992), pp. XIII-XXIV, here: p. XVIII.

6   State Treaty, Art. 1, para. 2, Art. 10; Annex I.

7   See State Treaty, Annex II, sect. II and sect. III.

8   State Treaty, Annex III, sect. I and sect. II.

9   Treaty on the German unification between the Federal Republic of Germany and the German Democratic Republic (the so-called "Einigungsvertrag") of August 3, 1990 (BGBl. II, p. 899), Art. 22, 23, 25.

10   Unification Treaty, Art. 26.

11   Unification Treaty, Art. 27.

12   Unification Treaty, Art. 21 - Art. 24.

13   Unification Treaty, Art. 22, para. 4.

14   Gesetz zur Privatisierung und Reorganisation des volkseigenen Vermögens (the so-called Treuhandgesetz - TreuhG, Treuhand Law) of June 17, 1990, GBl. DDR I 23, p. 300.

15   Unification Treaty, Art. 25, para. 1.

16   See § 2, para. 1 and para. 6 TreuhG, joint protocol on guiding principles, A II. 7 StVertr, and Treaty, Art. 25, para. 2.

17   TreuhG, § 8, para. 1, third mark.

18   Unification Treaty, Art. 25, para. 4.

19   § 1, para. 1 and 2, VermG; § 1 para. 1 and § 2, para. 2 c) AnmVO.

20   § 1, para. 6, VermG; § 1, para. 2 a) AnmVO.

21   Point 1, GemErkl., § 1, para. 5 a) AnmVO.

22   § 3, para. 1 VermG. Restitution of property was ruled out only when citizens of the GDR have honestly acquired proprietary or usufructary rights to it (Pt. 3 GemErkl.; § 4 para. 2 VermG), or if the nature of the matter renders restitution impossible (§ 4, para. 1 VermG).

23   § 6b VermG, esp. para. 1 and 2. Deconcentration was ruled out only in cases in which it makes no economic sense, i.e. if it were to lead to the loss of a sizable number of jobs (§ 6, para. 5 VermG).

24   § 3, para. 3 VermG.

25   See Unification Treaty, Art. 41, para. 2; § 1 and § 2 Gesetz über besondere Investitionen; § 3a VermG; § 7, § 19 InvVorG.

26   § 1, para. 1 Gesetz über besondere Investitionen.

27   See PrHBG of March 22; § 3a VermG; InVorG.

28   See Chapter 3.3.6 on this point.

29   See Chapter 2.1.

30   See Table 5.2.

31   See Chapter 2 for a definition of asset specificity.

32   For all flow variables, i.e. current liabilities like wages and salaries, pensions, scholarships, and leases, an exchange rate of one to one was chosen. The stock variables were differentiated for conversion: bank deposits of domestic natural persons born after July 1, 1976, were converted one to one up to an amount of 2,000 DM; this figure was 4,000 DM for persons born between July 2 1931 and July 1, 1976, and up to 6,000 DM for persons born before July 2, 1931. Larger amounts were converted at a rate of 2 to 1, and bank deposits made after December 31, 1989, were converted at a rate of three to one. Claims and liabilities of legal

persons were converted at the rate of two to one. Art. 10, para. 5 und Annex I, Article 6, para. 1 to 3, Vertrag über die Schaffung einer Währungs-, Wirtschafts- und Sozialunion zwischen der Bundesrepublik Deutschland und der Deutschen Demokratischen Republik (Treaty on economic and monetary union) of May 18, 1990, BGBl II, p. 537.

33 The exchange rate for flows entailed fixing an initial level for wages and salares of roughly 39 percent of the Western German level, while labor productivity following conversion was less than 30 percent of the Western German level. See 5.3.1.

34 In December of 1990 Eastern Germany's industry was producing only 45 percent of the volume it produced in 1989. After the First World War, in 1919, industrial production was 57 percent of what it had been in 1913, and in 1932, at the peak of the world economic crisis, German industry achieved 59 percent of its 1928 production levels. See ifo-Institut 1991, 39.

35 All data before the second semester of 1990 are based on calculations of the DIW. See DIW 1992c.

36 See Chapter 5.3.2.

37 See Table 5.3. The DIW had originally estimated that at a conversion rate of one to one labor costs would amount to 37 percent of the wage level in Western Germany (DIW 1990, 221).

38 Gross wage and salary incomes consist of the sum of gross wages and salaries plus the actual and assumed social insurance contributions made by employers; in other words, they are an suitable indicator for effective labor costs.

39 Author's calculations, based on data published by the Statistitisches Bundesamt und the Sachverständigenrat.

40 Author's calculations, based on DIW data on man-hour costs and labor productivity as measured in terms of real GDP per man-hour.

41 Economic and monetary union meant converting business-sector liabilities at a rate of one to one vis-à-vis the banking system, thus nominally cutting by half the interest and amortization burdens.

42 The data thus differ from those in Table 5.2; these indicate the average gross wage and salary sum for all persons employed in Eastern Germany.

43 100 (costs in the benchmark case) + (change in gross wage and salary sum in percent times 0.66) - (change in labor productivity times 0.66) = costs for the earning of 1 DM. $100 + (-11.84 \times 0.66)-(0 \times 0.66) = 92.19$; $1.84 \times 0.9219 = 1.696$.

44 $100 + (24.08 \times 0.66) - (6 \times 0.66) = 111.93$; $1.84 \times 1.1193 = 2.059$.

45 $100 + (51.1 \times 0.66) - (13.6 \times 0.66) = 124.75$; $1.84 \times 1.2475 = 2.2954$.

46 This extrapolation is based on two assumptions, that (1) all firms are equally affected by any change in average costs, and (2) the firms are distributed absolutely uniformly across the cost intervals.

47 Author's calculations, see Table 5.3.

48 Author's calculations, based on the Akerlof projection in Table 5.2.

49 Treuhandanstalt, Zentrales Controlling (March 1992, April 1991, August 1992, and November 1992); author's calculations. See Table 5.4.

50 See Chapter 7 for details.

Chapter 6

1 See Chapter 5.

2 § 1-15, TreuhG, see Chapter 5.1.

3 Treuhandanstalt, Abt. Dokumentation/Datenmanagement (1993).

4 The Deutsche Kreditbank AG is a successor organization of the state banking system of the GDR.

5 As per § 1 Vierte Durchführungsverordnung zum Treuhandgesetz, September 12, 1990, GBl. DDR I, p. 1465, Art. 21, para. 1, Treaty.

6 As per §§ 1 and 2 Zweite Durchführungsverordnung zum Treuhandgesetz, August 22, 1990, GBl. DDR I, p. 1260, Art. 21, para. 1, Treaty.

7 The Statistisches Jahrbuch (statistical yearbook) of the GDR indicated total basic assets of 1,202 GDR marks (at 1986 prices) (Statistisches Jahrbuch der DDR 1989, 107-108, 139). In Western terms, this value corresponds roughly to fixed assets minus real estate.

8 § 25 DMBilG.

9 See Chapter 3.2.

10 The Treuhandanstalt realized effective privatization revenues of 1.6 billion DM in 1990, 9.8 billion DM in 1991 (DIW 1992a, 65), and 7.846 million DM as of Nov. 30, 1992 (Treuhandanstalt, Zentrales Controlling (Nov. 1992), 56).

11 See Chapter 3.2.

12 See Chapter 5.1; preamble and § 2 Gesetz zur Privatisierung und Reorganisation des volkseigenen Vermögens (Treuhandgesetz - TreuhG) of June 17, 1990, GBl. DDR I 300.

Chapter 7

1   See Chapter 6.2.

2   "The vice-president of the Treuhandanstalt (Hero Brahms - H.B.) is (...) of the opinion that enforceability per se is in any case an empty word. The 'binding effect' results instead from the concept. But Brahms also made it clear the Treuhandanstalt is not interested forcing through agreements without consideration of the situation involved." In: Handelsblatt 1992e, 18; see also Handelsblatt 1993a, 4; FAZ 1992e, 15.

3   "The Treuhandanstalt is prepared to compromise in cases of noncompliance, President Birgit Breuel recently confirmed: 'If payment of a penalty means the end of the economic game, the Treuhandanstalt is prepared to discuss extending the guarantees agreed upon so as to safeguard jobs,'" in: Handelsblatt 1993b, 13.

4   For any $i > 0$ and all states of the world $\theta = \{l, h\}$ it is assumed that $b(\bullet)$ and $c(\bullet)$ are twice continuously differentiable and that $b(0) = 0$; $b(i) \leq b^{max}$, $b''(i) < 0$; $b'(0) > c'(0,h)$; $c(i,l) < c(i,h)$; $c'(i,l) < c'(i,h)$; $c''(i,l) \leq c''(i,h)$; $c(0,\theta) = 0$; $c'(i,\theta) > 0$; $c''(i,\theta) \geq 0$.

5   For any $i > 0$ it is assumed that $b(\bullet)$ and $c(\bullet)$ are twice continuously differentiable and that $b(0) = 0$; $b(i) \leq b^{max}$, $b''(i) < 0$; $b'(0) > c'(0,h)$; $c(i,l) < c(i,h)$; $c'(i,l) < c'(i,h)$; $c''(i,l) \leq c''(i,h)$; $c(0,\theta) = 0$; $c'(i,\theta) > 0$; $c''(i,\theta) \geq 0$.

6   For a formal proof see Schmidt 1991, 31-35.

7   "But Brahms also made it clear that the Treuhandanstalt is not interested in enforcing agreements with investors without taking consideration of the existing situation. The agency has no wish to behave like a bookkeeper, but is accessible in individual or difficult cases to talks on postponing commitments to later years." Handelsblatt 1992e, 18.

Chapter 8

1   See Chapter 6.1; § 2, para. 1, 6, Gesetz zur Privatisierung und Reorganisation des volkseigenen Vermögens (Treuhandgesetz - TreuhG) of June 17, 1990, GBl. DDR I 23, 300.

2   This is also proposed by the economic research institutes: "The better concept would be a purely knock-on type of rehabilitation or an approach that might be termed 'quasi-privatization'. (...) The Treuhandanstalt should generally assume the old burdens of all firms currently regarded as capable of rehabilitation and contribute to providing the share of equity capital appropriate to the industry or the size of firm concerned. But the crucial factor is that once this step is taken, the Treuhandanstalt should take on no further obligations and provide no further help whatever. (...) The firms, exposed in this way to the pressure of the market, will

have to act as if they were private enterprises (...)". Gemeinschaftsdiagnose 1992a, 224-225.

3   For any $i > 0$ it is assumed that in the two possible business states $\theta \in \{l,h\}$ the variables $c(\cdot)$ and $b(\cdot)$ are twice continuously differentiable and that: $b(0) = 0$; $b(i) \leq b^{max}$; $b''(i) < 0$; $b'(0) > c'(0, h)$; $c(0, \theta) = 0$; $c'(i,\theta) > 0$; $c''(i, \theta) \geq 0$; $c(i, l) < c(i,h)$; $c'(i,l) < c'(i,h)$; $c''(i,l) \leq c''(i,h)$.

4   Stipulation of a fixed wage w is not relevant for the implementation of an incentive-compatible mechanism; the stipulation of a wage is discussed below in connection with incentive problems.

5   To cede to the Treuhandanstalt manager a higher premium $z'(h) > z(h)$ (or $z'(h) > [b(i^{tha}(h)) - c(i^{tha}(h),h)] \div [b(i^{tha}(l)) + c(i^{tha}(l),h)])$ when the differential of the manager's utility is $\mu(i^{tha}(l)) - \mu(i^{tha}(h)) > z(h)$, would not be rational for the Treuhandanstalt, because in that case the information rent it is forced to cede to its manager would be higher than the benefit associated with revealing truthful information.

6   It is assumed for any $i > 0$ that for all business states $\theta \in \{l,h\}$) $b(i)$ and $c(i, \theta)$ are twice continuously differentiable and that: $b(0) = 0$; $b(i) \leq b^{max}$; $b''(i) < 0$; $b'(i) > (c'(0,h)$; $c(0,\theta) = 0$; $c'(i,\theta) > 0$, $c''(i,\theta) > 0$; $c(i,l) < c(i,h)$; $c'(i,l) < c'(i,h)$; $c''(i,l) \leq c''(i,h)$.

7   It is assumed that $p(a)$ and $\phi(a)$ are twice continuously differentiable and that: $\phi'(0) = 0$; $\phi'(a) \geq 0$; $\phi''(a) > 0$; $0 < p(a) < 1$; $p'(a) > 0$; $p''(a) < 0$; $a \geq 0$. The effort variable a was normalized in such a way that without an incentive the manager's activity level is zero.

8   As defined, the manager's activity level a cannot fall below zero, and thus $a = 0$ for all $z(h) > \mu(i^{tha}[l]) - \mu(i^{tha}[h])$.

9   It is assumed that $p(a^p)$ und $\phi(a^p)$ are twice continuously differentiable and that: $\phi'(0) = 0$; $\phi'(a^p) \geq 0$; $\phi''(a^p) > 0$; $0 < p(a^p) < 1$; $p'(a^p) > 0$; $p''(a^p) < 0$.

10 The same is of course true of the favorable cost conditions, because the manager's nonpecuniary benefits grow as the volume of investment is increased, i.e. $\mu(i^p(l)) > \mu(i^p(h))$, so that the utility stemming from truthful revelation is greater than that stemming from false information in the favorable business state l.

11 It is assumed that $\phi(a^m)$ and $p(a^m)$ are twice continuously differentiable and that: $\phi(0) = 0$; $\phi'(a^m) \geq 0$; $\phi''(a^m) > 0$; $0 < p(a^m) < 1$; $p'(a^m) > 0$; $p''(a^m) < 0$.

12 Treuhandanstalt, Zentrales Controlling 1991a.

13 Of an overall loan volume of 16.362 billion DM made available by Feb. 28, 1993, 7.462 billion DM was used to redeem global sureties within the framework of liquidation funding and 5.893 billion DM was used to reschedule old credits, liquidity credits/fresh money. Of the remaining 3.007 billion DM, 1.626 billion was used for liquidation, 1.150 billion DM was employed as shareholder loans to

finance rehabilitation investments, and 231 million DM was used for other measures. Treuhandanstalt, Zentrales Controlling 1993a.

14 Treuhandanstalt, Zentrales Controlling 1993a.

15 Treuhandanstalt, Zentrales Controlling 1993a.

16 This figure refers to a survey of 163 Treuhandanstalt's firms. Treuhandanstalt/ Zentrales Controlling 1993b, 8.11.

References

Akerlof, G.A. [1970], "The Market for "Lemons", Quality Uncertainty and the Market Mechanism", in: *Quarterly Journal of Economics*, Vol. 84, No. 3, pp. 488-500

Akerlof, G.A. / A.K. Rose / J.L. Yellen / H. Hessenius [1991], "East Germany In From the Cold, The Economic Aftermath of the Currency Union", Discussionpaper for the Presentation of the Brookings Panel on Economic Activity, Washington D.C., 4./5. April 1991, University of California, Berkeley 23. März 1991, published in: *BPEA*, No. 1, pp. 1-106

Alchian, A.A. [1969], "Corporate Management and Property Rights", *Economic Policy and the Regulation of Economic Policy*, ed. Henry G. Manne, Washington D.C.: American Enterprise Institute for Public Policy Research, pp. 337-360

- [1987], "Property Rights", in: *The New Palgrave - A Dictionary of Economics*, 1st edition, eds. Eatwell, John, Murray Milgate, and Peter Newman, London: McMillan, pp. 1030-1034

Alchian, A.A. / H. Demsetz [1972], "Production, Information Costs and Economic Organization", in: *AER*, Vol. 62, No. 5, pp. 777-795

Aleksashenko, S. / L. Grigoriev [1991], "Privatisation and the Capital Market", in: *Communist Economies and Economic Transformation*, Vol. 3, No. 1, pp. 41-56

Antal, L. [1979], "Development - with Some Digression, The Hungarian Economic Mechanism in the Seventies", in: *Acta Oeconomica*, Vol. 23, No. 3-4, pp. 257-273

Apáthy, E. [1991], "Case Study of the Ibusz Privatization", Diskussionspapier für die Konferenz der OECD zur Privatisierung, Pultrusk, August

Arbeitsgruppe Alternative Wirtschaftspolitik [1992], "Gegen den ökonomischen Niedergang - Industriepolitik in Ostdeutschland" (Memorandum 1992), Köln

Arrow, K.J. [1964], "The Role of Securities in the Optimal Allocation of Risk Bearing, in: Revue of Economic Studies", Vol. 31, No. 2, pp. 91-102

- [1969/1983], "The Organization of Economic Activity, Issues Pertinent to the Choice of Market Versus Nonmarket Allocation", in: *The Analysis of Public Expenditure*, ed. Joint Economic Committee, The PPB System 91st Congress, 1st Session, Vol. 1, Washington D.C., pp. 47-67, quotet after the version in: *Public Expenditure and Policy Analysis*, eds. Havemann, Robert H. and Julius Marglois, 3rd edition, Boston et al. 1983, pp. 42-55

- [1973], "Some Ordinal-Utalitarian Notes on Rawls' Theory of Justice", in: *The Journal of Philosophy*, Vol. 70, pp. 245-263

- [1978], "The Property Rights Doctrine and Demand Revelation under Incomplete Information", in: *Economics and Human Welfare*, ed. Michael J. Boskin, New York et al. 1978, pp. 23-39

- [1985], "Agency and the Market", in: *Agency, The Structure of Business*, eds. Richard Zeckhauser and John W. Pratt, Cambridge/Mass., quoted after the version of *Handbook of Mathematical Economics, Vol. III*, eds. Kenneth J. Arow and Michael D. Intriligator, Amsterdam et al. 1986, pp. 1183-1195.

- [1991], "Economic Theory and the Hypothesis of Rationality", in: *The New Palgrave - A Dictionary of Economics*, 3rd edition, eds. Eatwell, John, Murray Milgate, and Peter Newman, London: McMillan, pp. 198-211

Arrow, K.J. / L. Hurwicz [1960], "Decentralization and Computation in Resource Allocation", in: *Essays in Economics and Econometrics*, ed. Ralph W. Pfouts, Chapel Hill

Ashby, W.R. [1960], *Design for a Brain:* New York

Åslund, A. / Ö. Sjöberg [1992], "Privatisation and Transition to a Market Economy in Albania", in: *Communist Economies and Economic Transformation*, Vol. 4, No. 1, pp. 135-150

Ausubel, L.M. / R.J. Deneckere [1989], "A Direct Mechanism Characterization of Sequential Bargaining with One-Sided Incomplete Information", in: *Journal of Economic Theory*, Vol. 48, No. 1, pp. 18-46

Baltensperger, E. / T.M. Devinney [1985], "Credit Rationing Theory, A Survey and Synthesis", in: *ZfS*, Vol. 141, pp. 475-502

Barone, E. [1908/1935], "The Ministry of Production and the Collectivist State", in: *Collectivist Economic Planning*, ed. Friedrich A. Hayek, London 1935, pp. 245-290 (Original: "Il Ministro della Produzzione nelle Stato Colletivista", in: *Giornalo degli Economista* 1908)

Barro, R.J. / X. Sala-I-Martin [1991], "Convergence across States and Regions", in: *BPEA*, No. 1, pp. 107-182

Bauer, T. [1976], "The Contradictory Position of the Enterprise under the New Hungarian Economic Mechanism", in: *Co-Existence*, Vol. 13, No. 1, pp. 65-80

- **[1983]**, "The Hungarian Alternative to Soviet-Type Planning", in: *Journal of Comparative Economics*, Vol. 7, No. 3, pp. 304-316

- **[1984]**, "The Second Economic Reform and Ownership Relations. Some Consideration of the New Economic Mechanism", in: *Eastern European Economics*, Vol. 22, No. 3-4, pp. 33-87 (Original: "A második gazdasági reform és a tulajdonviszonyok, Szempontok az új gazdasági mechanizmus tevábbfejlesztéséhez", in: *Mozgó Világ, Budapest*, Vol. 8 [1982], No. 11, pp. 17-42)

- **[1987]**, "Perfecting or Reforming the Economic Mechanism?", in: *Eastern European Economics*, Vol., No. 4, pp. 5-34 (Original: "A gazdasági mechanizmus továbbfejlesztése vagy reformja?", in: *Közgazdasági Szemle*, Vol. 34 [1987], No. 5, pp. 527-546)

- **[1991]**, "The Microeconomics of Inflation Under Economic Reforms, Enterprises and Their Environment", in: ed. Simon Commander, *Managing Inflation in Socialist Economies in Transition*, Washington D.C.: Economic Development Institute of the World Bank, pp. 107-119

- **[1992]**, "Building Capitalism in Hungary", in: *The Transformation of Socialist Economies*, ed. Horst Siebert, Tübingen 1992, pp. 287-303

Baumol, W.J. [1952], *Welfare Economics and the Theory of the State*, Cambridge/Mass.

- [1982], "Contestable Markets, An Uprising in the Theory of Industry Structure", in: *AER*, Vol. 72, No. 1, pp. 1-15

Baumol, W.J. / J.C. Panzar / R.D. Willig [1982], *Contestable Markets and the Theory of Industry Structure*, San Diego

Bellinger, B. / G. Vahl [1984], *Unternehmensbewertung in Theorie und Praxis*, Wiesbaden, pp. 128-129

Ben-Ner, A. / E. Neuberger, [1988], "Towards an Economic Theory of the Firm in the Centrally Planned Economy", in: JITE, Vol. 144, No. 5, pp. 839-848

Berle, A.A. / G.C. Means, [1932], *The Modern Corporation and Private Property*, New York

Beschluß zur Gründung der Anstalt zur treuhänderischen Verwaltung des Volkseigentums [Treuhandanstalt] vom 1. 3. 1990, *GBl. DDR I,* p. 107

Börsig, C. [1993], Unternehmenswert und Unternehmensbewertung, in: zfbf, Vol. 45, No. 1, pp. 79-91

Boycko, M. / A. Shleifer / R.W. Vishny [1995], Privatizing Russia, Cambridge/Mass.

Bromley, D. [1989], Economic Interests and Institutions, The Conceptual Foundations of Public Policy, New York

Brücker, H. [1990], "Neuer deutscher Nationalismus und die Metaphysik des Wirtschaftswunders", in: *Neue Gesellschaft/Frankfurter Hefte,* Vol. 37, No. 4, pp. 314-324

- [1995], *Privatisierung in Ostdeutschland. Eine institutionenökonomische Analyse,* Frankfurt/New York: Campus

Buchanan, J. [1972], "Rawls on Justice as Fairness", in: *Public Choice,* Vol. 13, pp. 123-128

Buchanan, J. / W.C. Strubblebine [1962], "Externality", in: *Economica,* Vol. 29, No. 116, pp. 371-384

Bundesminister der Finanzen [1990], *Verhältnis der Treuhandanstalt zum Bundeshaushalt*, Erklärung, Bonn, 10/26/1990.

- **[1991]**, *Ein Jahr Tätigkeit der Treuhandanstalt*, Report, Bonn, 10/29/1991.

Carrington, S. [1992], "The Remonetarization of the Commonwealth of Independent States", in: *AER*, Vol. 82, No. 2, pp. 22-26

Cassel, D. [1987], "Inflation und Inflationswirkungen in Planwirtschaften", in: Geldtheorie, ed. H.J. Thieme, 2nd edition, pp. 263-294

Chandler, A.D., Jr. [1962], *Strategy and Structure*, Cambridge/Mass.

- **[1977]**, *The Visible Hand, The Managerial Revolution in American Business*, Cambridge/Mass.

Charap, J. / K. Dyba / M. Kupka [1992], "The Reform Process in Czechoslovakia, an Assessment of Recent Developments and Prospects for the Future", in: *Communist Economies and Economic Transformation*, Vol. 4, No. 1, pp. 3-22

Christ, P. / R. Neubauer [1991], *Kolonie im eigenen Land. Die Treuhand, Bonn und die Wirtschaftskatastrophe der fünf neuen Länder*, Berlin 1991

Coase, R.H. [1937], "The Nature of the Firm", in: *Economica*, Vol. 4, No. 12, pp. 386-405.

- **[1960]**, "The Problem of Social Cost", in: *Journal of Law and Economics*, Vol. 3, pp. 1-44

Coenenberg, A.G. [1984], "Entscheidungsorientierte Unternehmensbewertung und 'Ertragsschwäche'" in: *Betriebswirtschaftliche Forschung und Praxis*, No. 6, p. 496

Cooter, R.D. [1991], "Coase Theorem", in: *The New Palgrave - A Dictionary of Economics*, 3rd edition, eds. Eatwell, John, Murray Milgate, and Peter Newman, London: McMillan, pp. 51-57

Dabrowski, M. [1991], "Privatisation in Poland", in: *Communist Economies and Economic Transformation*, Vol. 3, No. 3, pp. 317-325

Dasgupta, P. / P. Hammond / E.S. Maskin [1979], "The Implementation of Social Choice Rule", in: *Review of Economic Studies*, Vol. 46, pp. 185-216

Davis, L. / D.C. North [1971], *Institutional Change and American Economic Growth*, Cambridge (Engl.) 1971

DeAlessi, L. [1980], "The Economics of Property Rights, A Review of Evidence", in: *Research in Law and Economics*, Vol. 2, No. 1, pp. 1-47

- **[1982]**, "On the Nature and Consequences of Private and Public Enterprises", in: *Minnessota Law Review*, Vol. 7, pp. 191-209

- **[1983]**, "Property Rights, Transaction Costs, and X-Efficiency, An Essay on Economic Theory", *AER*, Vol. 73, No. 1, pp. 64-81

Delhaes, K.v. [1992], "Privatisierung in Polen, Konzeptionen und Realität", in: *Privatisierungskonzepte im Systemwandel*, ed. Helmut Leipold, Marburg: Arbeitsberichte zum Systemvergleich der Philipps-Universität, No. 16, Juni 1992, pp. 39-75

Demsetz, H. / K. Lehn [1985], "The Structure of Corporate Ownership, Causes and Consequences", in: *Journal of Political Economy*, Vol. 93, No. 6, pp. 1155-1177

Dembinski, P.H. [1988], "Quantity versus Allocation of Money, Monetary Problems of Centrally Planned Economics Reconsidered", in: *Kyklos*, Vol. 41, No. 2, pp. 281-300

Demsetz, H. [1964], "Toward A Theory of Property Rights", in: *The Economics of Property Rights*, ed. Eirik G. Furubotn and Svetozar Pejovich, Cambridge/Mass. 1974, pp. 31-42 (Original in: *AER*, Vol. 57 (1967), No. 2, pp. 347-359)

- **[1964]**, "The Exchange and Enforcement of Property Rights", in: *Journal of Law and Economics*, Vol. 7, pp. 11-27

- **[1966]**, "Some Aspects of Property Rights", in: *Journal of Law and Economics*, Vol. 9, pp. 61-70

- **[1969]**, "Information and Efficency, Another Viewpoint", in: *Journal of Law and Economics*, Vol. 12, pp. 1-22

Der Spiegel [1991a], "Mischung zwischen Marx und Mafia", Vol. 45, No. 37, pp. 122-127

- **[1991b]**, "Außer Kontrolle", Vol. 45, No. 50, pp. 135-136

DIW [1990], "Quantitative Aspekte einer Reform von Wirtschaft und Finanzen in der DDR", in: *DIW-Wochenbericht*, Vol. 57, No. 17, pp. 221-245

- **[1991a]**, "Subventionierung und Privatisierung durch die Treuhandanstalt, Kurswechsel erforderlich", in: *DIW-Wochenbericht*, Vol. 58, No. 41, pp. 575-579

- **[1991b]**, "Zur Entwicklung des Produktionspotentials in Ostdeutschland", in: *DIW-Wochenbericht*, Vol. 58, No. 47, pp. 663-668

- **[1992a]**, "Zur Politik der Treuhandanstalt - Eine Zwischenbilanz", in: *DIW-Wochenbericht*, Vol. 59, No. 7, pp. 63-67

- **[1992b]**, "Arbeitsmärkte in Deutschland im Zeichen konjunktureller Schwäche", in: *DIW-Wochenbericht*, Vol. 59, No. 41, pp. 509-514

- **[1992c]**, "Ausgeprägte gesamtwirtschaftliche Verlangsamung", in: *DIW-Wochenbericht*, Vol. 59, No. 47, pp. 623-633

- **[1992d]**, "Strukturwandel im Prozeß der deutschen Vereinigung", in: *DIW-Wochenbericht*, Vol. 59, No. 48, pp. 641-652

DIW / IfW [1991a], "Gesamtwirtschaftliche und unternehmerische Anpassungsprozesse in Ostdeutschland", 3rd report, in: *DIW-Wochenbericht*, Vol. 58, No. 39-40, pp. 557-562

- / - **[1991b]**, "Gesamtwirtschaftliche und unternehmerische Anpassungsprozesse in Ostdeutschland", 4th report, in: *DIW-Wochenbericht*, Vol. 58, No. 51-52, pp. 716-718

- / - [1992a], "Gesamtwirtschaftliche und unternehmerische Anpassungsprozesse in Ostdeutschland", 7th report, in: *DIW-Wochenbericht*, Vol. 59, No.
52, p. 718

- / - [1993], "Gesamtwirtschaftliche und unternehmerische Anpassungsprozesse
in Ostdeutschland", 8th report, in: *DIW-Wochenbericht*, Vol. 60, No. 13,
pp. 131-157

Dluhosch, B. [1991], "Privatisierung in den neuen Bundesländern, Reaktionen
der Kapital- und Gütermärkte", in: *Wirtschaftsdienst*, Vol. 71, No. 8, pp.
416-422

Dornbusch, R. / H. Wolf [1992], "Economic Transition in Eastern Germany",
in: *BPEA*, No. 1, pp. 235-272

Dryll, I. [1989], "Forum przyszlych wlasciceli", in: *Zycie Gospodarcze*, No.
47, 11/19/ 1989, p. 3

Eggertsson, T. [1990], *Economic Behaviour and Institutions*, Cambridge/
Mass.

Einführungsgesetz zum Aktiengesetz [EGAktG] vom 6. September 1965,
BGBl. I, p. 1185

Engeleiter, H.J. [1970], *Unternehmensbewertung*, Stuttgart

Estrin, S. [1991], "Privatisation, Self-management and Social Ownership", in:
Communist Economies and Economic Transformation, Vol. 3, No. 3, pp.
355-366

Eucken, W. [1940/65], *Die Grundlagen der Nationalökonomie*, 8th edition,
Berlin et al. 1965 (1st edition 1940)

- [1952/75], *Grundsätze der Wirtschaftspolitik*, Tübingen, 5th edition, 1975
(1st edition 1952)

Fama, E.F. [1983], "Agency Problems and Residual Claims", in: *Journal of
Law and Economics*, Vol. 26, No. 2, pp. 327-349

Fama, E.F. / M.C. Jensen [1983], "Separation of Ownership and Control", in: *Journal of Law and Economics*, Vol. 26, No. 2, pp. 301-325

Farrell, J. [1987], "Information and the Coase-Theorem", in: *Journal of Economic Perspectives*, Vol. 1, No. 2, pp. 113-129

Feess-Dörr, E. [1991], *Mikroökonomie, Eine Einführung in die neoklassische und klassisch-ricardianische Preis- und Verteilungstheorie*, Marburg: Metropolis

Feldstein, M. / S. Horioka [1980], "Domestic Saving and International Capital Flows", in: *Economic Journal*, Vol. 90, pp. 314-329

Filip-Köhn, R. / U. Ludwig [1990], Dimensionen eines Ausgleichs des Wirtschaftsgefälles zur DDR, *DIW-Discussionpaper*, No. 3, Berlin: Deutsches Institut für Wirtschaftsforschung

Fischer, W. / H. Schröter [1993], Die Entstehung der Treuhandanstalt, in: *Treuhandanstalt. Das Unmögliche wagen*, eds. Fischer, Wolfram, Herbert Hax, and Hans K. Schneider, Berlin: Akademie

Fischer, W. / H. Hax / H.K. Schneider [1993], *Treuhandanstalt. Das Unmögliche wagen*, Berlin: Akademie

Frankfurter Institut für Wirtschaftspolitische Forschung e.V. (Kronberger Kreis) [1990], *Soziale Marktwirtschaft in der DDR, Wähungsordnung und Investitionsbedingungen*, Frankfurt a.M.: Schriftenreihe Band 20, January 1990

Frank, G. [1993], "Wirkungsanalyse der Subventionen für Investitionen in den neuen Bundesländern", in: *ZfB*, Vol. 63, No. 2, pp. 121-128

Frankfurter Allgemeine Zeitung (FAZ) [1990a], "Treuhandanstalt soll eine neue Organisation erhalten", No. 194, 8/22/1990, p. 13

- [1990b], "Die Treuhandanstalt wird neu organisiert", No. 201, 8/30/1990, pp. 13-14

- [1990c], "Rohwedder, Das Treuhandgesetz muß geändert werden", No. 278, 11/29/1990, p. 14

- [1991a], "Die Treuhand hat jetzt ihre endgültige Organisationsstruktur", No. 10, 1/12/1991, p. 12

- [1992a], "Treuhand soll mehr Kredit aufnehmen dürfen", No. 69, 3/21/1992, p. 11

- [1992b], "Erste Management KG der Treuhand steht kurz vor der Gründung", No. 83, 4/7/1992, p. 16

- [1992c], "Beanstandungen im Einzelfall nachgehen", No. 133, 6/10/1992, p. 16

- [1992d], "Treuhand benötigt bis zu 130 Milliarden DM", No. 226, 9/28/1992, p. 20

- [1993a], "Bisher hat die Mehrheit der Investoren die Vereinbarungen erfüllt", No. 142, 6/23/1993, p. 15

- [1993b], "Die Treuhand nimmt fast dreißig privatisierte Betriebe zurück", No. 165, 7/20/1993, p. 15

- [1993c], "Ermittlungen gegen Sachsenmilch ausgeweitet", No. 171, 7/27/1993, p. 14

Frankfurter Rundschau [1992], "Viele Ost-Investoren halten Zusagen nicht ein", No. 250, 10/27/1992, p. 9

Fromme, F.K. [1993], "Etwa 1,15 Millionen Anträge auf Klärung von Eigentumsverhältnissen", in: *Frankfurter Allgemeine Zeitung (FAZ)*, No. 100, 4/30/1993, p. 3

Fudenberg, D. / J. Tirole [1992], *Game-Theory*, Cambridge/Mass. et al., 2nd edition (1st edition 1991)

Furubotn, E.G. / R. Richter [1991], "The New Institutional Economics, An Assessment", in: *The New Institutional Economics, a Collection of Articles from the Journal of Institutional and Theoretical Economics*, eds. Furubotn, Eirik G. and Rudolf Richter, Tübingen: Mohr, pp. 1-32

Furubotn, E.G. / S. Pejovich [1972], "Property Rights and Economic Theory, A Survey of Recent Literature", in: *JEL*, Vol. 10, No. 4, pp. 1137-1162

Ganske, J. [1991], "Spaltung der Treuhandunternehmen", in: *DB*, Vol. 44, No. 15, pp. 791-797

Gemeinsame Erklärung der Regierungen der Bundesrepublik Deutschland und der Deutschen Demokratischen Republik zur Regelung offener Vermögensfragen [Gemeinsame Erklärung - GemErkl.] vom 15. Juni 1990, Anlage III, EVertr, *BGBl. II*, p. 889

Gemeinschaftsdiagnose [1991], "Die Lage der Weltwirtschaft und der deutschen Wirtschaft im Herbst 1991", in: *DIW-Wochenbericht*, Vol. 58, No. 42-43, pp. 587-622

- **[1992]**, "Die Lage der Weltwirtschaft und der deutschen Wirtschaft im Herbst 1992", Berlin: 22. Oktober 1992

- **[1994]**, "Die Lage der Weltwirtschaft und der deutschen Wirtschaft im Herbst 1994", Berlin: 27. Oktober 1994

- **[1995]**, "Die Lage der Weltwirtschaft und der deutschen Wirtschaft im Frühjahr 1995", in: *DIW-Wochenbericht*, Vol. 62, No. 15-16, pp. 299-326

Gesetz über besondere Investitionen in der Deutschen Demokratischen Republik vom 23. 9. 1990, Anl. II Kap. III Sachgeb. B Abschn. I No. 4 EVertr, *BGBL. II*, p. 1157

Gesetz über den Vorrang für Investitionen bei Rückübertragungsansprüchen nach dem Vermögensgesetz [Investitionsvorranggesetz - InVorG] vom 14.7.1992, BGBl. I p. 1268

Gesetz über die Eröffnungsbilanz in Deutscher Mark und die Kapitalneufestsetzung [D-Markbilanzgesetz - DMBilG], in der Fassung der Bekanntmachung vom 18. April 1991, *BGBl. I*, p. 971

Gesetz über die Spaltung der von der Treuhandanstalt verwalteten Unternehmen [Spaltungsgesetz - SpTRUG] vom 5. April 1991, *BGBl.*, p. 854

Gesetz zur Änderung des Vermögensgesetzes und anderer Vorschriften [Zweites Vermögensrechtsänderungsgesetz - 2. VermRÄndG] vom 14. Juli 1992, *BGBl. I,* p. 1257

Gesetz zur Beseitigung von Hemmnissen bei der Privatisierung von Unternehmen und zur Förderung von Investitionen [Hemmnisbeseitigungsgesetz - PrHBG] vom 22. März 1991, *BGBl. I*, p. 766

Gesetz zur Privatisierung und Reorganisation des volkseigenen Vermögens [Treuhandgesetz - TreuhG] vom 17. Juni 1990, *GBl. DDR,* I 23, p. 300

Gesetz zur Regelung offener Vermögensfragen [Vermögensgesetz - VermG] vom 23. September 1990, *EVertr, Anl. II, Kap. III, Sachgeb. B Abschn. I No. 5*

Gomulka, S. [1985/86], "Kornai's Soft Budget Constraint and the Shortage Phenomenon, A Criticism and Restatement", in: *Economics of Planing,* Vol. 19, No. 1; quoted after the version in: *Growth, Innovation and Efficiency,* ed. Gomulka, Stanislav, London 1986, pp. 73-90

Götz-Coenenberg, R. [1990], "Währungsunion in Deutschland, Alternativen und Konsequenzen", in: *Berichte des Bundesinstitutes für ostwissenschaftliche und internationale Studien [BIOST],* No. 20

Gresik, T.A. / M.A. Satterthwaite [1989], "The Rate at Which a Simple Market Converges to Efficiency as the Number of Traders Increases, An Asymptotic Result for Optimal Trading Mechanisms", in: *Journal of Economic Theory,* Vol. 48, No. 1, pp. 304-322

Grossmann, S.J. / O.D. Hart [1980], "Takeover Bids, the Free-Rider-Problem and the Theory of the Corporation", in: *Bell Journal of Economics,* Vol. 11, pp. 42-64

- / - [1986], "The Costs and Benefits of Ownership, A Theory of Vertical and Lateral Integration", in: *Journal of Political Economy,* Vol. 94, No. 4, pp. 691-719

Habermas, J. [1971], *Legitimationsprobleme im Spätkapitalismus,* Frankfurt a.M.: Suhrkamp

- **[1992]**, *Faktizität und Geltung. Beiträge zur Diskurstheorie des Rechts und des demokratischen Rechtsstaats*, Frankfurt a.M.: Suhrkamp

Hagemann, H. / H.D. Kurz / W. Schäfer (eds.) [1981], *Die Neue Makroökonomik. Marktungleichgewicht, Rationierung und Beschäftigung*, Frankfurt a.M.: Campus

Hahn, F. [1982], "Stability", in: *Handbook of Mathematical Economics*, eds. Arrow, Kenneth J. and Michael D. Intrilligator, Amsterdam et al.: North-Holland, pp. 745-793

- **[1984]**, "On the Notion of Equilibrium in Economics", in: Hahn, Frank, *Equilibrium and Macroeconomics*, Oxford, pp. 43-71

Hallenberger, R. [1993], *Die Theorie und Praxis der Unternehmensbewertung in den neuen Bundesländern*, Diplom-thesis, Frankfurt a.M.: Johann Wolfgang Goethe-Universität

Handelsblatt [1990a], "Diskussion um Zwischeninstanz", No. 167, 8/30/1990, p. 1

- **[1992a]**, "Prognose über Treuhand-Schulden von 250 Mrd. DM bis 1994 'ist realistisch'", No. 25, 2/5/1992, p. 3

- **[1992b]**, "Allzu üppige Versorgung der Führungskräfte gerügt", No. 85, 5/4/1992, p. 4

- **[1992c]**, "Altersversorgung und Bonussystem erneut kritisiert", No. 108, 6/5-6/1992, p. 8

- **[1992d]**, "Odewald, Privatisierung Ende 1993 abgeschlossen", No. 116, 6/28-29/1992, p. 16

- **[1992e]**, "Brahms, 'Die Behörde wird sich nicht wie ein Buchhalter verhalten'", No. 208, 10/27/1992, p. 18

- **[1992f]**, "Die meisten Investoren halten Zusagen ein", No. 250, 10/27/1992, p. 15

- **[1992g]**, "Rechnungshof mahnt gründliche Revision an", No. 244, 12/17/1992, p. 6

- **[1993a]**, "Privatisierte Betriebe werden nicht zurückgenommen", No. 51, 3/15/1993, p. 4

- **[1993b]**, "In besonderen Fällen nimmt die Treuhand auch Firmen zurück", No. 94, 5/17/1993, p. 13

- **[1993c]**, "Brahms, Investoren halten Zusagen ein", No. 118, 6/23/1993, p. 7.

- **[1993d]**, "Sequester Derra, Gesamtvollstreckung nicht Ursache für Südmilchvergleich", No. 144, 7/29/1993, p. 13

- **[1993e]**, "Sequester Derra hält Fortführung für gesichert", No. 150, 8/6-7/1993, p. 15

Hankiss, E. **[1989]**, *Kelet-euópai alternatívák* (Alternatives for Eastern Europe), Budapest

Hare, P. **[1989]**, "The Economics of Shortage in the Centrally Planned Economies", in: *Models of Disequilibrium and Shortage in Cantrally Planned Economies,* eds. Charamza, W. and C. Davis, Chapmann Hall 1989, pp. 49-81

Harsanyi, J.C. **[1956]**, "Approaches to the Bargaining Problem Before and After the Theory of Games, A Critical Discussion of Zeuthen's, Hicks', and Nash's Theories", in: *Econometrica,* Vol. 24, No. 2, pp. 144-157

- **[1991]**, "Bargaining", in: *The New Palgrave - A Dictionary of Economics,* 3rd edition, eds. Eatwell, John, Murray Milgate, and Peter Newman, London: McMillan, pp. 190-195

Härtel, H.-H. / R. Krüger / J. Seeler / M. Weinhold [1992], *Institutionelle Ursachen von Wettbewerbsverzerrungen in den neuen Bundesländern,* Hamburg: HWWA-Report No. 92

Hax, H. [1992], "Privatization Agencies, The Treuhand Approach", in: *Privatization, Symposium in Honor of Herbert Giersch,* ed. Horst Siebert, Tübingen: Mohr, pp. 143-155

Hayek, F.A. v. [1977], *Law, Legislation and Liberty. A new Statement of the Liberal Principles of Justice and Politicial Economy.* Vol. 1, Rules and Order, London-Henley

- **[1935/50]**, "The Present State of the Debate", in: *Collectivist Economic Planning*, ed. Hayek, Friedrich A. v., 4th edition, London 1950 (1st edition 1935), pp. 201-243

- **[1940/48]**, "Socialist Calculation, The Competitive 'Solution'", in: *Economica*, Vol. 7, No. 26, pp. 125-149; quoted after the version of Hayek, Friedrich A. v., *Individualism and Economic Order*, Chicago 1948, pp. 181-208

- **[1944/82]**, *The Road to Serfdom*, 1st edition London, quotet after the German version: *Der Weg zur Knechtschaft*, Landsberg am Lech 1982

- **[1945]**, "The Use of Knowledge in Society", in: *AER*, Vol. 35, No. 4, pp. 519-530

- **[1969]**, "Der Wettbewerb als Entdeckungsverfahren", in: Hayek, Friedrich A. v., *Freiburger Studien*, Tübingen 1969

Hinds, M. [1991], "Issues in the Introduction of Market Forces in Eastern European Socialist Economies", in: *Managing Inflation in Socialist Economies in Transition*, ed. Commander, Simon, Washington D.C.: Economic Development Institute of the World Bank, pp. 121-153

Hodjera, Z. [1991], "Privatisation in Eastern Europe, Problems and Issues", in: *Communist Economies and Economic Transformation*, Vol. 3, No. 3, pp. 269-282

Höffe, O. [1977], "Kritische Einführung in Rawls' Theorie der Gerechtigkeit", in: *Über John Rawls' Theorie der Gerechtigkeit*, ed. Otfried Höffe, Frankfurt a.M.: Suhrkamp

Hoffmann, L. [1991], "Preise, Politik und Prioritäten", in: *Frankfurter Allgemeine Zeitung (FAZ)*, No. 28, 2/2/1991, p. 13

Hoffmann, R. [1992], "Die erste Ost-Aktie dient der Finanzierung eines Milchwerks auf der grünen Wiese", in: *Handelsblatt*, No. 66, 4/2/1992, p. B5

Hohmeister, F.U. [1992], "Handlungsbefugnisse der Treuhandanstalt und Rechtsschutzmöglichkeiten Betroffener", in: *BB*, No. 5, pp. 285-290

Holler, M. / G. Illing [1993], *Einführung in die Spieltheorie*, 2nd edition, Berlin et al.: Springer

Holmstrom, B.R. / J. Tirole [1989], "The Theory of the Firm", in: *Handbook of Industrial Organization*, Vol. 1, eds. Schmalensee, Richard and Robert D. Willig, Amsterdam et al.: North-Holland 1989, pp. 63-133

Holt, C.A. [1979], "Uncertainty and the Bidding for Incentive Contracts", *AER*, Vol. 69, No. 4, pp. 433-445

Hurwicz, L. [1973], "The Design Mechanims for Resource Allocation", in: *AER*, Vol. 63, No. 2, pp. 1-30

ifo-Institut [1991], "Tiefer Produktionseinbruch in der ostdeutschen Industrie", in: *ifo-schnelldienst*, No. 16-17, pp. 39-45

IG-Metall [1991], *Zur solidarischen Finanzierung der sozialen Einigung*, Frankfurt a.M.: Schriftenreihe der IG-Metall No. 128, October

Institut der deutschen Wirtschaft (IW) [1990], *Möglichkeiten der breiten Streuung des volkseigenen Vermögens in der DDR im Zusammenhang mit seiner Privatisierung*, Köln: Gutachten für das Bundesministerium für Arbeit und Sozialordnung, June

Institut der Wirtschaftsprüfer in Deutschland (IDW) [1991], "Einzelfragen zum D-Markbilanzgesetz", in: *Fachnachrichten des IDW*, No. 6, p. 182

Institut der Wirtschaftsprüfer in Deutschland (IDW) [1992], *Wirtschaftsprüferhandbuch 1992.*

Institut für Angewandte Wirtschaftsforschung (IAW) [1990], *Die ostdeutsche Wirtschaft 1990/91*, Berlin: Gutachten, October 22.

- (IAW) [1991], *Privatisierung in den neuen Bundesländern - Bestandsaufnahme und Perspektive*, Berlin: IAW-Forschungsreihe No. 14/91

International Bank for Reconstruction and Development [1991], *The Transformation of Economies in Central and Eastern Europe, Issues, Progress, and Prospects*, Manuscript, Washington D.C.: The World Bank

International Monetary Fund/International Bank for Reconstruction and Development/Organization for Economic Co-operation and Development/European Bank for Reconstruction and Development [1991], *The Economy of the USSR. A Study Undertaken in Response to a Request by the Houston Summit*, Paris: OECD

Jacob, H. [1981], "Investitionsrechnung", in: Jacob, Herbert: *Allgemeine Betriebswirtschaftslehre - Handbuch für Studium und Prüfung*, 4th edition, Wiesbaden: Gabler, p. 710

Jasinski, P. [1992], "Transfer and Redefinition of Property Rights", in: *Communist Economies and Economic Transformation*, Vol. 4, No. 2, pp. 163-190

Jensen, M.C. [1986], "Agency Costs and the Free Cash Flow, Corporate Finance and Takeovers", in: *AER*, Vol. 76, pp. 323-329

Jensen, M.C. / W.F. Meckling [1976], "Theory of the Firm, Managerial Behaviour, Agency Costs and Capital Structure", in: *Journal of Financial Economics*, Vol. 3, pp. 305-360

Kachel, P. [1994], "Treuhandutnersuchungsausschuß und Bundesrechnungshof, Auf der Suche nach Treuhand-Altlasten", in: *Wirtschaftsbulletin Ostdeutschland*, Vol. 4, No. 4, pp. 38-42

Käfer, K. [1969], "Substanz und Ertrag bei der Unternehmensbewertung", in: *Betriebswirtschaftliche Information, Entscheidung, Kontrolle*, Wiesbaden: Gabler

Kaulmann, T. [1987], *Property rights und Unternehmenstheorie, Stand und Weiterentwicklung der empirischen Forschung*, München 1987

Kawalec, S. **[1989]**, Privatisation of the Polish Economy, in: *Communist Economies*, Vol. 1, No. 3, pp. 241-256

Kerber, M.C. / W. Stechow [1991], "Die Treuhandanstalt im Spannungsverhältnis zwischen öffentlichem und privatem Recht", in: *DWiR*, Vol. 1, No. 2, pp. 49-52

Kern, H. / C. Sabel [1993], "Die Treuhandanstalt, Experimentierfeld für neue Unternehmensformen", in: eds. Fischer, Wolfram, Herbert Hax, and Hans K. Schneider, *Treuhandanstalt. Das Unmögliche wagen*, Berlin: Akademie 1993, pp. 481-504

Kirzner, I. [1973], *Competition and Entrepreneurship*, Chicago 1973

- **[1984]**, "Economic Planning and the Knowledge Problem", in: *Cato Journal*, Vol. 4, No. 3, pp. 407-418

Kiss, K. [1991], "Privatisation in Hungary", in: *Communist Economies and Economic Transformation*, Vol. 3, No. 3, pp. 305-316

Klein, B. / R.G. Crawford / A.A. Alchian [1978], "Vertical Integration, Appropriatable Rents, and the Competitive Contracting Process", in: *Journal of Law and Economics*, Vol. 21, No. 2, pp. 297-326

Kloepfer, M. [1993], "Öffentlich-rechtliche Vorgaben für die Treuhandanstalt", in: *Treuhandanstalt. Das Unmögliche wagen*, eds. Fischer, Wolfram, Herbert Hax, and Hans K. Schneider, Berlin: Akademie, pp. 41-84

Knüpfer, W. [1990], "Wandlungen der Eigentumsverhältnisse durch die neue Wirtschaftsgesetzgebung in der DDR", in: *BB*, Appendix 20/No. 15, pp. 1-5

Konrad, G. / I. Szelenyi [1981] *Die Intelligenz auf dem Weg zur Klassenmacht*, Frankfurt a.M.: Suhrkamp

Koopmanns, T.C. [1957], *Three Essays on the State of Economic Science*, New York

Kornai, J. [1975], *Anti-Äquilibrium, Über die Theorien der Wirtschaftssysteme und die damit verbundenen Forschungsaufgaben*, Berlin et al.: Springer

- **[1980]**, *Economics of Shortage*, Amsterdam et al.: North-Holland

- **[1986a]**, "The Soft Budget Constraint", in: *Kyklos*, Vol. 39, No. 1, pp. 3-30

- **[1986b]**, "The Hungarian Reform Process, Visions, Hopes, and Reality", in: *JEL*, Vol. 24, No. 4, pp. 1687-1737

- **[1990]**, *The Road to a Free Economy. Shifting from a Socialist System, The Example of Hungary*, New York/ London: McMillan

- **[1991]**, "The Principles of Privatization in Eastern Europe", Discussionpaper No. 1567, Cambridge/Mass.: Harvard University, September

- **[1992]**, *The Socialist System. The Political Economy of Communism*, Princeton (New Jersey): Princeton University Press

Kosta, J. [1984], *Wirtschaftssysteme des realen Sozialismus*, Köln: Bund

Kühl, J. / R. Schaefer / J. Wahse [1992], "Beschäftigungsperspektiven von Treuhandunternehmen und Ex-Treuhandunternehmen im Oktober 1991", in: *MittAB*, Vol. 25, No. 1, pp. 32-50

Lange, O. [1936/37], On the Economic Theory of Socialism, in: *Review of Economic Studies*, Vol. 4, No. 1, pp. 60-66

Lavoie, D. [1978], *Rivalry and Central Planning*, Cambridge et al.

Leibenstein, H. [1966], "Allocative Efficiency Vs. 'X-Efficiency'", in: *AER*, Vol. 56, No. 3, pp. 392-415

Lenin, W.I. [1929/69], "Vorwort", in: Bucharin, Nikolai, *Imperialismus und Weltwirtschaft*, Wien; quotet after reprint: Frankfurt a.M.: Neue Kritik 1969, pp. 5-11

Lerner, A.P. [1937], "Statics and Dynamics in Socialist Economies", in: *Economic Journal*, Vol. 47, pp. 253-270

Lersmacher, R. [1979], *Handbuch der Unternehmensbewertung*, Wiesbaden: Gabler

Levitas, A. / P. Strzalkowski [1990], "What Does 'Uwlaszenie Nomen-klatury' ['Propertisation' of the Nomenklatura] Really Mean?", in: *Communist Economies*, Vol. 2, No. 3, pp. 413-416

Lewandowski, J. / J. Szomburg [1989], "Property Reform as a Basis for Social and Economic Reform", in: *Communist Economies*, Vol. 1, No. 3, pp. 257-268

Linhardt, P. / R. Radner / M.S. Satterthwaithe [1989], "Introduction, Symposium on Noncooperative Bargaining", in: *Journal of Economic Theory*, Vol. 48, No. 1, pp. 1-17

Lipinski, G. [1991], "Der Bürgschaftshahn wird zugedreht", in: Handelsblatt, No. 7, February 1991, p. 19

Lipp, E.-M. [1990], "Der Staat ist kein Sanierer", in: *Frankfurter Allgemeine Zeitung (FAZ)*, No. 85, 8/11/1990, p. 11

Lipps, W. [1991], "Gesetzgebungs- und Anwendungsfehler im Treuhandrecht der ehemals volkseigenen Wirtschaft", in: *BB, Beilage 9, Deutsche Einigung - Rechtsentwicklungen*, Vol. 46, No. 12, pp. 1-6

Lipton, D. / J.D. Sachs [1990], "Creating a Market Economy in Eastern Europe, The Case of Poland", in: *BPEA*, No. 1, pp. 75-133

- / - [1990], "Privatization in Eastern Europe, The Case of Poland", in: *BPEA*, No. 2, pp. 293-339

Malinvaud, E. [1967], "Decentralized Procedures for Planning", in: Malinvaud, Edmond and M.O.L. Bacharach, *Activity Analysis in the Theory of Growth and Planning*, London 1967, pp. 170-208

Manne, H.G. [1965], "Mergers and Markets for Corporate Control", in: *Journal of Political Economy*, Vol. 72, pp. 110-120

Markl, R., "Ökonomische Interpretationen des Wandels von Institutionen", in: *Frankfurter Volkswirtschaftliche Beiträge*, Working Paper No. 9, Frankfurt a.M.: Johann Wolfgang Goethe-University

Marx, K. / F. Engels [1948/1951], *Manifest der Kommunistischen Partei*, Berlin (1st edition: London 1948)

Maskin, E.S. [1992], "Auctions and Privatization", in: *Privatization, Symposium in Honor of Herbert Giersch*, ed. Horst Siebert, Tübingen: Mohr, pp. 115-136

Maskin, E.S. / J.G. Riley [1985], "Auction Theory with Private Values", in: *AER*, Vol. 75, pp. 150-155

Matschke, M.J. [1981], "Ertragswert", in: *Allgemeine Betriebswirtschafts-lehre - Handbuch für Studium und Prüfung*, ed. Herbert Jacob, 4th edition, Wiesbaden: Gabler

- **[1983]**, "Geschäftswert", in: Lück, Wolfgang, *Lexikon der Betriebswirtschaft*, Landsberg am Lech, p. 415

- **[1983]**, "Unternehmensbewertung", in: Lück, Wolfgang, *Lexikon der Betriebswirtschaft*, Landsberg am Lech, p. 1121

Maurer, R. / B. Sander / K.-D. Schmidt [1991], "Privatisierung in Ostdeutschland - Zur Arbeit der Treuhandanstalt", in: *Die Weltwirtschaft*, No. 1, pp. 45-65

McAfee, P.R. / J. McMillian [1987], "Auctions and Bidding", in: *JEL*, Vol. 25, pp. 699-788

Milgrom, P.R. / R.J. Weber [1985], "A Theory of Auctions and Competitive Bidding", in: *Econometrica*, Vol. 50, No. 5, pp. 1089-1122

Ministerium der Finanzen der DDR [1990], "Hinweise für die Bewertung von Unternehmen", in: *Bewertung von Unternehmen in der DDR*, ed. IDW, Düsseldorf: Institut der Wirtschaftsprüfer, p. 52

Mises, L. v. [1920], "Die Wirtschaftsrechnung im sozialistischen Gemeinwesen", in: *Archiv für Sozialwissenschaft und Sozialpolitik*, Vol. 47, pp. 86-123

- **[1936]**, *Socialism. An Economic and Sociological Analysis*, London (Original: Die Gemeinwirtschaft, Jena 1922)

- **[1992]**, *Die Gemeinwirtschaft*, Jena

Modigliani, F. / M. Miller [1958], "The Cost of Capital and Corporate Finance, and the Theory of Investment", in: *AER*, Vol. 48, pp. 261-297

Moxter, A. [1983], *Grundsätze ordnungsmäßiger Unternehmensbewertung*, 2nd edition, Wiesbaden: Gabler

- **[1985]**, "Zum neuen Bilanzrechtsentwurf", in: *BB*, Vol. 40, No. 17, pp. 1101-1103

Müller, J. [1993], "Strukturelle Auswirkungen der Privatisierung durch die Treuhandanstalt", in: *Treuhandanstalt. Das Unmögliche wagen*, eds. Fischer, Wolfram, Herbert Hax, and Hans K. Schneider, Berlin: Akademie, pp. 374-408

Münch, I.v. [1992], "Einführung", in: *Die Verträge zur deutschen Einheit*, Beck-Texte, 2nd edition, München 1992, pp. XIII-XXIV

Münstermann, H. [1970], *Wert und Bewertung der Unternehmung*, 3rd edition, Wiesbaden: Gabler

Murrell, P. [1983], "Did the Theory of Market Socialism Answer the Challenge of Ludwig von Mises? A Reinterpretation of the Socialist Controversy", in: *Journal of Political Economy*, Vol. 15, No. 1, pp. 92-105

Myerson, R.B. [1979], "Incentive Compatibility and the Bargaining Problem", in: *Econometrica*, Vol. 47, No. 1, pp. 61-73

- **[1983]**, "Mechanism Design By an Informed Principal", in: Econometrica, Vol. 51, No. 6, pp. 1767-1797

Myerson, R.B. / M.A. Satterthwaite [1983], "Efficient Mechanism for Bilateral Trading", in: *Journal of Economic Theory*, Vol. 29, No. 2, pp. 265-281

Nash, J.F. [1950], "The Bargaining Problem", in: *Econometrica*, Vol. 18, No. 2, pp. 155-162

- **[1953]**, "Two-Person Cooperative Games", in: *Econometrica*, Vol. 21, No. 2, pp. 128-140

Neubauer, R. [1992], "Quantensprung im Osten", in: *Die Zeit*, No. 22, 5/22/1992, p. 27

- **[1993]**, "Wort gebrochen. Ostdeutschland - Beschäftigungszusagen ohne Wert?", in: *Die Zeit*, No. 21, 5/21/1993, p. 18

Nolte, D. / R. Sitte / A. Wittig [1994], "Beschäftigungsbilanz der Treuhandanstalt", in: *Wirtschaftsbulletin Ostdeutschland*, 4. Vol., No. 2, pp. 28-35

North, D.C. [1981], *Structure and Change in Economic History*, New York

Nuti, D.M. [1991], "Stabilization and Sequencing in the Reform of Socialist Economies", in: *Managing Inflation in Socialist Economies in Transition*, ed. Somon Commander, Washington D.C.: Economic Development Institute of the World Bank, pp. 155-173

Nyers, R. / M. Tardos [1980], "Enterprises in Hungary Before and After the Economic Reform", in: *Public and Private Enterprise in a Mixed Economy*, ed. William Baumol, London

Olson, M. [1965], *The Logic of Collective Action, Public Goods and the Theory of Groups*, Cambridge/Mass.: Harvard University Press

Pareto, V. [1897], *Cours d'économique politique*, Vol. II, Lausanne

- **[1910]**, *Manuel d'économie politique*, Paris

Pejovich, S. [1982], "Karl Marx, Property Rights School and the Process of Social Change", in: *Kyklos*, Vol. 35, pp. 383-397

Pelikan, P. [1991], *Efficient Institutions for Ownership and Allocation of Capital.* Stockholm: Industrial Institute for Economic and Social Research, Working Paper 298

- **[1992]**, "The Dynamics of Economic Systems, or How to Transform a Failed Socialist Economy", in: *Journal of Evolutionary Economics*, Vol. 2, No. 1, pp. 39-63

Picot, A. / T. Kaulmann [1985], "Industrielle Großunternehmen im Staatseigentum aus verfügungsrechtlicher Sicht", in: zfbf, Vol. 37, No. 11, pp. 956-979

Picot, A. / E. Michaelis [1984], "Verteilung von Verfügungsrechten in Großunternehmen und Unternehmensverfassung", in: ZfB, Vol. 54, pp. 252-272

Pigou, A.C. [1952], *The Economics of Welfare*, 4th edition, London

Posner, R.A. [1977], *Economic Analysis of Law*, 2nd edition, Boston et al. 1977

Preu, P. [1992], "Wie wirksam schützt § 3 a VermG den Käufer eines Treuhandunternehmens vor Restitutionsansprüchen?", in: *DB*, No. 10, pp. 513-517

Priewe, J. [1991], "Sanieren, dezentralisieren, demokratisieren. Plädoyer für die Neufassung des Treuhandgesetzes", in: *Blätter für deutsche und internationale Politik*, No. 7, pp. 843-850

- **[1994]**, "Die Folgen der schnellen Privatisierung der Treuhandanstalt", in: *Aus Politik und Zeitgeschichte, Beilage zur Wochenzeitung Das Parlament*, 10/28/994, No. B 43-44/94, pp. 21-30

Priewe, J. / R. Hickel [1991], *Der Preis der Einheit. Bilanz und Perspektiven der deutschen Vereinigung*, Frankfurt a.M.: Fischer

Rawls, J. [1971], *A Theory of Justice*, Cambridge

- **[1992]**, *Die Idee des politischen Liberalismus, Aufsätze 1978-1989*, Frankfurt a.M.: Suhrkamp

Reese-Schäfer, W. / K.T. Schuon (eds.) [1991], *Ethik und Politik. Diskursethik, Gerechtigkeitstheorie und politische Praxis*, Marburg: Schüren

Richter, R. [1992], "A Socialist Market Economy - Can It Work?", in: *Kyklos*, Vol. 45, No. 2, pp. 185-207

Riese, H. [1990], *Geld im Sozialismus, Zur theoretischen Fundierung von Konzeptionen des Sozialismus*, Regensburg

- [1991], "Geld und Systemfrage", in: *Systemwandel und Reform in östlichen Wirtschaften*, ed. Jürgen Backhaus, Marburg: Metropolis, pp. 125-138

Riley, J.G. / W.F. Samuelson [1981], "Optimal Auctions", in: *AER*, Vol. 71, No. 2, pp. 381-392

Rob, R. [1989], "Pollution Claim Settlements Under Private Information", in: *Journal of Economic Theory*, Vol. 47, No. 2, pp. 307-333

Rubinstein, A. [1982], "Perfect Equilibrium in a Bargaining Modell", in: *Econometrica*, Vol. 50, No. 1, pp. 97-110

Sachs, J.D. [1991], *Accelerating Privatization in Eastern Europe*, Washington D.C.: World Bank Annual Conference on Development Economics, April 25/26, 1991

Sachverständigenrat zur Begutachtung der gesamtwirtschaftlichen Entwicklung (SVR) [1990], *Jahresgutachten 1990/91*, Bonn: Bundestagsdrucksache 11/8472

- [1991a], *Marktwirtschaftlichen Kurs halten. Zur Wirtschaftspolitik für die neuen Bundesländer*, Sondergutachten April 13, 1991, Bonn

- [1991b], *Jahresgutachten 1991/92*, Bonn: Bundestagsdrucksache 12/1618

- [1992], *Jahresgutachten 1992/93*, Bonn: Bundestagsdrucksache 12/3774

Scheifele, B. [1991], "Zur Anwendung des § 3 a Vermögensgesetz durch die Treuhandanstalt", in: *BB*, No. 20, pp. 1350-1356

Schmid-Schönbein / F.C. Hansel [1991], "Die Transformationspolitik der Treuhandanstalt", in: *Wirtschaftdienst*, Vol. 71, No. 9, pp. 462-469

Schmidt, K.M. [1991], *The Costs and Benefits of Privatization*, Discussionpaper, University of Bonn, February 1991

Schmidt, K.-D. [1993], "Strategien der Privatisierung", in: *Treuhandanstalt. Das Unmögliche wagen*, eds. Fischer, Wolfram, Herbert Hax, and Hans K. Schneider, Berlin: Akademie, pp. 211-240

Schmidt, R.H. [1981], "Grundformen der Finanzierung. Eine Anwendung des neo-institutionalistischen Ansatzes der Finanzierungstheorie", in: *Kredit und Kapital*, Vol. 14, pp. 186-221

- **[1988]**, "Neuere Property Rights-Analysen in der Finanzierungstheorie", in: *Betriebswirtschaftslehre und Theorie der Verfügungsrechte*, eds. Budäus, Dieter, Erwin Gerum, and Günther Zimmermann, Wiesbaden: Gabler

Schmieding, H. [1992], "Alternative Approaches to Privatization, Some Notes on the Debate", in: *Privatization, Symposium in Honor of Herbert Giersch*, ed. Horst Siebert, Tübingen: Mohr, pp. 97-108

Schnicke, C. [1991], "Überblick über die 'Hinweise für die Bewertung von Unternehmen'", in: *Probleme der Umstellung der Rechnungslegung in der DDR*, ed. Jörg Baetge, Düsseldorf

Schumpeter, J.A. [1954], Capitalism, Socialism and Democracy, 5th edition, New York: Harper 1942, pp. 122-125

Schwalbach, J. [1993], "Begleitung sanierungsfähiger Unternehmen auf dem Weg zur Privatisierung", in: *Treuhandanstalt. Das Unmögliche wagen*, eds. Ficher, Wolfram, Herbert Hax, and Hans K. Schneider, Berlin: Akademie

Seibel, W. [1993], "Die organisatorische Entwicklung der Treuhandanstalt", in: *Treuhandanstalt. Das Unmögliche wagen*, eds. Fischer, Wolfram, Herbert Hax, and Hans K. Schneider, Berlin: Akademie, pp. 111-147

- **[1994]**, "Das zentralistische Erbe", in: *Aus Politik und Zeitgeschichte, Beilage zur Wochenzeitung Das Parlament*, 10/28/1994, No. B 43-44/94, pp. 3-13

Selten, R. [1975], "Re-examination of The Perfectness Concept in Equilibrium Points in extensive Games", in: *International Journal of Game Theory*, Vol. 4, No. 1, pp. 25-55

Sen, A.K. [1970], *Collective Choice and Social Welfare*, San Francisco et al.

- **[1977]**, "Rawls versus Bentham, Eine axiomatische Untersuchung des reinen Verteilungsproblems", in: *Über John Rawls' Theorie der Gerechtigkeit*, ed. Otfried Höffe, Frankfurt a.M.: Suhrkamp, pp. 283-296

Sieben, G. [1992], "Zur Wertfindung bei der Privatisierung von Unternehmen in den neuen Bundesländern durch die Treuhandanstalt", in: *Der Betrieb*, Vol. 45, No. 41, pp. 2041-2051

Siebert, H. [1990a], "Die Wahlmöglichkeiten einer deutsch-deutschen Geld- und Währungspolitik", in: *Kieler Diskussionsbeiträge*, No. 159, April

- **[1990b]**, "The Economic Integration of Germany", in: *Kieler Diskussionsbeiträge*, No. 160, May

- **[1990c]**, "Die Treuhandanstalt darf nicht als ein Umstrukturierungsunternehmen fungieren", in: *Handelsblatt*, No. 190/91, 10/2-3/1990, p. B 16

- **[1991]**, "German Unification, The Economics of Transition", in: *Kiel Working Paper*, No. 468a, May

- **[1992]**, *Das Wagnis der Einheit. Eine wirtschaftspolitische Therapie*, Stuttgart: DVA, pp. 97-101

Siebert, H. / H. Schmieding / P. Nunnenkamp [1991], "The Transformation of a Socialist Economy - Lessons of German Unification", in: Kiel Workingpapers, No. 469, March

Simon, H.A. [1967], *Administrative Behaviour*, 2nd edition, New York

- **[1972]**, "Theories of Bounded Rationality", in: *Decision and Organization*, eds. C. McGuire and Roy Radner, Amsterdam, pp. 161-176

- **[1973]**, "Applying Information Technology to Organization Design", in: *Public Administrative Review*, Vol. 33, pp. 268-281

- **[1978]**, "Rationality as Process and as Product of Thought", in: *AER*, Vol. 68, No. 2

Singh, A. [1975], "Takeovers, Economic Natural Selection and the Theory of the Firm", in: *Economic Journal*, Vol. 85, No. 339, pp. 497-515

Sinn, G. / H.-W. Sinn [1991], Kaltstart, Die volkswirtschaftlichen Aspekte der deutschen Einheit, Tübingen: Mohr

Sinn, H.-W. [1991], Verteilen statt Verkaufen, in: *Wirtschaftswoche*, No. 5, 11/25/ 1991

Sirc, L. [1991], "The Revival of Entrepreneurship, Comments on the Draft of the Slovene Act on Privatisation", in: *Communist Economies and Economic Transformation*, Vol. 3, No. 3, pp. 375-382

Smith, A. [1776/1937], The Wealth of Nations, New York 1937 (1st edition 1776)

Smith, R. [1991], "Privatization Programms of the 1980s, Lessons for the Treuhandanstalt", in: Kieler Vorträge, No. 119

Soós, K.A. [1984], "A Propos Explanation of Shortage Phenomena, Volume of Demand and Structural Inelasticity", in: *Acta Oeconomica*, Vol. 33, No. 3-4, pp. 305-320

Sozialökonomische Strukturanalyse/Institut für Arbeitsmarkt- und Berufsforschung (Söstra/IAB) [1994], *Beschäftigungsperspektiven von Treuhandunternehmen und Ex-Treuhandunternehmen*, Memo, Berlin: February

SPD-Bundestagsfraktion (ed.) [1994], *Dokumentation Treuhanduntersuchungsausschuß, Zwischenbericht Oktober 1993 bis April 1994*, 2nd edition, Memo, Bonn

Staatssekretär beim Bundesminister der Finanzen [1990], *Brief an den Präsidenten der Treuhandanstalt*, Bonn: 10/9/1990

Stähl, I. [1972], *Bargaining-Theory*, Stockholm: Stockholm School of Economics

Staniszkis, J. [1991], Dylemati okresu przejsciowego, przypadek Polski, in: *Tygodnik Solidarnosc*, 6/1/1991

Statistisches Bundesamt, *Volkswirtschaftliche Gesamtrechnungen*, Fachserie 18, Reihe 3, various editions

- [1994], *Zur wirtschaftlichen und sozialen Lage in den neuen Bundesländern*, Vierteljahreszeitschrift, December

Statistisches Jahrbuch der DDR [1989], Berlin

Statut der Anstalt zur treuhänderischen Verwaltung des Volkseigentums [Treuhandanstalt] vom 15. März 1990, *Gbl. DDR I*, p. 167

Stiglitz, J. / A. Weiss, [1981], "Credit Rationing in Markets with Imperfect Information", in: *AER*, No. 3, Vol. 69, pp. 912-927

Suhr, H. [1991], *Der Treuhandskandal. Wie Ostdeutschland geschlachtet wurde*, Frankfurt a.M.: Fischer

Sutton, D. [1986], "Non-Cooperative Bargaining Theory, An Introduction", in: *Review of Economic Studies*, pp. 709-724

Svindland, E. [1990], *Möglichkeiten zu einer breiten Streuung des volkseigenen Vermögens in der DDR im Zusammenhang mit seiner Privatisierung*, Gutachten für das Bundesministerium für Arbeit und Soziales, Berlin: Deutsches Institut für Wirtschaftsforschung

Tardos, M. [1980], "The Role of Money, Economic Relations between the State and the Enterprises in Hungary", in: *Acta Oeconomica*, Vol. 25, No. 1-2, pp. 19-35

Taylor, F. [1938], "The Guidance of Production in a Socialist State", in: *On the Economic Thery of Socialism*, ed. Benjamin Lippincott, Minneapolis

Temkin, G. [1989], "On Economic Reform in Socialist Countries, The Debate on Economic Calculation Under Socialism Revisited", in: *Communist Economies*, Vol. 1, No. 1, pp. 31-59

Treuhandanstalt [1990], *Leitlinien der Geschäftspolitik*, Memo, Berlin: Treuhandanstalt, October

- [1991a], Arbeiten für die soziale Marktwirtschaft, Memo, Berlin: Treuhandanstalt

- [1991b], Auftrag, Zwischenbilanz, Grundsätze, Berlin: Treuhandanstalt, June

- [1991c], Fragen und Antworten zur Privatisierung, Berlin: Treuhandanstalt August

- **[1991d]**, Katalog der zustimmungspflichtigen Geschäfte eines Treuhandunternehmens, Fassung gemäß Beschluß des Gesamtvorstands der Treuhandanstalt vom 13.8.1991, Memo, Berlin: Treuhandanstalt

- **[1992a]**, "Erste Management-KG wird im April gegründet", in: *Treuhand-Informationen*, No. 12, 6.4.1992, p. 5

- **[1992b]**, *Monatsinformationen*, Stand: 3/31/992, Berlin: Treuhandanstalt

- **[1992c]**, *DM-Eröffnungsbilanz zum 1. Juli 1992*, Berlin: Treuhandanstalt, October

- **[1993a]**, Privatisierungshandbuch, Memo, Berlin: Treuhandanstalt

- **[1993b]**, *Jahresabschlüsse zum 31. Dezember 1991 und zum 31. Dezember 1992*, Berlin: Treuhandanstalt, December

- **[1994a]**, *Jahresabschluß zum 31. Dezember 1993*, Berlin: Treuhandanstalt, July

- **[1994b]**, *Daten und Fakten zur Aufgabenerfüllung der Treuhandanstalt*, Memo, Berlin: Treuhandanstalt, 12/30/1994

-, **Abt. Dokumentation/Datenmanagement [1993a]**, *THA-Unternehmensbestand*, Memo, Berlin: Treuhandanstalt, 6/1/1993

-, **Abt. Dokumentation/Datenmanagement [1993b]**, *THA-Unternehmensbestand*, Memo, Berlin: Treuhandanstalt, 7/1/1993

-, **Abt. P 14 [1993a]**, *Investitions- und Arbeitsplatzzusagen*, various editions, Berlin: Treuhandanstalt

-, **Abt. P 14 [1993b]**, *THA-Unternehmensbestand*, Memo, Berlin: Treuhandanstalt 4/6/1993

-, **Zentrales Controlling [1991a]**, *Monatsbericht April 1991*, Berlin: Treuhandanstalt

-, **Zentrales Controlling [1991b]**, *Monatsbericht Oktober 1991*, Berlin: Treuhandanstalt

-, **Zentrales Controlling [1991d]**, *Privatisierung, Stand 31.12.1991*, Memo, Berlin: Treuhandanstalt

-, **Zentrales Controlling [1992a]**, *Monatsbericht März 1992*, Berlin: Treuhandanstalt

-, **Zentrales Controlling [1992b]**, *Monatsbericht August 1992*, Berlin: Treuhandanstalt

-, **Zentrales Controlling [1992c]**, *Monatsbericht November 1992*, Berlin: Treuhandanstalt

-, **Zentrales Controlling [1992d]**, *Monatsbericht Dezember 1992*, Berlin: Treuhandanstalt

-, **Zentrales Controlling [1993b]**, *Monatsbericht Mai 1993*, Berlin: Treuhandanstalt

-, **Zentrales Controlling, [1993a]** *Monatsbericht Februar 1993*, Berlin: Treuhandanstalt

Tríska, D. [1990], *Privatization in Post-Communist Czechoslovakia*, Discussionpaper, Prag, October

Uechtritz, M. [1992], "Sicherer Erwerb restitutionsbelasteter Grundstücke trotz angefochtener Investitionsvorrangentscheidung?", in: *BB*, No. 9, pp. 581-588

Vaubel, R. [1992], "Comment on Holger Schmieding, 'Alternative Approaches to Privatization, Some Notes on the Debate'", in: *Privatization. Symposium in Honour of Herbert Giersch*, ed. Horst Siebert, Tübingen: Mohr, pp. 112-114

Veljanowski, C.G. [1982], "The Coase Theorems and the Economic Theory of Markets and Law", in: *Kyklos*, Vol. 33, No. 1, pp. 53-71

Verordnung über die Anmeldung vermögensrechtlicher Ansprüche [Anmeldeverordnung - AnmVO] vom 11. Juli 1990, *GBl. DDR I*, p. 718

Vertrag über die Schaffung einer Währungs-, Wirtschafts- und Sozialunion zwischen der Bundesrepublik Deutschland und der Deutschen Demokratischen Republik [Staatsvertrag - StVertr] vom 18. Mai 1990, *BGBl. II*, p. 537

Vertrag zwischen der Bundesrepublik Deutschland und der Deutschen Demokratischen Republik über die Herstellung der Einheit Deutschlands [Einigungsvertrag - EVertr] vom 3. August 1990, *BGBl. II*, p. 899

Vickers, J. / G. Yarrow [1988], *Privatization. An Economic Analysis*, Cambridge/Mass. et al.

Vickrey, W. [1961], "Counterspeculation, Auctions and Competitive Sealed Tenders", in: *Journal of Finance*, Vol. 16, No. 1, pp. 44-61

Vossel, H. [1991], "Spaltung der von der Treuhandanstalt verwalteten Unternehmen", in: *Deutsches Steuerrecht*, Vol. 29, No. 16, pp. 519-520

Vuylsteke, C. [1988], *Techniques of Privatization of State-Owned Enterprises*, Vol. I, Washington D.C.: World Bank Technical Paper No. 88

Wagener, H.-J. [1979], *Zur Analyse von Wirtschaftssystemen. Eine Einführung*, Berlin et al.: Springer

Wegehenkel, L. [1981], *Gleichgewicht, Transaktionskosten und Evolution*, Tübingen: Mohr

Weimann, J. [1991], *Umweltökonomik. Eine theorieorientierte Einführung*, 2nd edition, Berlin et al.: Springer

Weimar, R. [1990], "Treuhandanstalt und Treuhandgesetz", in: *BB*, Beilage 40, Deutsche Einigung-Rechtsentwicklungen, No. 35, pp. 10-15

- [1991], "Zum Wirkungsbereich der Treuhandanstalt gegenüber ihren Gesellschaften", in: *Neue juristische Wochenschrift*, Vol. 44, No. 14, pp. 105-108

- [1992], "Wegfall des Abhängigkeitsberichts bei treuhandeigenen Aktiengesellschaften?", in: *DB*, No. 39, pp. 1969-1970

Wienecki, J. [1991], "Theoretical Underpinnings of the Privatisation of State-owned Enterprises in Post-Soviettype Economies", in: *Communist Economies and Economic Transformation*, Vol. 3, No. 4, pp. 397-416

Wieser, F.v. [1899], *Der natürliche Werth*, Wien

Williamson, O.E. [1985], *The Economic Institutions of Capitalism*, Yale: Yale-University Press

- [1988], "Corporate Finance and Corporate Governance", in: *Journal of Finance*, Vol. XLIII, No. 3, pp. 567-591

- [1990], A Comparison of Alternative Approaches to Economic Organization, in: *JITE*, Vol. 146, pp. 61-71

Windsberger, J. [1983], "Transaktionskosten in der Firma", in: *ZfB*, Vol. 53, No. 9, pp. 889-903

Wissenschaftlicher Beirat beim Bundesministerium für Wirtschaft [1991], *Gutachten zu "Problemen der Privatisierung in den neuen Bundesländern"*, Memo, Bonn, 2/16-17/1991

Wöhe, G. [1986], *Einführung in die allgemeine Betriebswirtschaftslehre*, 16th edition, München

Wysocki, K. [1990], *Die D-Markeröffnungsbilanz von Unternehmen in der DDR*, Stuttgart

Yarrow, G. [1986], "Privatization in Theory and Practice", in: *Economic Policy*, Vol. 2, pp. 323-379

Zeuthen, F. [1930], *Problems of Monopoly and Economic Welfare*, London

Ziller, P. [1994], "Ein Schuß Hoffnung garantiert die Arbeitsplatzzusagen in Ostdeutschland", in: Frankfurter Rundschau, No. 88, 4/161994, p. 9

Zivilgesetzbuch der DDR vom 19. Juni 1975, *GBl. DDR I*, p. 465

For Product Safety Concerns and Information please contact our EU representative GPSR@taylorandfrancis.com Taylor & Francis Verlag GmbH, Kaufingerstraße 24, 80331 München, Germany

T - #0089 - 160425 - C0 - 229/152/17 - PB - 9780714643359 - Gloss Lamination